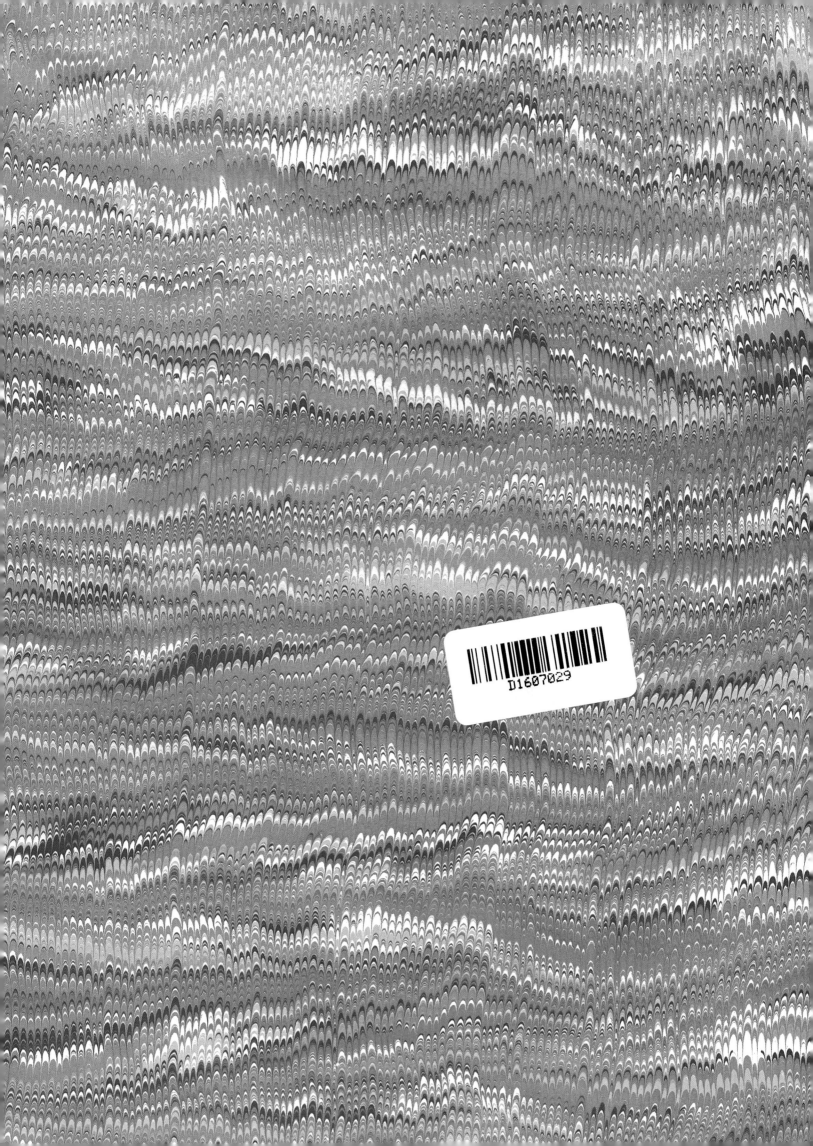

American Wristwatches
Five Decades of Style and Design

Edward Faber and Stewart Unger
with Ettagale Blauer

77 Lower Valley Road, Atglen, PA 19310

This book is dedicated to the memory of Arnold F.T. Kotis

"A Collector of People"

The authors acknowledge that there may be errors in fact or omission. We
would greatly appreciate any and all comments that will help correct and
further the legacy of American wristwatches.

Revised price guide 1996
Copyright© 1996 by Stewart Unger, Edward Faber, and Ettagale Blauer.
Library of Congress Catalog Number: 88-62691.

Printed in The United States of America.
ISBN: 0-7643-0171-3

Published by Schiffer Publishing, Ltd.
77 Lower Valley Road
Atglen, PA 19310
Phone: (610) 593-1777
Fax: (610) 593-2002
Please write for a free catalog.
This book may be purchased from the publisher.
Please include $2.95 for shipping.
Try your bookstore first.

We are interested in hearing from authors with book
ideas on related subjects.

Contents

Acknowledgments

For their support and commitment to this project we sincerely thank: Patricia Kiley Faber and Douglas Congdon-Martin.

For their generous help in sharing memories, memorabilia and wristwatches for this book, we gratefully acknowledge: Richard Arbib, Peter Beaumont, William Bennett, Irvin Gruen Bieser, Gus Bozzo, A. Brown, Judith Blumberg, Charles N. Cleves, Kenneth Derr, Jack Feldman, Ira Fickes, Peter Fossner, Henry Fried, Eugene T. Fuller, Paul Graehling, John Gruen III, Robert D. Gruen, Jeff Hess, Harry B. Henshel, Steve Jacobson, Werner Koeningsberger, Robert Lesser, Ted Lisnow, Mr. and Mrs. S. Manolis, Stanley D. Marx, Jesse Medlock, Bettye Miller, Jeff Morris, the National Association of Watch and Clock Collectors (N.A.W.C.C.), Molly Orr, Osvaldo and Madeleine Patrizzi, Sandra Pezzulli, Marco dePlano, Mark Pollack, Henry Polissack, Kurt Rothner, Daryn Schnipper, Kenneth Schoenrock, Michael Schub, Irving Sherman, Sig Shonholz, Jonathan Snellenburg, Jerry Solin, Kenneth Specht, Ron Starnes, Harry Stecker, Tami Steiner, the staff of Aaron Faber Gallery, the staff of Time Will Tell, Haskell C. Titchell, Robert Weber, Harvey Whidden, Jean Wuischpard, and Elaine Wnukowski. Thanks to Dr. Richard Smith for the revision and updating of the Illinois section and photography.

For their enthusiasm, support and development of the American wristwatch market, we thank: Libardo Alvarez, Jaeder Barracca, Massimo Barracca, Marilyn and Shari Bembenek, Semion Bronsztejn, Ilene Chasanof, John Cole, Tony Curatola, Joe Demesy, Steve Dubinsky, Paul Duggan, Roy Erhardt, Jr., Alan Ehrlich, Ruth Faber, Joe and Cindy Fanelli, Mike FitzSimmons, Keith Gray, Brad Gold, George Gordon, Doug Gruenberg, Warren Haber, Governor Jim Thompson, former Governor of Illinois, Spencer and Carol Hodgson, Gordon and Carol Hyatt, P.J., Ken Jacobs, Claudia Kable, Stan King, Jeff Knepper, Alan and Seth Larrabure, Joe Levine, Harvey Marcus, Gil Margolis, Bill Marin, Fred Mayer, Warren Messing, Richard Moss, Dave Mycko, Dennis and Linda Nickerson, Pia, Peter Planes, Nathan Reiskin, Terry Rhodes, Adam Ross, David Sandler, Oscar Schwenk, Owen Sercus, Marc Shaffman, Jack and Joan Stanton, Diana Sandstrom Thomas, Lawrence Unger, Philip Welsh, Dave Williams, Paul Wing, Robert Wingate, Eve Wolfson, Ruth Zandberg. The sketches by Richard Arbib in the Chapter on the Hamilton *Electric* are provided through the courtesy of Jeff Hess. The photographs were taken in New York by Don Manza and in Pennsylvania by Lyngerda Kelley.

E. Faber
S. Unger
E. Blauer

Preface I

What is This Phenomenon About?

by Edward Faber

Why does a mechanical wristwatch that was manufactured in 1929 by Hamilton, and that sold as recently as four years ago for its gold value, now bring a fair market price of upwards of $4000 (Hamilton *Spur*)? Why does a gold-filled Gruen *Curvex* which had virtually no value four years ago currently sell upwards of $600-800? Why are there countless examples of previously valueless granddad wristwatches bringing record prices? Gresham's law. The 16th century economist, Sir Thomas Gresham realized that "when you withdraw something from circulation (stop production), its value goes up." In his day it was silver coins. In ours it is mechanical wristwatches.

Worldwide production of wristwatches by the end of the '70s was 200 million pieces per year, almost exclusively mechanical. By 1988, worldwide production is approaching 500 million units, with virtually 80% being quartz variations.

All the ingredients are in place for a *bona fide* collectible to flourish:

1. A willing and aggressive group of collectors anxious to pursue informed purchases.

2. A rather large and growing group of individuals who wish to own one or two watches as fashion statements or for nostalgic reasons, who will wear and enjoy a single piece.

3. The liquidity that comes from the ability to dispose of or trade items through dealer networks, flea markets, and ultimately auction houses.

4. A reasonable supply of material.

5. A growing source of information that intelligently describes and discusses the wristwatch.

The globalization of the market adds energy and a dynamic force that partially account for the rapid rise in prices. What began in Italy in the late '70s, traveled to Germany and England, and took root in America as early as 1979 or 1980, is now flourishing on three continents as well as Japan. As the field rapidly expands to include a growing number of collectors, dealers, and auctions, more opportunities present themselves. The European bias toward high grade European products has created a vacuum, and an opportunity for fine American products. Hamilton,

Gruen, Illinois, Elgin, Bulova, and Waltham give us the basis for an exciting collectible.

This book hopes to explain the development of the American industry, how it quickly changed from its European parentage, became a leader of industrial design throughout five decades, and has produced a rare and desirable product. It far exceeds the European product in design. American watches, more than European, synthesize all the currents of industrial design in all the periods covered, and dramatize the excitement and leadership that America has given the world vis-a-vis its industrial design.

Genuine opportunity exists to find enameled bezel watches, unusual case materials such as 18k gold and platinum, the great decorative watches of the '20s, doctors' watches, *Reversos* and *Curvexes* of the '30s, wild and pink varieties of the '40s, fantastic asymmetrics of the '50s, and, of course, the *Space View*, the truly post-modern series, the *Accutrons* of the '60s.

It is the fashion aspect of these periods that motivates many of those who are excited by these watches, and it is the secret of the phenomenal success that wristwatches have experienced in the last few years. Stylists and fashion editors in the major international press are promoting the intriguing and versatile designs of former periods as a necessary component of the complete wardrobe. Hundreds of thousands of willing buyers are being cultivated worldwide, ready to be unleashed on the market.

Otherwise conservative people will indulge in this tasteful display of "luxe". The phenomenon is explained by the reality of the conservative nature of the American businessperson. The men and women who make up the middle and upper middle classes are the newly wealthy in this country. Aged 30-50, and employed in the financial and banking industries, they dress carefully for their success, avoiding the ostentation of previous generations of the *nouveau riche*. We do not see the men of this generation wearing large diamond rings. They are no longer draped in heavy gold chains about the neck. Their jewelry is limited to their cuff, and now their wrist.

Style and status, wealth and powers, and all other

signals of success can be read with the flick of a wrist, the bringing back of a cuff. The wearer can express himself any way he or she chooses, whether it is an exaggerated style or a $5000, $10,000 or even $100,000 wristwatch. It's a subtle expression of pleasure. It can be worn and carried with the owner, for the owner's pleasure and a small circle of friends and knowledgeable people. It is not kept locked in a box, in a desk drawer, or hanging on a wall.

As with any collectible, the knowledge and experience available from dealers can be invaluable. They have been trading wristwatches for many years, and they have built up a vast inventory of knowledge and price information. They have the service of restorations and repair and stand behind each piece they sell, usually with a year's warranty. They advise estates and individuals, bring their experience to bear as auction agents, and are available to the seasoned and new collector and to the people who want to give one watch as a gift for a special occasion or the collector who passionately seeks them by the dozens. Their advice and counsel can help the collector reach his or her own goals of enjoyment, value and personal taste.

Preface II
Historical Development of the Wristwatch

by Stewart Unger

The wristwatch has always been a marriage of form and function. While its function is as a timekeeping device, its form is a piece of jewelry. As a jewelry form it traces its roots back to the bracelet which has adorned the human wrist for many millennia. Bracelets are found as funerary jewelry from antiquity. They are seen on statuary and other portrayals of human adornment and fashion from nearly every era and from around the world. The form of the wristwatch has its beginning in the bracelet.

Its function begins much later. Mechanical means of marking time began in the late thirteenth century. Large movements were used and they were bound by their size to the place they stood. But the clockmakers were constantly refining their skills and coming up with more accurate and smaller timepieces.

The antecedent of the wristwatch is the Renaissance ring watch. This early blend of jewelry form and timekeeping function is a testament to the skill of the early watchmaker, and may have opened the way for the development of the wristwatch.

While there is no one date for the "invention" of the bracelet watch, some significant steps in its development are traced to the late 18th and early 19th centuries. We have several examples of bracelet watches from this period. The most famous of these is a pair of bracelet watches presented by Empress Josephine to her daughter-in-law in 1806. These were key wound watches set in bracelets and emphasized jewelry rather than time. One of the pair told the time, while the other watch gave the date and month.

The trend continues in the 19th century. Examples of jewelry-oriented decorated bracelets can be found occasionally in flea markets, dealer shows, stores or at auction. Generally they employed small pocket watch movements in a case designed for the wrist. They were not mass-produced, being, instead, designed for specific persons by specific jewelers.

The production of wristwatches by watchmaking companies in the United States would wait until the twentieth century. In Europe, however, small levels of production began as early as 1850 and grew toward the end of the century.

Most of the early bracelet watch production utilized the cylinder watch movement, though the lever escapement with both pin and crown set is also employed. The crown set lever movement becomes the predominant movement for wristwatches through the 20th century up to the 1960s and 1970s. Toward the latter part of the 19th century very inexpensive movements were used, similar to the one-jewel pin that Timex would use in the twentieth century.

In the late 1880s and early 1890s "watch bracelets" as they were then called began appearing in English catalogues. J.W. Benson, an English dealer, began advertising them in the 1880s.

The major Swiss watch companies began experimental manufacturing of bracelet watches in the mid-1800s. Patek Philippe manufactured a bracelet watch in 1868, Omega started to convert pocket watches to watch bracelets in the late 19th century, and Girard Perregaux of Switzerland produced wristwatches for Berlin naval officers in the 1880s.

On the other side of the Atlantic there was an established pocket watch industry in the 1850s. Elgin and Waltham were very active and would become major manufacturers of wristwatches early in the 20th century.

Early American wristwatches were conversions of other watch forms. Many were simply women's pendant watches with solid lugs soldered at the top and bottom for the attachment of a bracelet or strap.

In the 1890s the Waterbury Watch Company introduced a form of wristwatch. This construction incorporated a leather watch holder/strap which allowed a small inexpensive pocket watch to be inserted into the holder and then affixed to the wrist.

While entering into the wristwatch field in only a very limited way in the late 19th century, America was making progress in a technology whose impact would be felt throughout the coming decades. In the late 1800s Americans developed the processes called gold filled and rolled gold plate. Basically these processes involve the fusing of two layers of gold with a middle layer of suitable supporting base metal. This sandwich of metal is fused into a laminate through the controlled application of heat, time, and pressure.

In the gold filled process the gold is 10k or better and is 3 thousandths of an inch thick. In the rolled gold plate the gold is also 10k or better and is 1.5 thousandths of an inch thick. In watch cases the amount of gold varies from 25 microns in the rolled gold plate to 50 microns in gold filled. The gold, however, is applied in such a way as to be much denser than the electroplating process. In addition it has a softer look. It was not the bright, "costume jewelry" look as so often happens with electroplating.

Besides the aesthetics of these products of American technology there were some practical advantages. Gold filled and rolled gold cases are less porous and because of their density they will resist corrosion and the effects of body oils more than electroplated cases. They also enable much deeper stamping and tooling in the manufacturing, allowing many more possibilities in design. This technology was applied to American and Canadian wristwatch cases after 1918 and became one of the prime reasons for the emergence of that specialized North American style and design.

Meanwhile the European watch industry was going through an interesting evolution. Wristwatches were developed by more and more pocket watch firms. Around the turn of the century Patek Philippe, Vacheron and Constantin, Audemars Piguet, Longines, Omega, Tissot, Girard Perregaux and numerous others had begun production of wristwatches.

Specialization was an important part of the market both in Europe and the United States, with one company producing the case and another the movement (ebauche). Gruen in Switzerland, for example took its famous #877 doctor's wristwatch movement and with slight modifications manufactured it for the #300/500 series Rolex *Prince* wristwatches.

This has been an accepted industry practice going back to pocket watches and clocks. Instead of manufacturing their own movements, a watch firm would have them made by an ebauche manufacturing company according to the watch firm's specifications. In 1926, 16 major ebauche makers including A. Schild S.A., Eta S.A., and Fontainemelon grouped themselves together to form Ebauche S.A. and began manufacturing movements for watch companies throughout the world.

Some American companies such as Bulova and Benrus purchased most of their movements from Swiss ebauche makers. Gruen USA had its own sister company in Switzerland manufacturing movements and sending them to the U.S. In another variation, Swiss parent companies such as LeCoultre, Longines, Movado and others set up distributors in the U.S. which would case Swiss movements in American cases.

Most American watch companies, however, produced their own movements. Elgin, Waltham, Hamilton, Illinois, South Bend, and others all manufactured the movements for their wristwatches, and marketed a complete wristwatch. The design process, while directed by the watch companies was shared with the watch case sub-contractors which manufactured most of the cases.

This book is devoted to the uniquely American contribution to the style and design of wristwatches, although it cannot ignore the European influence. In addition to some function of telling time, wristwatches fall into one or more of several categories. Specific wristwatches are investments, collectibles, fashion statements or design innovations. The wristwatches we have selected reflect America's changing tastes and its developing technology. They reflect the United States' growing maturity after the First World War, its emergence from isolation into world responsibilities. This new America is seen in its people, its music, its architecture and in the multitude of manufactured products. Cars, trains, washing machines, toasters and, yes, wristwatches all reflect the American coming of age. And, at least in the case of wristwatches, the beauty and vitality of America is also captured. The genius of the country is being reflected in the designs, the styles and the outpouring of exquisite and exciting wristwatches.

It is to the ingenuity of the American wristwatch that this book is directed and dedicated. We hope you will enjoy this book, its photos and story, as much as we and the publisher have enjoyed researching and preparing it for you.

Chapter One
Transition:
Out of the Pocket

1915-1925 The first decade

of the American wristwatch

As America, and the world, saw the dawning of the new century, the very concept of time entered a new era. The pace of the world became faster; the style of time changed. The transition from the era of the pocket watch to that of the wristwatch was symbolic of the change. The pocket watch belongs to the 19th century and its less hurried sense of time. The wristwatch clearly speaks of the faster pace of the 20th century.

The image of the portly man, in a three-piece suit, gold chain stretched across his considerable girth, pulling a watch out of his pocket, captures our view of the 19th century businessman. Deliberate in his motions, measuring time in an obvious, even ostentatious way, he stood on the factory floor, or in a board room, and went through all the motions attendant to checking on the time.

What is false about this image, what makes it into a stereotype, is the association of the pocket watch with wealth and power. It was not limited to gold models for the elite. Indeed the genius of the American watch industry was in making it available to everyone. This "democratization" of time began in the mid-1800's, says Paul Graehling, a watch aficionado, when "An American visited the Springfield Rifle Works and figured you could make a watch in the same way, [using standard, duplicate parts]. That was the beginning of the Waltham Co."

Inexpensive pocket watches became widely available, thanks to the precision tool and die workers who enabled American industry to set the highest standards in the manufacturing community. Mass-produced parts for modestly priced pocket watches met much finer tolerances than were possible in Europe. As a result, parts for pocket watches were interchangeable with only minor adjustments, a crucial fact that paved the way for the mass-produced wristwatch.

Women, too, owned timepieces, but they were not as limited in form. Watches were worn as lapel pins or on chains around the neck. Thus the function of timekeeping was combined with the form of jewelry.

In 1915, Waltham patented the *Disappearing Eye*, an attachment to the bottom of a pocket watch used to connect it to a bracelet. The other end of the bracelet attached to the bail at the top where the watch chain was usually clipped on. When the watch was being worn as a pocket watch, the "eye" folded up behind it and disappeared from view. The watch could be worn in five ways: on a metal link bracelet, on a leather strap, pinned on the lapel, with an elastic strap, or on a chain around the neck. It was "the modern girl's watch—one watch for all occasions". It was a very reasonable way to use a watch, and quite attractive. But it was detrimental to the development of the wristwatch, especially for men.

The male mind being what it is, wearing a wristwatch was associated with effeminacy. While the concept of the wristwatch was well advanced in

WALTHAM, ca 1912. With its hook eyelet at 6:00, this is a typical example of a convertible lady's watch. The case is 14k gold with enamel on the bezel and a matching expandable spring bracelet. The movement is 6/0 size and has 17 jewels. This type of wristwatch is rarely found with the enamel in good condition and with the original band.

HAMPDEN, ca 1920-24. This gold filled convertible wristwatch is boxed in its presentation case. The Hampden movement has a 7 jewels.

ELGIN, ca 1912-16. An early example of a lady's convertible watch, it changes from a pendant watch to a wristwatch by fastening the ribbon band to the lug wire at 6:00. The gold filled case is engraved, and the dial is metal. The Elgin lever movement has 7 jewels.

Europe, American watch manufacturers were facing stiff opposition to their marketing efforts. Evidence of that resistance comes from an early Waltham brochure. It was published just after the First World War and addresses the difficulty that American men were having with the idea of the wristwatch. The brochure is selling "Waltham Military Wristwatches" and heralds them as being for soldiers, sailors, hunters, golfers, motorists, tennis players, sportsmen, and "all real men". The copy hits the source of resistance head on: "Manly watches for manly men—any man so out-of-date as to consider the wristwatch effeminate need only learn the kind of men who use the Waltham. They are fighting men—the soldiers in the World War, the military and naval men the world over, the big game hunters, the aviators, the sportsmen, motorists, yachtsmen, the college man.

"Strong, virile, two-fisted men wear the Waltham Wrist Watch... before the perfection of the Waltham there may have been grounds for the charge of effeminacy against the wristwatch. But the Waltham itself and the men who use it now make the charges as outworn as the humor is flat."

As the brochure implies, modern warfare changed the image of the wristwatch by putting it on the most masculine of men, the soldier in the trenches. Who could claim a wristwatch was effeminate if a soldier's life depended on it—for coordination with his mates and his superior officers, for timing artillery, for winning a war? For the British, the war that marked the change in attitude came before 1900—the Boer War in South Africa. But for America, it was not until soldiers went over to Europe to fight in the First World War that American men came into contact with the wristwatch as a practical, masculine timepiece. The soldiers accepted the wristwatch in the same spirit as they greeted a more accurate weapon. It gave them a degree of mastery over their perilous situation.

The Americans' exposure to the wristwatch during the First World War translated into a new demand for them when the soldiers returned home. Companies such as Waltham capitalized on this new market, and used the association with the war to overcome the wristwatch's previous image. The wristwatch found a new acceptability.

WALTHAM, ca 1918. The hinged, gold filled case of this transitional Waltham has solid wire lugs attached at 9:00 and 3:00 with the crown at 12:00. The porcelain dial has Arabic numerals with red minute numerals at five-minute intervals. 15 jewels. Waltham movement.

WALTHAM, ca 1918. The case of this Waltham is by the Dennison Watch Case Company and is of sterling silver with a screw back and front and a coin edged bezel. The crown is brass, though it may once have been silverplated. Though large and designed like a pocket watch, steps have been taken to transform this watch including moving the crown to 3:00 and placing the strap attachments at 12:00 and 6:00. The dial is porcelain with silhouette numbers, skeleton hands, and a subsidiary seconds chapter at 6:00. Waltham 7-jeweled movement.

WALTHAM, ca 1922. The luminous paint on this porcelain dial has been removed, exposing a very handsome design with silhouetted numerals and pierced hands. The 14k gold filled case has angled lugs. 15 jewels. Waltham movement.

WALTHAM, ca 1918. The porcelain dial of this Waltham features red minutes indicators at five-minute intervals. 7 jewels.

ELGIN, ca 1917. The pierced case protects the porcelain dial of this soldier's watch. The dial has outlined Arabic numerals and black outlined hands, with a subsidiary seconds chapter at 6:00. The anodized case has its original khaki adjustable strap. This original wristwatch is highly collectible and rare. In the 1980s there has been an attempt to duplicate this wristwatch in quartz, but it fails to achieve the same look. 7 jewels.

WALTHAM, ca 1917-19. A rare and unusual watch, this pierced case soldier's wristwatch is highly sought after by military and fashion collectors. The cushion-shaped sterling silver case sets it apart from most of the other military wristwatches of the period. The dial is white porcelain with fired enamel Arabic numerals. 15 jewels, Waltham movement.

They also capitalized on the design of the soldier's wristwatch. A pierced top cover had protected the crystal and hands of the wristwatch during a soldier's day-to-day activities. This idea of protection was also appealing to civilians, for whom the unprotected watch, exposed to the hazards of being worn on the wrist, was too vulnerable. The wristwatch had established a beachhead on the American market from which it would never retreat.

The American watch manufacturer was well-positioned from a mechanical standpoint to meet this new demand for wristwatches. The earliest such items were all fashioned from small pocket watch movements fitted into a case and affixed to a band of some type. But styling the wristwatch called for a different mentality and an understanding that the timepiece had now become decorative as well as functional. It is the resolution of this marketing challenge that laid the foundation for the success of the American wristwatch industry.

The look of the transitional American wristwatch owed its basic form to the pocket watch. Cases were made of silver, gold, gold filled and rolled gold plate, gunmetal, nickel and other base metals. Most wristwatches had lever mechanisms although cylinder movements were used up to the 1930s. These new wristwatches were round because the movements were taken from the round pocket watch; pocket watches did not call for rectangular movements. Until Movado, a Swiss firm, created a three-part rectangular movement in 1912, the *Polyplan*, the commitment to making a wristwatch required only the skills of the case-maker, not the innovations of the watch manufacturer. A movement specially designed for the wristwatch did not become the industry standard until the late 1920s.

INGERSOLL, 1920s. The *Wrist Radiolite* has a round nickel silver case and wire lugs. The black dial has white luminous Arabic numerals. The hands of this wristwatch are set by depressing the crown and turning it. Ingersoll pin-lever movement.

INGERSOLL, ca 1914. This transitional wristwatch has its crown at 12:00, but has adopted the more comfortable 12:00 and 6:00 band attachments. The dial is painted cardboard with luminous numerals. To set the hands on this wristwatch the crown is depressed and rotated. Ingersoll movement

SOUTH BEND, 1920s. While South Bend made many pocket watches, they did not make many wristwatches. This rare example is gold filled and evokes its pocket watch ancestry. The two-toned porcelain dial features Arabic numerals and a minutes chapter of gold-toned dot and star markers. The porcelain has a crazing crack. South Bend movement, 15 jewels.

WALTHAM, 1920s. Bold Arabic numerals dominate the porcelain dial of this gold filled wristwatch. The red 12 gives the wristwatch a touch of color. Solid wire lugs at 11:00 and 5:00 give the wristwatch an offset position, permitting what is essentially a pocket watch to be more conveniently read and wound. 7 jewels.

ELGIN, ca 1915. The W.F. Hackett Company of Rochelle, Illinois, marketed this Elgin as a private label watch. The gold filed case was manufactured by B & B Case Company, and houses a 7-jeweled Elgin movement. The porcelain dial features an hours chapter and a minutes chapter with red numerals at the five minute intervals. The integrated linked expansion band is original.

Dials were made predominately of porcelain which gives a beautiful, durable surface for the numbering system. While inexpensive wristwatches were made with metal dials, porcelain was the material of choice for better watches. When wristwatches began to surpass pocket watches in volume in the late 1920s, the porcelain dial gave way to enamel paint on a metal base. Both for economic and practical reasons the desirability of the porcelain dial was suspect for the more vulnerable wristwatches. In the pocket, well protected and often covered, the porcelain dial wears well; out of the pocket, and required to meet the production demands of the small case, the porcelain dial proved to be too subject to the everyday hazards. It also simply became too expensive an element.

The hours were fully indicated by figures; markers in lieu of numerals had not yet made their appearance. The hours chapter was nearly always on the dial although a few rare examples exist where it has been placed on the bezel. Most wristwatches have a minutes chapter outside the hours chapter, often with five minute indicators in a second color. When a seconds hand is present, it is placed in a subsidiary position, generally at 6:00. The sweep seconds hand has yet to appear.

Nearly all the dials of the early wristwatches conformed to the overall shape of the watch, but experimentation began before 1920. A lady's wristwatch featured a tonneau-shaped dial within an elongated marquise-shaped case of silver with white enamel designs. The severity of the Roman numbers is at odds with the softly tapered case. Other early models show the beginnings of design experimentation. The round dial is placed within a cushion-shaped case, then changes entirely as in these examples.

WALTHAM, ca 1917. The case is what Waltham called "20 Year Gold Filled." Usually used for pocket watches, the term referred to a 20 year warranty for the case material, and underscores the transitional nature of this watch. The case was also available in silver. The stylized numerals and the hands give a well-defined, bold read-out to this early American wristwatch. 15 jewels, though available with 7 jewels.

WALTHAM, Ca. 1915. Indicative of its early creation, this Waltham has the crown above the twelve and solid wire lugs at 3:00 and 9:00. The porcelain dial has Arabic numerals and red numbers in the minutes chapter. The case is gold filled and the movement has 15 jewels.

SWISS, ca 1925. This early decorative lady's wristwatch has a sterling silver case with inlaid white enamel. It was imported into the United States in the late 1920s. 15 jewels.

S. KIRK & SON, ca 1925. Samuel Kirk was a Maryland silversmith. This is an early example of the introduction of spring bars in the lugs. A white porcelain dial with luminous Arabic numerals is housed in a sterling silver case. The Swiss movement has 15 jewels.

WALTHAM, 1920s. This 14k gold cushion-shaped wristwatch has a porcelain dial with luminous numerals and hands. A subsidiary seconds chapter is at 6:00. 17 jewels. Waltham movement.

ELGIN, ca 1926. The cushion-form case of this early Elgin wristwatch is yellow gold filled and has an oversized brass crown. The brushed white metal dial has luminous Arabic numerals.

ELGIN, ca 1917. A lady's pocket watch has been converted to form this fine example of the transitional period. The gold filled cushion-shaped case has solid wire lugs at 3 and 9. The crown is at 12:00. Elgin has simply taken its 15 jewel lady's pocket watch movement and cased it for the wrist.

ELGIN, ca 1918. A handsome example of an early American wristwatch , this Elgin was cased in England by the Dennison Watch Case Co. The very heavy case is 9k gold, in a cushion design. It has solid wire lugs. The dial is porcelain with Roman numerals and a red XII. A subsidiary seconds chapter is at 6:00. 15 jewels.

ELGIN, Ca. 1920. With its star minute markers and its eagle standing guard over the "Elgin, U.S.A.," this wristwatch is well suited to its early use as a military watch. The gold-filled cushion-shaped case holds a round dial with outlined Arabic numerals. The wristwatch has black hands and a subsidiary seconds chapter. 7 jewels. Elgin movement.

NEW HAVEN WATCH CO., ca 1930. The *Tip Top* has an octagonal case and a round dial. The decorative painting in the center of the dial and around the subsidiary seconds chapter picks up the octagonal motif. The case is nickel-plated with a chromium plated back. Solid lugs set at the 5:00 and 11:00 positions give the wristwatch an offset configuration. Pin-lever movement.

WALTHAM, ca 1918. This gold filled case has unusual offset lugs. By keeping the crown at 12:00, the designer solved some of the problems of the transitional wristwatch without radically changing the design of the pocket watch. The dial is porcelain with luminous skeleton hands. 7 jewels.

WALTHAM, 1920s. An offset lug arrangement permits the crown to stay at 12:00 on this wristwatch. The angled solid lugs are at 5:00 and 11:00. The porcelain dial is housed in a steel case. 17 jewels.

Despite these experiments with design, the transitional wristwatch generally had the look of a pocket watch that has simply been attached to a band. Its relationship to the band was tenuous. The size of the wristwatch was too large for the band. There were attempts to modify the pocket watch, to take its familiar features and fit them on the wrist often with awkward results. Style and function were sometimes at odds with one another.

Waltham, Elgin, Illinois, and Hamilton are among the American watch companies of the transitional period that endured, along with Bulova and Gruen which imported movements from Switzerland and cased them here. These early wristwatches reveal their ancestry in easily recognizable details. Their crowns are bulbous, fluted and ridged, the correct proportion for a pocket watch but out of scale for the smaller wristwatch.

There were no guidelines for manufacturers, nothing to tell them how to adapt the position of the dial in relation to the wrist. The winding stem and crown often remain in the 12:00 position, indicating that the movement is a pocket watch model. The band was usually attached at 3:00 and 9:00 on these early models. This was an awkward position for reading the time, and one is surprised that it took so long for the dial to be redesigned. A 90 degree turn was needed if the time was to be read easily on the wrist and this forced the crown to move to the 3:00 position, and the band to 12:00 and 6:00. The crown seems to be physically resisting the move in this delightful Elgin model which dates from the late teens/early '20s.

HAMPDEN, 1920s. A hinged gold-filled case, bulbous crown and porcelain dial mark this as a transitional watch. Hampden movement.

ELGIN, ca 1917-18. The off-set position of this early Elgin wristwatch marks it as one of the transitional efforts. The crown is at twelve o'clock and the subsidiary seconds chapter at six, as was typical of pocket watches. The solid lugs, however, are attached to the flat side of the cushion case between 9 and 12, making the crown accessible for winding and setting, and the wristwatch easier to read. The wristwatch is gold filled with a round porcelain dial and outlined numerals which were fired into it. 7-jeweled Elgin movement.

PATRIA, 1920s. Embossed numerals inlaid with enamel adorn the bezel of this English rolled gold plate case. The case opens by pressing the crown. The dial is porcelain with outlined numbers and hands. Both originally had luminous paint. Swiss movement, 15 jewels.

SWISS. This sterling silver hunting case wristwatch has a porcelain dial. The case is spring loaded with a push button and opens to allow viewing of the dial. While closed, it protects the dial. The dial is black with a subsidiary seconds chapter at 6:00. A Swiss movement with 15 jewels powers the watch. Inside the case is engraved "925 Brevet +71363" and "A.G.R. 663743 J".

LIVERPOOL, 1920s. A sterling silver hinged case demi-hunter, this English wristwatch has enameled Arabic numerals on the bezel. At 6:00 there is a button for releasing the spring-loaded cover, which reveals a white porcelain dial and subsidiary seconds chapter. The hands are probably not original. The case construction features a screw-off back. Swiss movement, 15 jewels.

DUBLIN, 1920s. Left-handed people will appreciate this unusual wristwatch designed to be worn on the right wrist. This demi-hunter styled wristwatch features the crown at 9:00 for easy winding. The hinged pink translucent enamel bezel sets off the blue enameled Roman numerals centering around the small crystal. The sterling silver case was manufactured in England and houses a Swiss movement. 15 jewels.

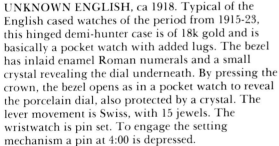

UNKNOWN ENGLISH, ca 1918. Typical of the English cased watches of the period from 1915-23, this hinged demi-hunter case is of 18k gold and is basically a pocket watch with added lugs. The bezel has inlaid enamel Roman numerals and a small crystal revealing the dial underneath. By pressing the crown, the bezel opens as in a pocket watch to reveal the porcelain dial, also protected by a crystal. The lever movement is Swiss, with 15 jewels. The wristwatch is pin set. To engage the setting mechanism a pin at 4:00 is depressed.

ROLEX, 1920s. Hans Wilsdorf established casemaking facilities in England for the Rolex movements he manufactured in Switzerland. This 9k gold case is an example of the English cased watches that Wilsdorf and Davis (W&D) produced during the early 20th century. The dial is porcelain with full Arabic numerals in black, with a red 12. 15 jewels, Swiss movement.

Actually, part of the solution was ready at hand; the hunting case watches already placed the crown at 3:00. Hunter and demi-hunter cases made their way onto the wrist, helping to wean the wearer away from the pocket watch while still giving the familiar protection of the cased watch. The wristwatch crystal clearly needed protection; not only had the watch come out of the pocket, it was now exposed to hazards with every movement of the wearer's wrist. The variations show the effort to bridge the gap between the pocket and the wrist.

The transitional wristwatch is marked by distinctive identifying characteristics in addition to the crown placement and the orientation of the wristwatch on the band. During this period the lugs were soldered to the case, making a change of band very difficult. A distinctive red 12 marks Omega and Rolex wristwatches of the period. Virtually all wristwatches from this period feature Arabic numbers, often elongated to stretch around the dial evoking the languorous feeling of the Art Nouveau period in which these wristwatches were made. A few models are marked with Roman numbers.

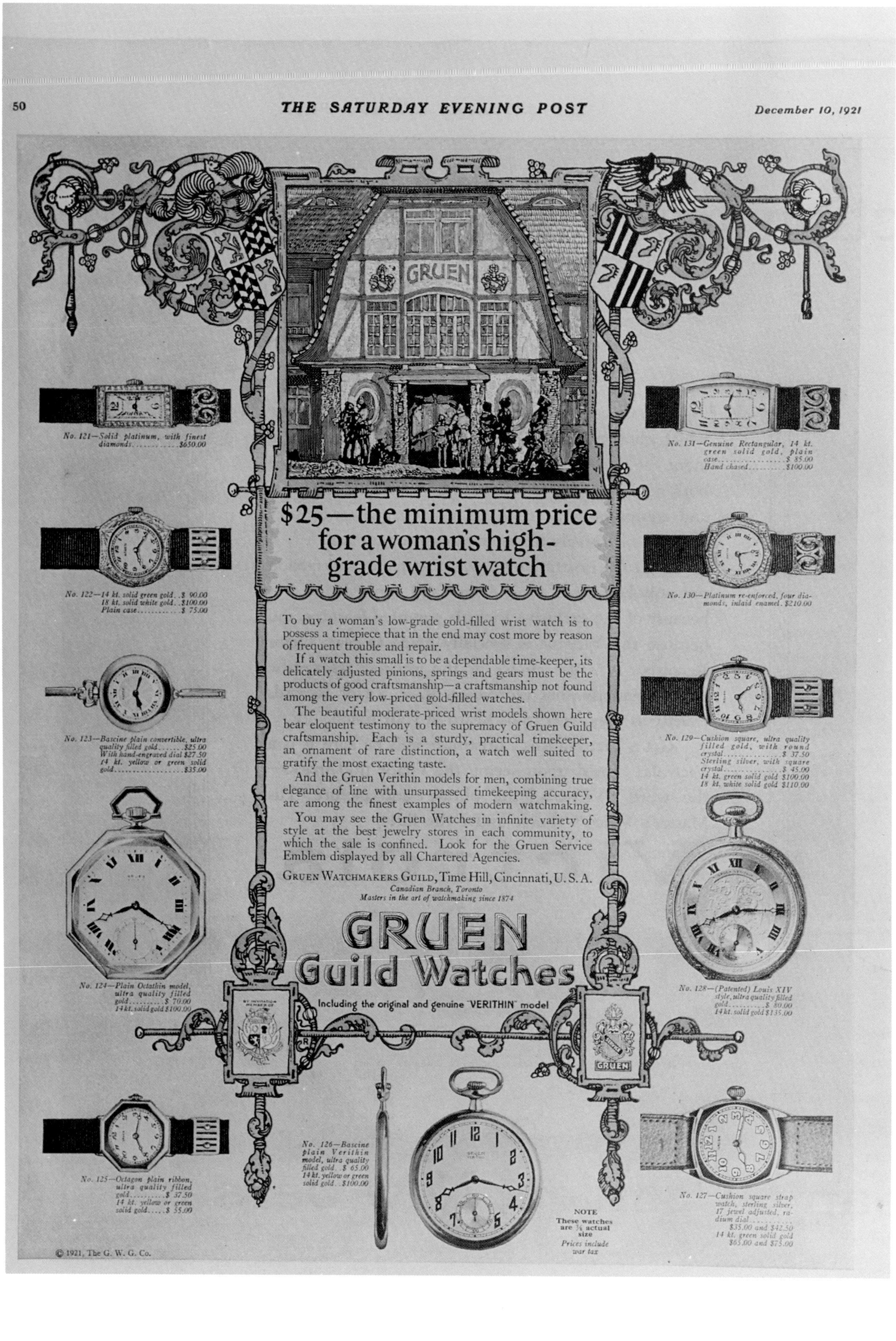

No. 121—Solid platinum, with finest diamonds..........$650.00

No. 122—14 kt. solid green gold..$ 90.00
18 kt. solid white gold..$100.00
Plain case...........$ 75.00

No. 123—Bascine plain convertible, ultra
quality filled gold........$25.00
With hand-engraved dial $27.50
14 kt. yellow or green solid
gold....................$35.00

No. 124—Plain Octathin model,
ultra quality filled
gold............$ 70.00
14 kt. solid gold $100.00

No. 125—Octagon plain ribbon,
ultra quality filled
gold...........$ 37.50
14 kt. yellow or green
solid gold.....$ 55.00

No. 131—Genuine Rectangular, 14 kt.
green solid gold, plain
case.................$ 85.00
Hand chased.........$100.00

No. 130—Platinum re-enforced, four diamonds, inlaid enamel. $210.00

No. 129—Cushion square, ultra quality
filled gold, with round
crystal.................$ 37.50
Sterling silver, with square
crystal.............$ 45.00
14 kt. green solid gold $100.00
18 kt. white solid gold $110.00

No. 128—(Patented) Louis XIV
style, ultra quality filled
gold.............$ 80.00
14 kt. solid gold $135.00

No. 126—Bascine
plain Verithin
model, ultra quality
filled gold..$ 65.00
14 kt. yellow or green
solid gold...$100.00

No. 127—Cushion square strap
watch, sterling silver,
17 jewel adjusted, ra-
dium dial.
$35.00 and $42.50
14 kt. green solid gold
$65.00 and $75.00

NOTE
These watches
are ¾ actual
size
Prices include
war tax

$25—the minimum price for a woman's high-grade wrist watch

To buy a woman's low-grade gold-filled wrist watch is to possess a timepiece that in the end may cost more by reason of frequent trouble and repair.

If a watch this small is to be a dependable time-keeper, its delicately adjusted pinions, springs and gears must be the products of good craftsmanship—a craftsmanship not found among the very low-priced gold-filled watches.

The beautiful moderate-priced wrist models shown here bear eloquent testimony to the supremacy of Gruen Guild craftsmanship. Each is a sturdy, practical timekeeper, an ornament of rare distinction, a watch well suited to gratify the most exacting taste.

And the Gruen Verithin models for men, combining true elegance of line with unsurpassed timekeeping accuracy, are among the finest examples of modern watchmaking.

You may see the Gruen Watches in infinite variety of style at the best jewelry stores in each community, to which the sale is confined. Look for the Gruen Service Emblem displayed by all Chartered Agencies.

GRUEN WATCHMAKERS GUILD, Time Hill, Cincinnati, U.S.A.
Canadian Branch, Toronto
Masters in the art of watchmaking since 1874

GRUEN Guild Watches

Including the original and genuine "VERITHIN" model

© 1921, The G. W. G. Co.

MOVADO, 1920s. This large, tonneau-shaped wristwatch was made for a dealer named Berthoud. The case is of sterling silver and is curved to fit the wrist. The case is held together by four screws in its sides. The stylized Roman numerals conform to the shape of the watch, emphasizing the curves. 17 jewels. Swiss.

LONGINES, 1920s. This bold, stylized Art Nouveau wristwatch has a sterling silver case. A large watch, it features elongated Arabic numerals in black, except for the red 12. This is a good example of the transition from Nouveau to Art Deco styles. Swiss movement, 17 jewels.

No sooner had miniaturization and repositioning the crown been accomplished than the wristwatch manufacturers had to turn their attention to the problem that had inhibited many of them from designing wristwatches in the first place: wristwatches inherently were more subject to wear, to shock, and to dirt, all the hazards that come with increased exposure and affect the accuracy of the timepiece. The need for both shock and water resistance was clear; the solutions were not.

Some solutions were being explored in England and elsewhere in Europe with varying degrees of success. John Harwood, a British soldier during the First World War, devised an automatic winding system to seal the wristwatch more tightly against dirt. His solution was to eliminate the need for the stem and crown used to both wind and set the wristwatch. Harwood experimented with a movable bezel which took the place of a movable crown. Working with an A. Schild movement, by 1926 he had succeeded in making the first truly automatic wristwatch. His success was far from perfection although the cases he made were exquisite and are very desirable today. But an improved system would have to wait until the '30s. The A. Schild movement he used employs a bumper system, bumping from one side to the other. This puts an untenable stress on the movement, inevitably causing problems. Omega also tried a bumper movement which they retained into the 1960s. LeCoultre also used a bumper system.

Many approaches to achieving automatic winding were tried during the period. LeRoi et Cie, a French firm, took the automatic weight movement it used in its pocket watches and fitted it to a wristwatch. Some firms made wristwatches with a hinged flap in the back; as the wrist moved, the flap opened slightly and a gear was wound. But only excessive wrist action could keep this watch wound sufficiently. In 1930, the *Rolls* employed a system in which the dial moved back and forth in response to the movement of the wearer's arm. The *Auto-Wrist*, by Harwood, set its lugs on hinges; the motion of the wrist caused the lugs to move up and down, and in the process, wound the watch. Bulova made an automatic with a hammer and weight system similar to that of LeRoi. But it fell to Rolex to create a truly successful automatic. Rolex used a 360 degree rotor that swiveled both ways to wind the watch.

HARWOOD, 1920s. An example of the
Harwood automatic, the case of this one is
yellow-gold plated.

HARWOOD, 1920s. One of the early automatic
watches, this Harwood has a white gold plated
die struck case with embossing and enamel work
on the bezel and the lugs. The wristwatch was
manufactured in England using modified A.
Schild movements with 17 jewels. The hands are
set by moving the bezel. There is a small round
window above the six that indicates with a red
dot whether the wristwatch is in the winding or
setting mode.

HARWOOD, 1920s. This decorated Harwood
combines several shapes. The decagonal bezel
sits on a tonneau case and surrounds a round
dial. Both the bezel and the case are heavily
embossed gold plate. The dial is also gold
embossed pattern, reflecting the motif of the
bezel. The movement has 17 jewels and is from
A. Schild of Switzerland. This is the first
automatic movement designed for a wristwatch.

OYSTER WATCH COMPANY. The precursor of the Rolex *Oyster* series, this English wristwatch features a 3-piece case with the bezel and back screwing into the body, providing a waterproof seal. This waterproofing is further enhanced by attaching the crown to the body of the wristwatch through a tube. The case is sterling silver with a porcelain dial and Roman numerals. The Rolex *Viceroy* model (the first waterproof chronometer) is very similar to the one shown here. Swiss movement, 15 jewels.

Rolex introduced the *Oyster*, the first water resistant wristwatch, in 1927, contracting the design from the Oyster Watch Company in England. With a screw-in back and crown, plus the automatic movement, the Rolex *Oyster Perpetual*, introduced in 1931, embraces virtually all the technical improvements the wristwatch wearer can ask for...or nearly all.

In addition to design challenges, American manufacturers faced other problems. It was difficult to decide to commit working capital for the new equipment that was needed to successfully miniaturize the wristwatch parts. Many in the American watch industry still saw the wristwatch as a fad, and a passing one at that.

There is no documented moment, similar to the "Dr. Watson, come here" story about the first telephone message, to describe the moment when any of the watch companies decided to turn a pocket watch movement into a wrist model. It is clear that between roughly 1907 and 1914, Elgin, Illinois, Waltham and Hamilton began offering wristwatch adaptations. (By comparison, in 1902, according to contemporary records, 93,000 wristwatches were sold in Germany.)

"There wasn't much to invent about a watch," Paul Graehling says, referring to the pocket watch technology that was available to any firm that had the money to get going. But money was always the problem, and never more so than with Waltham. "They got a few watches out before the Civil War before they went broke. At the close of the Civil War they got on their feet. That was the beginning of all the watch companies. Once Waltham got started, early in the industrial revolution, they grew a lot of good, talented people. Good mechanics like to be associated with good companies. They really refined the industry and the watch making business in America."

Illinois may have been the first American watch company to begin wristwatch production, according to Graehling. He estimates they produced a total of 820,000 wristwatches from the beginning, about 1905, until 1933. Working with an 0/size pendant watch movement, Illinois simply adapted a lug on the opposite side of the wristwatch, the way Waltham did with its *Disappearing Eye*.

WALTHAM, 1920s. This gold filled wristwatch has solid lugs at the 12:00 and 6:00 positions. The bulbous crown is at three o'clock and the enamel painted dial has a subsidiary seconds chapter at 6:00. While its shape is still strongly influenced by the pocket watch, it has made some significant steps toward being a genuine wristwatch. 7-jeweled Waltham movement.

Gruen, one of America's premier watch companies, advertised its *Wristlet* watch in 1912 issues of the weekly *Saturday Evening Post.* Capitalizing on what they recognized as a real trend, Gruen's wristwatch sat sideways on the wrist, the band sections affixed at the 3:00 and 9:00 positions, with the winding stem at 12:00. There is no understanding or acceptance of the need to re-orient the dial to make it easier for the numbers to be read when the watch is positioned on the wrist. One had to be a contortionist to read the time, but the concept was moving ahead, spurred on by Gruen's recognition of the trend. "All Europe is wearing them now and their practicability and convenience, as well as their beauty, are rapidly making them the most popular watch in America."

Gruen also showed its *Veri-Thin* pocket watch; it used a new design in escapements which permitted the movement to be compressed to half its former height. It would take another engineering effort to reduce the dimensions of the pocket watch movement to suit a wristwatch, but efforts were already underway.

No sooner had the American watch industry begun to work seriously on wristwatches than many of its prominent makers, along with many other industries, were called on to convert to war production. Although Europe had faced the same challenge even earlier than the Americans, the Swiss who were already preeminent in wristwatch manufacture, were officially neutral during the war, and were able to continue their regular production at the expense of the emerging American wristwatch industry. This gave them a distinct, though momentary advantage.

European manufacturers had taken the lead in experimenting with case design. Movado developed an elliptical dial and then, about 1912, it addressed the real challenge of designing to fit the wrist and anticipated Gruen's celebrated *Curvex* by two decades. Its *Polyplan,* a three-part movement curved to fit the natural curve of the wrist, was an attempt to re-shape the interior, to move the wristwatch's vital organs into a line rather than arranged in the familiar round. A new case was designed that followed the same three-part plan, but the crown remained at the 12:00 position.

ILLINOIS, ca 1918. A lady's 14k gold convertible watch in its original presentation box, it has a matching bracelet. The dial is enamel painted, and the 6/0 movement has fifteen jewels.

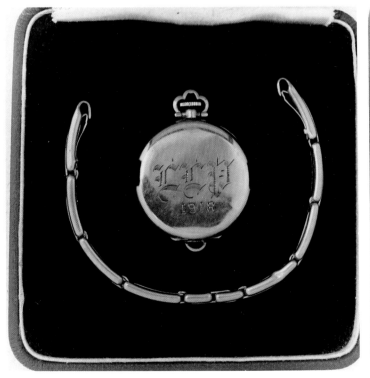

1920s. This unique wristwatch has a German case formed from a military medal. The round dial has Roman numerals, with the XII colored red. The hands are blued steel. 15 jewels.

Much of the Swiss production was "cottage industry" with small groups of skilled workers making one particular part and supplying it to a number of watchmakers. Because the Swiss used this method, the American industry was able to develop after the First World War and overtake the Swiss in the American market during this period. American production techniques saved the industry, but this story of war, neutrality, and wristwatch production in Switzerland would repeat itself during the Second World War, with very different results. By then, Switzerland had changed over to mass production techniques as well. After the Second World War, America never regained the wristwatch manufacturing industry it had before the war.

While America was still struggling to make a wristwatch in the quantities the market required, the Swiss were well ahead in styling and design. By 1912, Vacheron & Constantin had a variety of wristwatch styles with the crown placed at 3:00, and the watch turned 90 degrees so that the 12:00 and 6:00 positions coincided with the placement of the band sections. In this position, the dial could be easily read. Rolex in 1914 had also moved to this configuration, as indeed had the Swiss watch industry in general. Rolex leapt into wristwatches vigorously. By 1910 according to Ken Specht, Rolex, which was founded by Hans Wilsdorf in 1905, had obtained the world's first official timing certificate for a wrist chronometer.

During this period, the culmination of the Edwardian age, European wristwatches featured the styling ideas that were the hallmark of dress, jewelry and ornamentation of all types. Patek Philippe's production from the teens included models with diamond set, lacy, openwork bands that epitomized the airy designs of the period. But these designs had solid underpinnings. Technological advances had enabled designers to pierce metal with precision, and set it with myriad, small gems.

SWISS, 1920s. Dramatic in its oval shape, this 14k gold wristwatch takes its style from the Art Nouveau period. The enamel painted dial, correctly refinished features luminous Nouveau Arabic numerals. 17 jewels, Swiss movement.

OMEGA, ca 1920s. The cushion case of this wristwatch is of sterling silver and has solid lugs. The dial is enamel painted. Both the case and movement are Swiss. 17 jewels.

ROLEX, 1920s. A graceful, small man's watch, this Rolex was cased in England for the English market. The tonneau-shaped case is of 14k white gold and has a solid lug. The dial features highly stylized Roman numerals and stylized arrow hands that complement the overall design. 15 jewel, Swiss movement.

OMEGA, 1918-20. The hexagonal case of this Swiss wristwatch is in 18k gold. The enamel painted dial has Nouveau styled Arabic numerals. 17-jeweled Swiss movement.

OMEGA, ca 1918. A most unusual and beautiful wristwatch, this Omega is an early example of the use of juxtaposed shapes in design. A square dial is set within a round bezel, while the overall case is tonneau-shaped and rises cone-like to the bezel. The Swiss case is hinged and has solid lugs. The dial is porcelain with Roman numerals fired into it. 17 jewels, Swiss movement.

SOPRA, ca 1920. The bold black and white dial of this Swiss wristwatch resembles the railroad style both in the use of large, unadorned numbers and in overall design. The Arabic numerals and minutes chapter stand out against a black background. The center of the wristwatch is white, as is the subsidiary seconds chapter. The case is chrome plated and has solid wire lugs and a fluted winding crown.

PATEK PHILIPPE, ca 1908. The hinged bezel of this lady's wristwatch is serrated. The case is 18k gold with an 18k gold expansion bracelet. The Arabic numerals are all circled in gold to bring out the stylized porcelain dial. Swiss movement, 15 jewels.

The European influence on wristwatches was in technology as well as design. Their models made those of the American firms look exactly like what they were: tentative forays into a strange new world. The American output looked naïve and unsophisticated, more straightforward. Design was secondary to technology in the United States. As Henry Ford was fond of saying of his auto production, "You can have any color as long as it's black."

While the Europeans had already begun to grapple with designing a specific wristwatch movement, the American wristwatch had yet to make the leap from modified pocket model to the genuine article, a movement completely redesigned to suit the size, shape and action of the wrist. The transitional period covered two major leaps: the watch came out of the pocket and moved onto the wrist, and the wristwatch that was first developed in Europe made the transition across the ocean to America. Now the watch manufacturers could devote themselves to improving both the inside and the outside of these timepieces.

By the 1920s, the American wristwatch industry was in full swing and was overwhelming the Europeans in the American market. The American wristwatch had achieved variety, design, and quality. When we solved the problems inherent in the transition, we entered one of the great periods of design. The Europeans remained in a refined, rather staid mode; the Americans jumped into the excitement of Art Deco. They were able to translate the same elements that made them successful at the end of the 19th century. Using individualized case-makers and huge movement facilities, they put together endless varieties of well-made, attractive wristwatches, and responded quickly to the ever-changing demands of style. Design had caught up with technology. It was the dawn of the decorative period in wristwatches.

BLANCPAIN, ca 1910. This attractive wristwatch is a precursor of the decorative period. Its 14k gold case is in an octagon shape with engraving on the bezel and an integrated, pierced link bracelet. The dial is a sunburst design. Swiss movement, 15 jewels.

AUDEMARS PIGUET, ca 1915. Calibrated French-cut sapphires surround the diamond-set rectangular bezel of this platinum wristwatch. 8 ligne, 18-jeweled movement.

Chapter Two
The Decorative Period
1925-1936

The end of the First World War marked the end of America's isolation from the world, the end of the first phase of the industrial revolution, and the beginning of the end of the pocket watch. The pocket watch continued to outsell the newfangled wristwatch until about 1929 but the acceptance of the wristwatch by the soldier in the trenches of Europe set the scene for a timepiece that was in step with the other changes taking place in style, in society, and in manufacturing.

"The war to end all wars" wrought undeniable changes in American design; everything soft and tender that was epitomized by the look of Art Nouveau came to an abrupt end. The nation, and its products, took on a thoroughly modern and hard-edged look. The tendrils and curves of the first decade of the 20th century gave way to the glorious design period known to us as "Art Deco". This short, catchy name was derived from *L'Exposition des Arts Decoratifs*, an international fair held in Paris in 1925.

Curves were out, geometry was in. In jewelry, the freeing up of materials that had been restricted for use by the war effort combined with technology to create the brilliant pieces that so summed up this period. Platinum, strong and sleek, formed the settings for tiny, calibre-cut gems. The look extended to the spare, boyish dress of the flappers, the sophistication of black and white.

The sources of the ornamentation of the period were several. Prime among them was the opening of the tomb of King Tutankhamen in Egypt in 1922. This widely reported event was the sensation of the early 1920s and with it came a mania for anything that looked remotely Egyptian. These motifs came to be incorporated into all ornamental products. Turquoise and coral, colors associated with the artifacts found in the tomb, were used extensively during the period. In jewelry and on wristwatch bezels, these colors were represented by gems or by enamels.

Oriental motifs, especially Chinese carvings in mother of pearl, jade and other gemstones, were bought up in huge lots and incorporated into Cartier's Deco period jewelry and *objets d'art*. Carved rubies, emeralds and sapphires from India created the "fruit basket" motif, as well as the technicolor look of jewelry. These and other design influences came to bear on the wristwatch.

African motifs were strongly imitated in the cubist paintings of the period. Sharp edges in art and architecture were echoed in the sharp and jazzy syncopations of the music of the time. The 77-story Chrysler Building in New York City was stylized as magnificent Art Deco structure. It was the American age in music and George Gershwin's "Rhapsody in Blue" set the tone.

In the American wristwatch, modern methods permitted mass production of these precise designs so as to keep prices within the reach of many. The

ELGIN, ca 1929. The extreme Art Deco design of Elgin's *Parisienne* is by Callot. It features black and white enamel on a 14k gold case, and is set with two diamonds. A rare and sought after wristwatch. Elgin movement, 15 jewels.

SWISS, 1920s. A group of highly decorative lady's wristwatches exported to the United States from Switzerland to compete with American Companies to fill the growing U.S. demand for enamel styled watches. The cases are of silver, gold, or steel.

GRUEN, 1920s. Both the bezel and the case of this 14k white gold filled wristwatch are inlaid with polychrome enamel. A chain of black and green enamel encircles the case while triangles surround the dial. White enamel painted dial with luminous Arabic numerals. 17 jewels, Swiss movement.

GRUEN, 1920s. The Deco period is evoked in this cut-corner rectangular wristwatch with an oval dial. The white gold filled die struck case is embossed and has a decorative enamel bezel. The crown has an inlaid sapphire. The enamel painted dial has an oval minutes chapter surrounded by an hours chapter with highly stylized Arabic numerals. Swiss movement, 15 jewels.

GRUEN, ca 1926. Part of the Gruen *Guild* series, this Precision is in 18k white gold. The bezel is set with four diamonds and sapphires. These surround an oval engraved dial. 17 jewels. This is an example of a high-fashion jeweled lady's wristwatch. A grosgrain ribbon band attaches to fixed wire lugs. Swiss movement, 15 jewels.

ELGIN, ca 1928. The *Madame Alpha* features a 14k white gold-filled embossed case with monochrome enamel on the bezel. The dial is enamel painted with a decorative center design. The case is by Illinois Watch Case Company and houses an Elgin movement with 15 jewels. Rare.

ELGIN, Ca. 1928. The case of the Elgin *Madame Premet*, Model 103, was made by the Illinois Watch Case Company and is 14k white gold filled. The rectangular case houses a dial in the shape of a parallelogram. The case was available with different colored enamel designs on the bezel. Elgin movement, 15 jewels. (Courtesy Aaron Faber Gallery)

GRUEN, 1920s. This rectangular 14k gold filled lady's wristwatch has an embossed bezel with an attached 14k gold filled band. The enamel painted dial is also embossed with a floral design around the oval hours chapter. Swiss movement, 15 jewels.

ELGIN, ca 1929. The white gold filled case of this Elgin features an orange and cobalt blue enamel geometric design. Created by Lucien Lelong, it was advertised in the *Ladies Home Journal* in 1929. The case is by the Illinois Watch Company. It has 7 jewels.

GRUEN, 1920s. Geometric enamel motifs decorate a 14k gold die struck case. It is rectangular and has embossing on the bezel and sides. The dial is square with full Arabic numerals and an inside minute track. 15 jeweled Swiss movement.

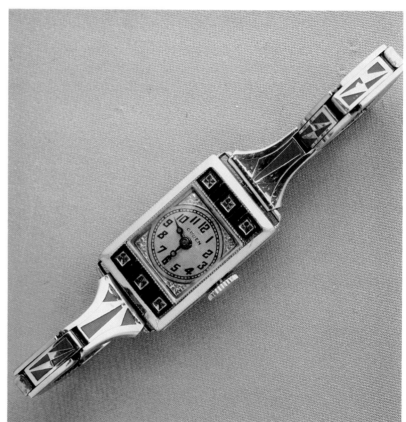

GRUEN, 1920s. This 14k gold rectangular case holds a round enamel painted dial. At the lug ends of the case, black enamel forms the setting for six diamonds, three at each end. The link bracelet is enameled in orange. Swiss movement, 15 jewels.

ELGIN, 1920s. This gold filled tonneau case has die struck embossing and multi-colored enamel work. The movement has 15 jewels.

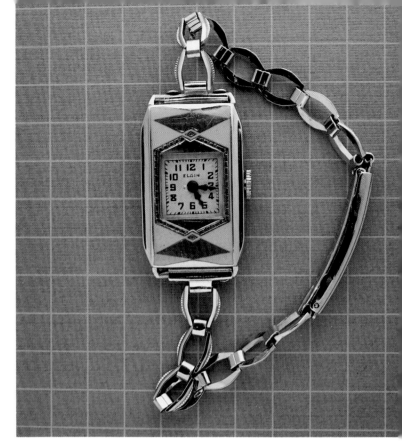

ELGIN, ca 1930. This lady's wristwatch has a gold filled case with turquoise enamel geometric patterns made by the Illinois Watch Case Company, and an attached band. 15 jewels.

WALTHAM, 1920s. Stripes of turquoise and black enamel decorate the embossed gold filled case of this lady's watch. The cut-corner octagonal case houses a square dial. 17-jeweled Waltham movement.

ELGIN, ca 1928. An inlaid enamel bezel adorns this 14k gold rectangular case. The sterling silver dial has an unusual design for the minutes chapter. The square it forms within the rectangular dial includes the 2,3,4,8,9, and 10 numerals within and leaves the others outside its perimeter. 15 jewels.

ELGIN, 1925. The Elgin *Lady 'N Tiger* was designed by Lucien Lelong. The embossed design features enamel figures on the bezel. This 14k white gold case is by the Illinois Watch Case Company. A rare yellow gold case also exists. This 15mm x 25mm wristwatch has 15 jewels. It is very rare. (Courtesy: Time Will Tell)

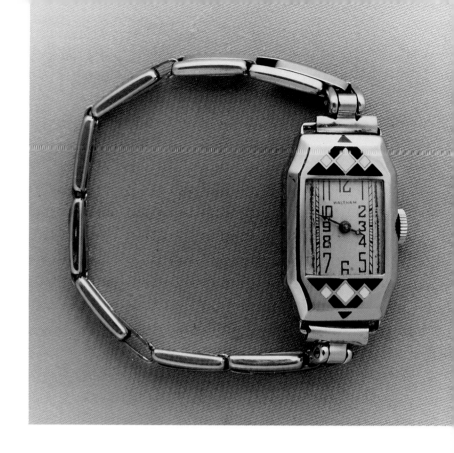

WALTHAM, 1920s. This lady's wristwatch is decorated with diamond and triangular enameled sections forming pyramids at the top and bottom of the bezel. The case is 14k gold filled. 17 jewels.

The Waltham movement does not belong in this case, as is apparent by the way the minutes chapter is lost. Obviously this was recased after manufacture.

ELGIN, ca 1928. The *Lanvin 104* features a visually dramatic inlaid enamel bezel on the gold filled case, framing an unusual hexagonal dial with an outer minutes chapter. Star Case Company manufactured the case. 7 jewels.

ELGIN, ca 1928. The diamond-shaped dial of this *Madame Agnes* model is very unusual for the period. The case is 14k white gold filled with copper enameled designs on the bezel. 15 jewels.

HARWOOD, 1920s. Developed by John Harwood, this was the first automatic winding wristwatch. It uses a 17 jewel A. Schild Swiss movement with a bumper style rotor. The rotating bezel is used to set the hands. The red dot on the dial indicates whether the movement is in the winding or setting position. The case is gold plated with embossed lugs.

BENRUS, 1920s. Embossing decorates this rectangular 14k gold-filled case. The dial is a modified octagon with a minutes chapter and gold Arabic numerals. Swiss movement, 15 jewels.

ELGIN, 1920s. This rare 14k gold-filled die stamped case features figures of mermaids and seahorses on the bezel. A rectangular enamel painted dial is set in a tonneau case. 15 jewels.

SWISS, 1920s. The die struck case of this wristwatch is of base metal with applied gold belts over the lugs. There is embossing on the bezel. Swiss movement, 15 jewels.

LONGINES, 1920s. The round dial is set within the tonneau gold filled case. There is an enameled bezel with a ring of engraving around the dial. The dial features stylized Arabic numerals in the hours chapter, an outer minutes chapter, and a subsidiary seconds chapter. 17 jewels, Swiss movement.

BENRUS, 1920s-30s. The elaborate embossed gold filled case is typical of the period. The hinged case has curved lugs. The dial is a cut-corner rectangle with outlined painted luminous numbers and luminous skeleton hands. 15 jewels, Swiss movement.

GRUEN, 1920s. The highly stylized dial of the Gruen Precision captures the spirit of the Deco period. The case is 14k gold with an embossed bezel. It has oval hours and minutes chapters set within the overall rectangular shape of the watch. Swiss, 15 jeweled movement.

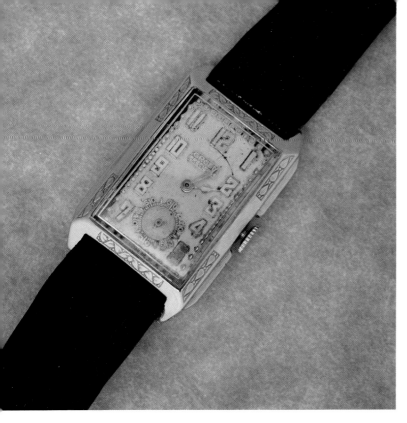

GRUEN, ca 1928. A fine example of a 1920s Gruen wristwatch, it uses bold numerals and a large subsidiary seconds chapter on its enamel painted dial. The 14k white gold die-struck embossed case houses a 17-jeweled Swiss movement.

BULOVA, 1930s. Although not particularly rare, this design is very sought after by collectors. The gold filled tank case is slightly curved, with a step form and an embossed motif along the sides of the bezel. The enamel painted dial is white with applied Arabic numerals. The 10AX Swiss movement has 15 jewels.

GRUEN, 1920s. An embossed bezel highlights this rectangular gold-filled Gruen. The enamel painted dial has outlined Arabic numerals and skeleton hands. 15 jeweled Swiss movement.

ELGIN, 1920s. This two-toned 14k gold-filled case features embossing in white gold-filled in a rope pattern on the bezel. The remainder of the case is yellow gold-filled. The enamel painted dial features highly stylized Arabic numerals and an outer minutes track. 15 jewels.

ELGIN, 1920s. This 14k gold die struck case features embossing and enamel. The enamel painted dial features decorative designs in gold. 17 jewels.

ELGIN, 1920s. This Elgin Model 401 features a chromium plated nickel case, with a round dial. The corners of the bezel and the sides of the case are decorated with embossing in the deco style. The dial has Arabic numerals and a subsidiary seconds chapter at 6:00. The Elgin movement has 7 jewels.

ELGIN, 1920s. This 14k wristwatch is highly decorated with an embossed bezel and lugs. The movement is Elgin, 17 jewels.

GRUEN, ca 1928. This square 14k gold case has embossing around the bezel. The numerals are luminous and silhouetted. The case by Gruen and the 17 jewel movement is Swiss. (Courtesy Time Will Tell)

ELGIN, 1920s. This is one of the finest overall examples of the Elgin wristwatch. The embossed case is by the Illinois Watch Case Company. On the dial, Arabic numerals follow the shape of the bezel, which is repeated again in the round seconds chapter. This rare and beautiful wristwatch is a fine example of the Deco period. Elgin movement, 15 jewels.

detailed cases with their chased bezels and edges, and sometimes backs, were made possible by die striking. This method, also known as stamping, allowed the designers to enhance cases with sharply incised, ornate engraving. It also compresses the metal used, for a sleek, dense look unobtainable by other metalsmithing techniques.

The transitional period was clearly over; these wristwatches broke the ties to the pocket watches that had spawned them. The proof was in the shapes. A pocket watch was always round but wristwatches embraced all shapes. They were squared, stretched into rectangles both long and wide. They were pulled wider at the middle, sliced into hexagons, anything, it would seem, but round. In fact, there were round watches made during this period, but they bear the other distinctive style elements that mark them as wristwatches of the decorative rather than the transitional period.

HAMILTON, ca. 1928. Oval case, 14k white gold. 17-jewel movement. (Courtesy of Aaron Faber)

ELGIN, 1930s. The dial of this Elgin Model 1602 is two-toned and has an outer minutes track, an hours chapter with stylized Arabic numerals and a subsidiary seconds chapter. The tonneau-shaped case is 14k gold. 15 jewels. (Courtesy Time Will Tell)

GRUEN, 1920s. The hinged, square case of this Gruen Precision has extended lugs and is decorated with black enamel on the bezel. The dial is enamel painted with an outer minute track and Arabic numerals. 17 jeweled Swiss movement.

BENRUS, 1920s. This rectangular case has a round enameled bezel containing the hours chapter. It is rolled gold plate and has decorative embossing on the lugs. There are four open triangles between the bezel and the rectangular case. The Swiss movement has 17 jewels.

ELGIN, ca 1931. The stylized Arabic numerals of the hours chapter are on the enameled bezel of the white gold-filled case. The tonneau shape is echoed on the enamel painted dial which has a minutes chapter and subsidiary seconds chapter. 15 jeweled Elgin movement.

ELGIN, 1920s. The chrome plated case is by Osco Quality Watch Case Company. It has an engraved, inlaid enamel bezel which is highly unusual. It is one of approximately ten enameled-bezel designs of the late '20s that have become necessities for the serious American collector. 7 jewels.

ELGIN, Ca. 1931. The Elgin *Clubman* has a wide tonneau case with embossing on the bezel. The case was manufactured by the Illinois Watch Case Company and is 14k gold filled. The dial has hours, minutes, and subsidiary seconds chapters. 17 jewel Elgin movement.

INGRAHAM, late-1920s. Embossed tonneau case and dial, matching bracelet. Pin-lever movement. (Courtesy of Harry Stecker)

DUEBER HAMPDEN, 1920s. This 14k gold filled tonneau case has a decorative enameled bezel. The dial has an hours chapter between two minutes tracks, and uses blue steel hands. 15 jewels, Hampden movement.

BENRUS, 1920s. This unusual case is rolled gold plate and features a
white enamel bezel with black numerals for the hours chapter. The lugs
are decorated with enamel. The crown ends with a synthetic sapphire.
The dial has a minutes chapter and a subsidiary seconds chapter. The
Swiss movement has 7 jewels.

GRUEN, 1920s. One of the only entries by Gruen into the decorative
enameled bezel era. This 14k yellow gold square wristwatch is rare and
desirable as an American collectible. Swiss movement, 17 jewels.

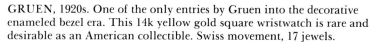

PATEK PHILIPPE, 1920s. Made for Tiffany & Co.,
as marked on the dial, this wristwatch has an 18k
gold hinged case. The enamel painted dial has
luminous Arabic numerals and skeleton hands.
Subsidiary seconds chapter above 6:00. 18-jeweled
Swiss movement.

Round or rectangular, square or tonneau, these wristwatches had one characteristic in common: the solid lug, a continuous wire to which the strap attached. Not until the late '20s or early '30s was the spring bar developed, a fiendishly simple improvement that permits a new strap to be attached in seconds. Until then straps were made with open ends, which allowed the strap to slip through the solid lug, wrap around and be closed. Closing the strap required a rivet, or two steel pins that came out from one side of it, went through two slits, and then were bent over so the strap was secured to the wristwatch.

Although the term "digital" is associated with the quartz wristwatch of the '70s, the ancestor of this style was developed in the '20s. One catalogue of the day called them "Handless Chronoscopes". Essentially the watch manufacturers substituted discs with numbers on them for the more familiar hands. As the discs revolved, the hours, minutes and sometimes seconds would show in windows on the dial. The hour window would expose three hours, the minute cut-out five or ten minutes. These digitals proved very difficult to read and remained a novelty. With an analog watch, the hands "tell" the time as an image that needs no further translation by the brain. But the mechanical digital required that extra step. The eyes took in the numbers, then sent the information to the brain to be assembled into the time. Still, watch companies from the most prestigious such as Patek Philippe and Audemars to the mass market such as Bulova made digital models.

The exquisite analog dials of early '20s wristwatches were of porcelain, a very durable and beautiful material. Except in extreme temperature changes, hot or cold, when the porcelain can craze or crack, porcelain dials were very durable, although they remained vulnerable on the wrist. Most were white, though a few were black.

ELGIN, 1920s. This cushion-shaped Elgin is decorated with embossing around the sides of the gold filled die struck case. The black enamel painted dial contrasts dramatically with the gold Arabic numerals, hands and subsidiary seconds chapter. The Elgin movement has 15 jewels.

BULOVA, 1920s. The highly stylized 14k gold filled stepped case of this mechanical digital wristwatch has embossed bezel and lugs. The 17 jewel Swiss movement turns three enamel painted discs which reveal hours, minutes and seconds through their respective windows.

BULOVA

T-A-T MADDUX PLANES

BULOVA presents *The Sky King—Standard Bearer in the New Winter Presentation!*

The Sky King is named in honor of a great event — for now all T. A. T. Maddux Planes, flying in conjunction with the Pennsylvania Railroad, spanning the continent in forty-eight hours, fly via Bulova time.

The
SKY
KING
$42.50
17 JEWELS

THE PRESIDENT: 17-jewel; curved to fit the wrist; beautifully engraved; smart link band $50.00

ENVOY: 15-jewel; radium dial; neat, popular shape, smart woven mesh band $24.75

SKY KING: The handsomely engraved two-tone case is enhanced by a link band to match. 17-jewel, radium dial . . . $42.50

BY NIGHT
PENNSYLVANIA RAILROAD
BY DAY
T. A. T. MADDUX PLANES

San Francisco
Fresno
Bakersfield
Los Angeles
San Diego   Albuquerque   Clovis
Agua Caliente
Wichita
Waynoka

LISTEN NIGHTLY FOR BULOVA RADIO TIME ANNOUNCEMENTS

A colorful advertisement of unusual beauty, introduces the Bulova Sky King in t... will dominate the issue! It will hold the attention of every reader — and t...

WATCHES

FLY ON BULOVA TIME

This great air lane, mapped out by Colonel Charles A. Lindbergh, Chairman, Technical Committee, T. A. T.; Consulting Aeronautical Engineer Pennsylvania Railroad, now has all its planes equipped with Bulova timepieces.

See The Sky King at your Jewelers—and the many other smart new Bulova watches with bands or bracelets to match. Priced from $25 to $2500, they vary in price only as they vary in design. They are alike in dependability.

BULOVA WATCH COMPANY, FIFTH AVENUE, NEW YORK
In Canada, Sterling Tower, Toronto

LONG EAGLE: 15-jewel; radium dial; handsomely engraved; flexible link band to match $37.50

MISS AMERICA: 15-jewel; 4 simulated sapphires or emeralds; flexible bracelet . . $37.50

ISOBEL: 15-jewel set with 2 diamonds, 4 simulated sapphires $49.50

New York
Philadelphia
Baltimore
Pittsburgh
Columbus
Washington
Indianapolis
St. Louis
Kansas City
Norfolk

BY NIGHT
PENNSYLVANIA RAILROAD

BY DAY
T. A. T. MADDUX PLANES

LISTEN NIGHTLY FOR BULOVA RADIO TIME ANNOUNCEMENTS

...ber 18th issue of the Saturday Evening Post. Here is an advertisement that ...ns about fifteen million persons, or one out of every ten people in America.

ILLINOIS, 1930s. Called the *Speedway*, both the bezel and lugs of this wristwatch are embossed. The wide tonneau-shaped case is 14k gold filled. The hands and numerals are luminous and there is a subsidiary seconds hand at 6:00. A 15 jewel manual wind movement powers the watch.

ILLINOIS, ca 1929. This *Ensign* model is in 14k yellow gold filled, though the design was also available in white gold filled. The case has an unusual tonneau shape that is almost hexagonal, and is embossed on the bezel and sides. The enamel painted dial has luminous hands and a subsidiary seconds chapter which reflects the tonneau shape of the case. 15-jeweled, 601 grade, 6/0 size Illinois movement.

ILLINOIS, ca. 1928, the *Bennett*. This modified octagonal wristwatch was made in 14k white or yellow gold filled, and has embossing on the bezel. The enamel painted dial has luminous hands and a subsidiary seconds chapter at 9:00. The 6/0 movement is a 907 grade and has 19 jewels. (Courtesy Dr. Jerry Solin)

A singular element of '20s dials were the numbers and hands which glowed in the dark, especially attractive to the period's night club goers. These spectral touches, whether green, white or yellow, owed their glow to radium. While safe and convenient to those who wear these wristwatches, it was a tragedy of the watch industry that the deadly effects of radium were not known at the time workers were applying the solution to the dials. Many workers' deaths resulted from its use.

The look of the period spread quickly around the world. In part this is due to the growing influence of radio. Though not a visual medium, its programming and advertisements had a strong influence on listeners, establishing styles, setting trends, and bringing recognition to brandnames. The other public factor in spreading the Art Deco look was motion pictures. In 1926, a weekly audience of 100 million flocked to the nation's movie houses to see newsreels along with two feature films. Styles became truly international, thanks to this powerful communications medium.

It was an age looking for heroes and there was none more widely recognized than Charles Lindbergh. In 1927, barely a quarter century after the Wright Brothers' first flight, Lindbergh flew non-stop from New York to Paris, and into the pages of history. He was flooded with presents including more pocket watches than he had pockets for. It was Bulova, however, that received his endorsement and was able to market the Lindbergh wristwatch. (See ad on pages 48 and 49)

Marketing and advertising were becoming American institutions and were more and more important to a product's success or failure. Mechanically, there was little to distinguish the wristwatches produced by the companies that were active during this period. Movements were basic, and basically the same. Because cases were produced by specialized case-makers at the direction of the watch firms, the quality was fairly constant across the industry. As Paul Graehling says, "It wasn't the art of making

BULOVA, ca 1927. This rectangular case has embossed rope patterns on the bezel and lugs. This rare example is 14k white gold. Typically the case was produced in gold filled. The dial has luminous numerals and hands with a subsidiary seconds chapter at six o'clock. Swiss movement, 15 jewels.

BULOVA, 1930s. An unusual round case stepped at the top and bottom surrounds a horizontal tonneau-shaped dial. The case is gold filled and the enamel painted dial is two-toned. The hours chapter has Arabic numerals at 12, 3, 6, and 9 surrounded by a minutes chapter. Swiss movement, 15 jewels.

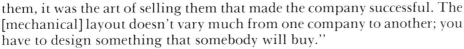

them, it was the art of selling them that made the company successful. The [mechanical] layout doesn't vary much from one company to another; you have to design something that somebody will buy."

After creating a good design, the challenge was to bring it to the public's attention in a consistent and continuous way. With enough repetitions, the name began to take on an image quite separate from the quality of the product. In the beginning, there was certainly nothing to differentiate the mechanism of the Bulova wristwatch from the Elgin, Waltham or Illinois product. It was essentially a round ebauche.

Bulova had come into the watch business quite by accident, according to one former employee. Joseph Bulova was a small jewelry maker located on Maiden Lane, in New York's old jewelry district. He had on staff a street-smart office boy from Brooklyn, John H. Ballard, who had come to work for Bulova at the age of fourteen. In payment of a bad debt, Bulova accepted a quantity of watches and young Ballard persuaded Bulova to let him try to sell them. After successfully disposing of them, he urged Bulova to buy more and more, and eventually to put the Bulova name on the watches in the early 1920s. Ballard became first a salesman, then sales manager, and ultimately president of Bulova for nearly three decades. He remained with the firm into the Accutron era. According to Haskell Titchell, Bulova's long-time public relations director, Ballard and Arde Bulova (Joseph's son) worked as an incomparable duo. "Arde Bulova made the product, John Ballard sold the product. They were equally responsible for the success of the company."

It was also Ballard who persuaded Joseph Bulova to change the firm's distribution method. Rather than selling through middlemen, which was customary, he sold directly to retailers. He split the savings with the merchants, giving them a bigger profit when they sold a Bulova watch, and applied Bulova's portion of the savings to advertising. When Arde Bulova

BULOVA, 1920s-30s. This gold filled die stamped case features an embossed, stepped bezel and a hinged case. The dial features a window with a digital seconds display. The movement is Swiss and uses 17 jewels.

THE SATURDAY EVENING POST   June 28, 1930

BULOVA

PRESIDENT
$50
17 JEWELS

THE PRESIDENT: A man's watch of unusual beauty. 17 jewels. Curved to fit the wrist. A beautiful engraved motif distinguishes the watch and its smart link band. A handsome ensemble—$50.00

...*If* you appreciate beautiful things
be sure to see the *new Bulova Presentation*

The new showing of Bulova models by your jeweler is more than a presentation. It is a *style event!*

There are many new, smart models from which to choose—each with its flexible band or bracelet specially designed to complete the ensemble.

For the man, there is the handsome Bulova President . . . for the lady, the exquisite Miss America . . . standard-bearers in the most extensive presentation of models ever offered by your jeweler.

But never forget that Bulova beauty is only outward evidence of dependability within. Whether you pay $25 or $2500, Bulova Watches vary in price as they vary in design. Each is a trustworthy timepiece.

BULOVA WATCH COMPANY,   FIFTH AVENUE, NEW YORK   In Canada: Sterling Tower, Toronto

RONA: 15 jewel movement; exquisitely engraved; mesh band to match $24.75

MISS LIBERTY: 15 jewel, 6 simulated sapphires or emeralds; flexible bracelet to match $37.50

BULOVA OBSERVATORY

ATOP 580 FIFTH AVENUE
New York . . .

FEATURED   BY   THE   BETTER   JEWELERS . . . EVERYWHERE

THE SATURDAY EVENING POST · June 28, 1930

WATCHES

ENVOY: 15 jewel; radium dial; popular shape; smart woven mesh band to match **$24.75**

BANKER: 15 jewel movement; radium dial; smart woven mesh band to match **$24.75**

CYRANO: 15 jewel; radium dial; inlaid enamel case; woven mesh band **$29.75**

BRUNSWICK: 15 jewel; handsomely engraved; flexible link band to match . . **$29.75**

AMBASSADOR: 15 jewel; handsomely engraved; radium dial; flexible band . . . **$37.50**

LONE EAGLE: 15 jewel; radium dial; handsomely engraved; flexible link band . . . **$37.50**

TREASURER: 17 jewel; richly engraved; inlaid with enamel; mesh band to match **$42.50**

SPENCER: 17 jewel; radium dial; curved to fit wrist; wafer thin; flexible link band **$60.00**

Ladies' Sports Watches

COLLEGIATE: 15 jewel; radium dial; beautifully engraved; flexible link band **$29.75**

Broadcasting stations nation-wide bring B·U·L·O·V·A time signals to you

WELLSLEY: 15 jewel; radium dial; enamel inlaid; curved to fit wrist; leather strap **$37.50**

LISTEN NIGHTLY FOR BULOVA RADIO TIME ANNOUNCEMENTS

BULOVA, 1930s. This tonneau case has an embossed bezel and lugs. It has a subsidiary seconds chapter at 6:00 and an outer minutes chapter. The Swiss movement has 17 jewels.

BULOVA, 1930s. This 10k gold-filled case features embossing and enamel work. It has an enamel painted dial with a subsidiary seconds chapter. The movement is Swiss, 17 jewels. (Courtesy Time Will Tell)

BULOVA, 1920s-30s. The ribbed lugs and embossed bezel adorn the cushion-shaped, gold-filled case of the Bulova *Excellency*. The dial has a subsidiary seconds chapter, hours and minutes chapters. 17 jewels, Swiss movement. (Courtesy Time Will Tell)

BULOVA, ca 1929. This good example of the Deco case features yellow gold-filled trim on a white gold-filled, die struck case. The square dial features a subsidiary seconds chapter at 6:00.

BULOVA, 1920s. This gold filled rectangular wristwatch has a hinged case with an embossed bezel. The hands and numerals are luminous. 17 jewels, Swiss movement.

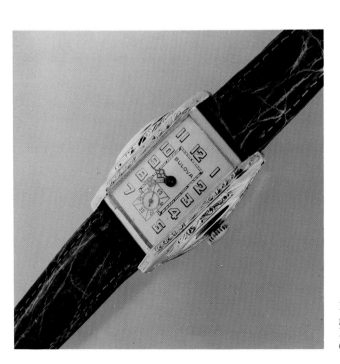

BULOVA, 1920s. This unusual two-toned case is yellow and white gold-filled. It is of a stepped design with embossing on the bezel and lugs. The enamel painted dial has a subsidiary seconds chapter at 6:00. The 15-jeweled movement is Swiss. (Courtesy Time Will Tell)

WALTHAM, 1920s. An early example of the use of a seconds window with a digital disc. The window is at the 9:00 position. The dial of this gold filled rectangular wristwatch features Arabic numerals. 17 jewels.

WALTHAM, ca. 1930s. Five-stepped deco yellow gold-filled case. Subsidiary second. (Courtesy of Harry Stecker)

WALTHAM, 1920s. The 14k gold case has the Arabic hours chapter enameled onto the bezel. The case is tonneau-shaped with a round enamel painted dial. Waltham movement, 15 jewels.

died in 1958, Ballard wrote of Bulova's legacy and his role in it: "In 1926, with radio in its infancy, Arde and I planned the first radio spot advertising. I travelled the country purchasing radio time, and we became the first watch company to advertise with national spot announcements. 'B-U-L-O-V-A...9:00 p.m., Bulova Watch Time' was heard and remembered by countless millions of Americans." Ballard's longevity with the firm virtually spanned the history of the American wristwatch.

But while Bulova dominated the airwaves with its simple and brilliant time announcement ads, it also was heavily invested in the print medium, along with its competitors. The popular *Saturday Evening Post* became a prime outlet for advertising wristwatches in this era. This weekly magazine, with its readership in the millions, was a key to the growth of the American watch companies. Long before the advertising man was the subject of master's theses, watch firms were practicing the idea known today as "image" advertising. The story of the period is spelled out in opulent advertisements that promote not just style and quality but morals, virtues, and philosophies.

Bulova's full-color, two-page spreads covered a variety of points within the lavish scroll-and-wave borders that framed each ad. In 1925, for example, along with displays of men's and women's wristwatches priced from $37.50 to $750, the copy discusses the reliability of the movement as it describes and illustrates the hair spring. A slogan sums up the combination: "Aristocrat of Beauty, Autocrat of Time." No one need sacrifice accuracy to the demands of style, this advertisement implies, a clear reminder that the wristwatch still suffered in comparison with the pocket watch that was well-protected against shock. A 1922 advertisement offers another slogan with the same implication: "As Serviceable As They Are Beautiful." Each advertisement reminds the reader that "The best jewelers in your community will gladly show you original and distinctive Bulova designs."

The role played by case-makers was significant throughout the development of the American wristwatch, and they were known to advertise directly to the consumer as well. In an advertisement timed for the 1922 Christmas selling season, Wadsworth Watch Case Co. of Cincinnati, Ohio, depicted wrist and pocket watches of the period without any brand names

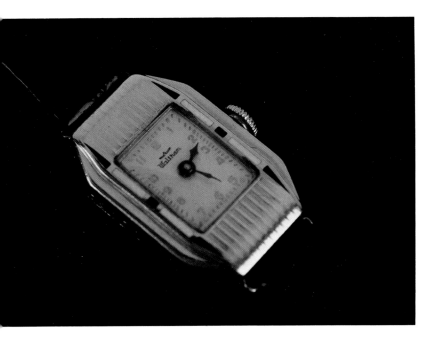

WALTHAM, 1920s. The rectangular dial of this Waltham is framed in a decorated 14k die-struck case. It features embossed stripes on the lug ends of the bezel and black and white inlays along the sides of the bezel. 15 jewels.

WALTHAM, 1920s. The two-toned dial of this Waltham features highly stylized Arabic numerals. The subsidiary seconds chapter at 6:00 competes with the numeral 6 which remains on the hours chapter. The hands are luminous. The case is gold filled and has moveable lugs. 15 jewels. Waltham movement.

on the dials. One would like to have eavesdropped on the conversations that went on between Wadsworth and the watch companies it serviced after this advertisement appeared: "For more than thirty years Wadsworth Cases have dressed and protected the leading watch movements. Many of the most beautiful, most popular watch-case designs with which you are acquainted are Wadsworth creations. When you buy a watch select a movement that your jeweler will recommend and see that it is dressed in a Wadsworth Case." This was an American practice, and was not done in Europe where pocket watches were cased at the factory. In fact there is little evidence that this pocket watch practice carried over into wristwatches, but that did not stop Wadsworth from bundling the two ideas together.

At this stage of the development of the American wristwatch, there were numerous companies producing the cases (see appendix for listing). Waltham's *Royalty Series*, for example, comprised Waltham movements housed in cases from Star Watch Case Co. and Keystone Watch Case Co. To confirm the change in policy from the pocket watch days, Waltham's trade advertisement in the September 5, 1929 issue of *The Jeweler's Circular* is headlined "New Waltham Factory-Cased Strap Watches."

Waltham is an interesting story; it is a company that lived its long life in or on the brink of bankruptcy. It is the "Perils of Pauline" of the watch business. Waltham was dragged and pulled, kicking and screaming, into each phase of its perilous, century-long existence. The key figure for good and evil during the decorative period was Frederic C. Dumaine. He came to a company that was heavily weighted toward the production of pocket watches. With a nominal capacity of 2500 watch movements a day (pocket watches mainly), it was turning out only 800. Although the demand after the First World War was already moving toward wristwatches, resistance at Waltham was strong. The wristwatch was still seen as a fad, not part of the "staple watch trade". In 1926, the firm was still producing more pocket watches than wristwatches by roughly a two-to-one ratio. But under Dumaine, an abrupt change was made. In 1927, the ratio reversed exactly: two wristwatches were made for every pocket watch produced. By 1930, the ratio was three to one. Then production of all watches plummeted, recovering to 1930 levels only in 1935.

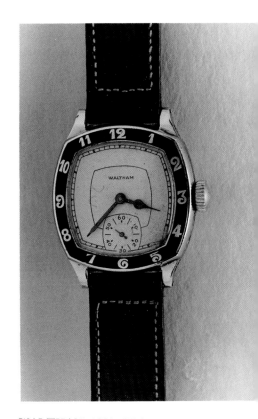

WALTHAM, 1920s. This Waltham has a black enamel bezel with Arabic numerals forming the hours chapter. The dial has a minutes chapter and a subsidiary seconds chapter in the same cushion shape. 15 jewels.

WALTHAM, 1928.
Tonneau(Courtesy of Dr. Richard
Smith)

ILLINOIS, 1930. *Manhattan.*
(Courtesy of Dr. Richard Smith)

ILLINOIS, 1931. *Futura.* (Courtesy
of Dr. Richard Smith)

ILLINOIS, 1930. *Townsman.*
(Courtesy of Dr. Richard Smith)

ILLINOIS, 1930. *Manhattan.*
(Courtesy of Dr. Richard Smith)

ILLINOIS, 1932. *Ensign.* (Courtesy
of Dr. Richard Smith)

ILLINOIS, c. 1930. (Courtesy of Dr.
Richard Smith)

ILLINOIS, 1933. *Larchmont.*
(Courtesy of Dr. Richard Smith)

ILLINOIS, 1933. *Derby.* (Courtesy of
Dr. Richard Smith)

ILLINOIS, 1927. *Marquis.* (Courtesy
of Dr. Richard Smith)

ILLINOIS, 1929. *Guardsman.*
(Courtesy of Dr. Richard Smith)

ILLINOIS, 1933. *Derby.* (Courtesy of
Dr. Richard Smith)

ILLINOIS, c. 1930. *Consul.* (Courtesy of Dr. Richard Smith)

ILLINOIS, 1932. *Cavalier.* (Courtesy of Dr. Richard Smith)

ILLINOIS, 1930. *Blackstone.* (Courtesy of Dr. Richard Smith)

ILLNOIS, 1932. *Commodore.* (Courtesy of Dr. Richard Smith)

ILLINOIS, 1932. *Cavalier.* (Courtesy of Dr. Richard Smith)

ILLINOIS, 1931. *Viking.* (Courtesy of Dr. Richard Smith)

ILLINOIS, 1933. *Chesterfield.* (Courtesy of Dr. Richard Smith)

ILLINOIS, 1932. *Beau Royale.* (Courtesy of Dr. Richard Smith)

ILLINOIS, ca. 1928. Rectangular case with clipped corners. Subseconds, white gold filled. (Courtesy of Aaron Faber Gallery)

ILLNOIS. *Champion.* (Courtesy of Dr. Richard Smith)

ILLINOIS, 1925. *Art Deco.* (Courtesy of Dr. Richard Smith)

WALTHAM, 1920s. This lady's wristwatch is of 14k white gold. It has a blue enamel bezel containing the hours chapter. The enamel painted dial has a minutes chapter. The wristwatch has moveable lugs. Waltham movement, 17 jewels.

WALTHAM, ca 1930. An early example of an incentive or premium wristwatch, Waltham made this wristwatch for Chevrolet. The octagonal case is chrome plated. It has a luminous silver matte dial with a Butler silver center, and a subsidiary seconds chapter. A 6/0 size, 7 jewels, 12 ligne Waltham movement.

ILLINOIS, Ca. 1930. This *Beau Brummel* has a 14k gold filled embossed case in the Deco style. It is tonneau-shaped with a curved back and bezel. The movements for this wristwatch had 17 or 19 jewels. The *Beau Brummel* also came in 14k white gold filled. (Courtesy Aaron Faber Gallery)

Dumaine was installed as chief executive of Waltham in 1922, by the banks who were reorganizing the firm. He succeeded in changing production and making the company profitable at the expense of virtually everyone except the Class A stockholders. He owned half the Class A stock, having invested in the company when he joined it. He cut wages, allowed equipment to age, neglected to provide funds for a much-needed new plant. Instead of providing for the company's future, he saw to his own. As soon as the company was in a profitable position, he channeled money to the stock, sold his shares, and left.

Waltham appears to have had more difficulty than most companies in producing a quality wristwatch with the new, desirable, smaller movement although it always drew attention to the size of the movements it produced. In 1931, Waltham introduced its new baguette model #400, advertised as the smallest watch made in America. (Watchmakers disliked working on this small movement.) A much earlier advertisement by Jacques Depollier & Sons, in the *Jeweler's Circular-Weekly* of 1919, shows the smallest American watch movement, "the size of a ten cent piece," by Waltham.

But its styling was staid; in an era of great drama and exquisitely detailed wristwatches, Waltham's styles look like grudging concessions to the prevailing mode. Its most distinctive design is an echo of Hamilton's *Piping Rock*, introduced in 1928. It limped through the Thirties, only to be saved by the Second World War.

The Illinois Watch Company of Springfield, Illinois produced wristwatches which best exemplify the feeling and the look of the decorative period. Where Waltham was a poor follower, Illinois was a savvy leader, clearly in touch with the style and mood of the times. In a 1929 catalog, the company emphasizes both the quality and the styling of the product: "Many fine features of railroad watch construction may be found in these

ILLINOIS, 1920s. This Illinois *Piccadilly* has a very unusual elliptical case and dial. It is 14k gold filled with an enamel painted dial. The subsidiary seconds chapter is at 9:00. It has a 17 jewel Illinois movement.

small wristwatch movements. The selection of cases to enclose these fine Illinois strap watch movements has received the same care and attention as the movements themselves. There is a smart beauty, a deftness, a modern air in their design that betokens the touch of the artists. Their sturdiness, their dust and shock-resisting qualities show the work of a skilled manufacturer." The series shown features engraved and geometric-patterned bezels, some in gold filled, others in karat gold. Prices range $42.50 for a 17-jeweled gold-filled style to $90 for the 14k gold, 21-jeweled model. Many of these feature the subsidiary seconds dial in the nine o'clock position, an indication that the round movements they contained dated back to the pocket watch era.

As a startling precursor to today's trends, the same catalog offers *The Tuxedo*, a unisex style. "*The Tuxedo* has a wide appeal among both men and women and is quite popular with both sexes." Illinois was clearly moving briskly into the modern age. The 1929 catalogue also offers *The Medalist* fitted with its new, rectangular wristwatch movement, which it says "sets the pace in American watch design." "The construction of this rectangular movement permits the use of very large and sturdy moving parts for a watch of this small size. To both the jeweler and the consumer this is a vital feature. It is now possible to secure a really fine men's strap watch in the popular 12/0 size without sacrificing durability and accuracy." Attention is also drawn to its extreme thinness and its curved back "which fits the wearer's wrist snugly." This foreshadows the coming of the curved wristwatches in the 1930s, the leader being Gruen's *Curvex*. Illinois was at the height of its success when it was sold to Hamilton Watch Co. in 1929, after the death of Jacob Bunn, Jr. in 1926. The family owned business was now in the hands of the Hamilton Watch Company of Lancaster, Pennsylvania.

ILLINOIS, 1920s-30s. This hexagonal wristwatch has an embossed bezel on its 14k gold-filled case. The subsidiary seconds chapter is at 9:00 and it has profile metal hands. Illinois, 17-jeweled movement.

ILLINOIS, ca 1925. The cut-corner rectangular case of this Illinois was manufactured by the Star Case Company and is 14k gold filled. The enamel painted dial has the subsidiary seconds chapter at 9:00. The hands and numerals are luminous. The 903 grade Illinois movement has 15 jewels.

ILLINOIS, Ca. 1928. Exquisite polychrome stepped enamel work on the bezel of this lady's ribbon wristwatch is quite unusual. The rectangular case tapers as it approaches the solid wire lugs. The dial is hexagonal and is painted in two tones. 17 ruby and sapphire jewels. Examples of this decorative wristwatch are still available.

ILLINOIS, 1930s. The *Trophy* has a simple stepped rectangular 14k white gold filled case. It was also available in yellow gold filled. Applied gold Arabic numerals are on a matte silvered dial with luminous hands. A 12/0 size, 17-jeweled, grade 207 movement powers the *Trophy*. This is a late example of an Illinois wristwatch.

ILLINOIS, ca 1933. The *Beau Geste* has an embossed bezel on a two-level stepped tonneau 14k gold-filled case. The dial is painted in a pin wheel design and has stylized raised gold numerals. 15 jewels, 6/0 size, grade 607 Illinois movement.

ILLINOIS, ca. 1929. Known as Special Model #178, has a decorative embossed case typical of the Deco period. It was manufactured by the Keystone Watch Case Company and came in 14k gold filled or green gold filled. The dial is sterling painted in two tones and has luminous Arabic figures and a subsidiary seconds chapter. 17 jewels.

ILLINOIS, 1920s. This cushion-shaped case is 14k gold-filled, and decorated with embossing on the bezel. The dial is two-tone enamel painted with luminous numbers. The style name is *Jolly Roger*, and it has a 17-jeweled Illinois movement.

ILLINOIS, ca 1930. The *Chieftain* is a remarkable example of high Deco design. The tonneau-shaped case features an elaborate embossed motif. The silvered dial has luminous figures and hands and features the 9:00 placement of the subsidiary seconds chapter. The 6/0 Illinois movement is a #607 and has 15 jewels. The *Chieftain* is a rare wristwatch, available in yellow or white gold filled.

ILLINOIS, ca 1929. This model is almost identical to the Illinois *Marquis,* but has no subsidiary seconds chapter. The 14k gold-filled case has an engraved bezel and lugs. The enamel painted dial has luminous Arabic figures and black hands. Illinois movement, 17 jewels.

ILLINOIS, ca 1930. The tonneau stepped case of the *Ritz* is a modified hexagon and is one of the most dramatic silhouettes available in the Deco period. It is two-toned 14k gold filled with white gold around the bezel. The enamel painted dial has applied numerals. A subsidiary seconds chapter follows the tonneau shape of the case. 15 jewels. This wristwatch is a very rare design.

ILLINOIS, 1920s. This 15-jeweled wrist-watch is cushion-shaped with an embossed bezel. Note the bulbous crown, a carry over from the earlier era. The subsidiary seconds chapter is at 6:00. The hands are skeletonized, and the numbers are luminous.

ILLINOIS, 1920s. This tonneau-shaped wristwatch is 14k gold filled, and has an embossed bezel. The enamel painted dial uses Arabic numerals and has a subsidiary seconds chapter at 6:00. 15 jewels.

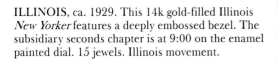

ILLINOIS, ca. 1929. This 14k gold-filled Illinois *New Yorker* features a deeply embossed bezel. The subsidiary seconds chapter is at 9:00 on the enamel painted dial. 15 jewels. Illinois movement.

HAMILTON, ca 1930. The *Greenwich* comes in 14k white or yellow gold. It has a stepped bezel with rounded corners. The dial has applied gold numbers on a painted silver background. A 6/0 grade 987 Hamilton movement with 17 jewels.

HAMILTON, ca 1930. An elegant example of a decorative Hamilton case, the cushion form case has an embossed bezel. In 14k white gold filled, it was also available in 14k green and yellow gold filled and 14k white, green and yellow gold. A 987 grade Hamilton movement, with 17 jewels. There is some question whether the dial and hands are original.

Robert E. Miller, then vice president of Hamilton, left Lancaster for Springfield, Illinois to become general manager of the Illinois operation. But by late 1932, the depression forced Hamilton to economize and operating two factories was no longer possible. In November of that year, the Springfield factory was shut down and Illinois's inventory was moved to Lancaster. Until that move, Illinois had produced a total of 800,000 wristwatch movements. To the public, there was no indication of change. Advertisements carried the Illinois name well into the 1930s. For years after the closing of the factory, movements were put together from the inventory of left over parts, and were still marked "Illinois Watch, Springfield." Hamilton continued to sell wristwatches under the Illinois name through the 1950s although these later models were of Hamilton design. Many dealers and collectors believe the original Illinois product to be the most collectible of all mechanical wristwatches made in America.

By 1931, production of wristwatches had far surpassed that of pocket watches throughout the industry. The energy that was given over to wristwatch design made it clear that this was the product of the future.

The wristwatch was a fitting symbol of this new age of speed. Although few people traveled by air, the automobile had begun to be more than simply a means of transportation. It was becoming an emblem of our culture. We were becoming the nation we are today, obsessed with time and speed, with setting records and saving time. The ever-present wristwatch, easy to read at a glance, became part of that mood, the sense of the importance of each second.

Although very few people truly lived the lifestyle we now associate with the "Roaring '20s", many shared a part of it through their ownership of a Deco style wristwatch. In its attention to opulent decoration, to embellishment on such a small surface as the bezel of a wristwatch, the period was dedicated to the consumer.

HAMILTON, 1920s. Styled as a horizontal tonneau, this 14k gold-filled case features an embossed bezel. The painted silver dial has a subsidiary seconds chapter at 6:00. 17 jewels.

HAMILTON, 1920s. Embossing decorates this cut-corner square Hamilton. The case is 14k gold filled with a painted silver dial featuring luminous Arabic numerals and hands, an hours chapter and an outside minutes chapter. 17 jewels.

Chapter Three
Streamlining the Thirties

GRUEN, ca 1938. Part of the 311 series, this is a classic Gruen tank. The tonneau case is curved to the wrist and has a curved two-tone dial. 14k yellow gold case and a 17-jeweled Precision Swiss movement.

Time can be measured in many ways—by minutes, by hours, by days. Or it can be measured by world events—by wars, the reigns of kings or economic woes. Two decades measure the time between the two World Wars, with the dividing line standing out clearly as the stock market crash of October, 1929. In the depression that followed the crash there was a discernIble change in the nation, and in the world. The decorative period in wristwatches—the frivolous and beautiful colored enamels, the engraved, chased, and embossed surfaces that had expressed the optimistic times in which they were made—came to an end in every sense. By 1932, the depression was at its nadir. Half the working population of Cleveland was out of work; 80% of Toledo was jobless. Every week across the nation, 100,000 workers on average were fired from their jobs.

As production of wristwatches surpassed that of pocket watches some time between 1927 and 1931 (the date varying with each company's dedication to capturing the emerging wristwatch market) product design of all sorts shifted to the dramatic streamlined look introduced by industrial designer Raymond Loewy, the king of contemporary engineering design, and designer of the streamlined locomotive.

Aerodynamics scientists found that stripping away unnecessary exterior decoration cut wind drag and enabled vehicles of all sorts to travel more efficiently. This real advantage soon found itsway into products that didn't have anything whatsoever to do with speed and the effects of wind. Even the homely family toaster became streamlined by the simple trick of changing its silhouette. Streamlining was the symbol of the age, and it fit the mood of the times very well. Streamlined designs were modern, and modest. They were forward looking and forward thinking, stripped of excess decoration and embellishment.

It is in this creative atmosphere that the management of one watch company began to develop a wristwatch that was not only startling in its design but innovative in its movement. The feeling was sleek, modern, no-frills, hard-edged. It would come to symbolize the streamlined look of the period. The company was Gruen; the wristwatch was the *Curvex*.

Gruen had had its share of economic ups and downs, and had been in the hands of the banks more than once since its founding in 1874. But Eugene Fuller, a devoted Gruen hobbyist and author of *The Priceless Possession of a Few*, says "Elgin and Gruen were two of the strongest companies when the depression hit. That's why they survived." But survival meant many changes, among them the end of their intensive advertising program. There was little point in advertising high quality wristwatches when total domestic consumption of watches had dropped from more than five million in 1929 to 854,000 in 1932 and 821,000 in 1933.

At the helm of the company was president Frederick G. Gruen, son of the founder Dietrich Gruen, and a unique figure in the watch world. Though rigorously trained as a watchmaker at the Royal Horological Institute in Glashutte, Germany (graduating in 1893), he also had a keen eye for marketing and had organized Gruen's method of distributing its watches to a limited number of select dealers. It was under his management of the firm that Henri Thiebaud, head of manufacturing in Bienne, Switzerland, oversaw the design of the elongated, curved movement that became model #311, the first *Curvex*. The new concept was introduced to the public in the October 26, 1935 issue of *Saturday Evening Post*, the preferred advertising medium of the day.

ILLINOIS, ca. 1931. 14k solid gold tonneau case. (Courtesy of Harry Stecker)

The advertising copy, while correct on the technical aspects, took poetic license in crediting the "creators" of the *Curvex*. While Count Alexis deSakhnoffsky is cited as the case designer, he was in fact the artist who illustrated the ad. The movement is credited as having been created "at Time Hill by Gruen Engineers." Gruen engineers, yes; Time Hill (Cincinnati), no. In a 1949 issue of *Gruen Time*, the employee magazine, Henri Thiebaud is cited as "director-general of the Swiss plant; his skill created the *Curvex* and the *Veri-Thin* movements." The actual Swiss patent was in the name of Emile Frey, a principal of the Frey Watch Company. Eugene Fuller surmises that Gruen purchased exclusive rights to the Frey patent. The concept was then developed and refined under the direction of Henri Thiebaud.

There may well have been input from Time Hill. There was a group of German-speaking watchmakers laboring in "the Attic", as the top floor of Time Hill was called, according to Charles Cleves, a dedicated Gruen collector. "Dietrich Gruen went over to Glashutte where they were trained and brought them back here some time in the 1930s." So vigorous was the training at the school in Glashutte that for their test, prospective graduates had to make an entire watch from scratch. This was the training that Frederick Gruen had successfully completed as well.

Cleves says "Gruen was looking for a marketing idea. Curved wrist-watches were beginning to get popular in the '20s. In the '30s, the demand came increasingly for a curved wristwatch." Certainly some of the demand was coming from Gruen's own dealers, the fine jewelers across the country who also provided market research data from their daily customer contact.

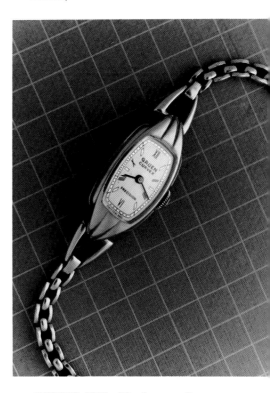

GRUEN, 1930s. The famous Gruen *Curvex* was marketed to women in the late '30s as the ultimate example of streamlined design. This Countess was available in 14k yellow or white gold filled. It has a 17-jeweled Gruen Precision Swiss movement. The original issue price was $42.50. The bracelet on this example is not original.

But it wasn't just the design idea that Gruen liked. They were also looking for a bigger and better movement. "The others were using a small, round movement," says Cleves. "It was a woman's movement in a curved case and was so small that it got dirty easily and stopped." The result of their efforts was the #311 *Curvex* movement. The soaring curves of the *Curvex* owe their shape not just to a design concept but to a partnership between case-maker and movement maker, a relationship little known before.

The *Curvex's* shape was honestly earned. Gruen engineered a new, mitered movement by cutting the plates in such a way as to fit into the case in a thinner, curved construction. This new curving movement fit into a case that curved around the wrist. The idea of engineering the inside and the outside of the wristwatch in this way marked the final stages of the transition from the pocket watch to the wristwatch. The *Curvex* was the logical extension of Gruen's late 1920s models with their elongated feeling. The style caught on because it so perfectly captured the design mood of the period. It remained a successful model in part because the movement was sound.

Robert Gruen, nephew of Frederick, grandson of Dietrich Gruen, and devoted keeper of the flame, worked on two of the *Curvex* ads during a summer stint at the company's advertising agency. He describes the many movements that followed the #311 which curved only at the top. "On October 3, 1936, the lady's *Curvex* (#420) was introduced." The advertising copy takes cognizance of the competition's efforts in this subtle rebuke:

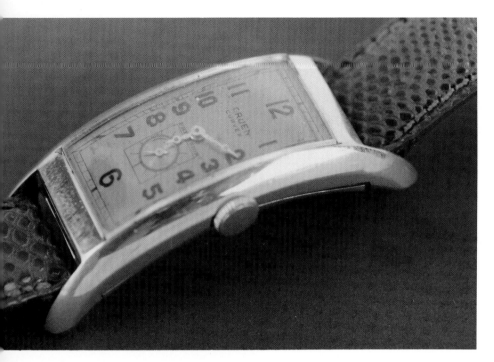

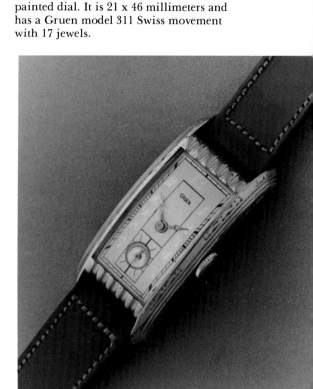

GRUEN, ca 1937, This Gruen *Curvex* has a ridged and engraved bezel and an enamel painted dial. It is 21 x 46 millimeters and has a Gruen model 311 Swiss movement with 17 jewels.

GRUEN, ca 1938. The ultimate example of the Gruen *Curvex*, the General had an extremely curved elongated tank case large enough to cover the entire wrist. It is pictured in 14k yellow gold filled, with a pink dial and Arabic numerals. Originally available with a flexible bracelet, the issue price was $59.50. 17-jeweled Precision movement.

GRUEN, ca 1935. Part of the *Ristside* series, the *Baylor* was meant to be worn on the edge of the wrist, and was promoted as a driver's wristwatch. This is an unusual *Curvex* design with an integrated gold filled band. Variations include hooded lugs and leather bands. The case is 14k yellow gold filled with a steel back. 22 x 36 mm with a 15-jeweled Swiss movement.

"*Curvex* is a principle—a revolutionary advance in watch construction, conceived and made by Gruen. There is no imitation and there is no substitute. Despite other curved cases of pleasing style and design, remember that only *Curvex* has the genuine curved movement entirely filling the wristform case, and even the new, dainty feminine *Curvex* has this sturdy movement which gives in the men's and women's *Curvex* alike, precision pocket watch accuracy."

On October 2, 1937, the #330 made its appearance. This one curved at both top and bottom. This was an extreme curve, as the headline described it: "four times as much curve as before!...permitting, for the first time, 'custom curved' wristwatches." "Custom curved" did not mean that each wristwatch was individually fitted to the wrist. It was just a catchy slogan to differentiate this version from the earlier models. Clearly Gruen was fighting back against the parade of imitators who knew a good thing when they copied it. The advertisement featured a crowd of fashionably dressed men and women peering into a case filled with *Curvexes*. It also offered approval from a wide variety of celebrities of the day ranging from Veloz and Yolanda, "the premiere dance team," to Omar Kiam, designer for Samuel Goldwyn movie productions.

Having curved the wristwatch as far as it could go, Gruen now changed its placement on the wrist. On October 15, 1938, Gruen introduced the side-of-the-wrist *Curvex*, using the #330 model. "This innovative design did not prove very popular," says Robert Gruen, "and not too many were sold." A look at the illustrations in the advertisement points up the problem: both the man's and the woman's wrists appear to have been turned sideways to support wearing the wristwatch in this position.

GRUEN, 1930s. Of all the driver's wristwatches this *Curvex* design is the most extreme and desirable. Pictured in yellow gold filled, it is also available but extremely rare in 14k gold. The exaggerated hooded lugs have embossed graphic detail. The form fitting back plate is screwed into place. The dial is painted in black enamel with painted numerals. 20mm x 36mm. 17-jeweled Swiss Precision movement.

GRUEN, ca 1938. This Gruen 10k gold filled side-of-the-wrist driver's watch, has a vertical tonneau case suspended between sculpted wire lugs. It is ultra-curved to fit the edge of the wrist. The clean and simple design is typical of the streamlined style. 17-jeweled Swiss Gruen Precision movement.

FORTUNE May 1947

GRUEN CURVEX . . . so truly Beautiful . . .

truly Accurate . . . truly Curved

● Inside and outside the *only* watch of its kind in the world . . . the *one* watch with the exclusive, patented Gruen Curvex* Precision movement . . . curved to permit large, accurate working parts. The *one* watch in which both case and movement are curved to fit the wrist. Gruen Curvex . . . truly the greatest watch *of all time!* Gruen . . . official time-piece of Pan American World Airways, from $33.75 to $4000 including federal tax.

GRUEN CURVEX
THE PRECISION WATCH

*T.M. Registered
U. S. Pat. Office
© 1947, The Gruen Watch Company

GRUEN • THE PRECISION* WATCH • AMERICA'S CHOICE SINCE 1874

Courtesy: Robert Gruen

HAMILTON, ca. 1933. Tonneau 14k gold case with subsidiary second and 19-jewel movement. (Courtesy of Harry Stecker)

GRUEN, "Curvex," ca. 1938. Convertible "edge of wrist" watch, gold-filled with flexible lugs. Very rare. (Courtesy of Time Will Tell)

GRUEN, "Precision", ca. 1930s. Tonneau case with subsidiary subsecond. 14k white gold. (Courtesy of Harry Stecker)

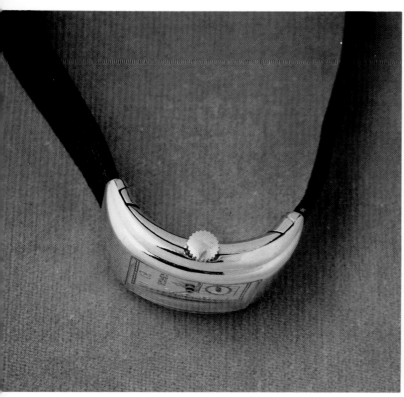

GRUEN, ca 1937. The American case of this *Edge-of-Wrist* watch is 14k gold filled. The extreme curve was designed to be worn only on the edge of the wrist. The style was known as the driver's watch. 17-jeweled Gruen Precision movement.

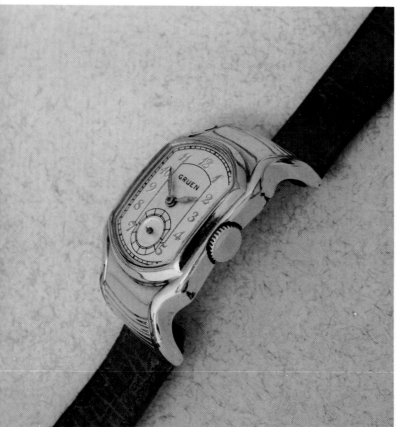

GRUEN, ca 1940. A part of the *Edge-of-Wrist* series, this *Curvex* is yellow gold-filled. The case has the extreme curve seen only in the edge of wrist models, and is unusual in its fluted lug covers. 17-jeweled Swiss movement.

GRUEN, Late 1930s. The modified teardrop lugs distinguish the streamlined case of this 14k gold Gruen *Curvex*. The very handsome two-toned dial has a well-defined hours chapter. 17-jeweled Precision Swiss movement.

GRUEN, ca 1940. The two-toned black and gray dial and the wedge-shaped lugs make this *Curvex* unusual and desirable to collectors. The case is by the Wadsworth Watch Case Company and is 14k gold filled. The movement is 17-jeweled Swiss. This wristwatch is difficult to find in the marketplace.

In 1940 Gruen introduced model #440, the *Compact Curvex*. This model featured less of a curve than the #330 and tapered at the sides. Finally, leaping over the Second World War, Gruen brought out the *Curvametric* in 1948, model #380. Eugene Fuller says, "They kept using the name *Curvex* to maintain the trademark, even though they weren't as extreme a curve. It was just a gentle curve like everybody else's. It was a very desirable concept and they wanted to protect the name."

It took the technical innovation of Henri Thiebaud and his staff to conceive the curved movement but it required the style leadership shown by Gruen during this period to follow through with the curved cases. While other watch manufacturers were still resisting the wristwatch and treating it as a passing fad, by 1931, 90% of the cases produced by Gruen's own plant were for wristwatches. Those who didn't adapt didn't survive. Fuller writes, "By the end of the twenties the wristwatch invasion had left a number of notable casualties in its wake [including] Howard, Hampden, Dudley, South Bend, and New York Standard."

Curvex cases, as well as all Gruen cases, were made not only in the company's own Cincinnati plant but also by Star Case Company, Wadsworth and other smaller firms. According to Robert Gruen, "In the initial days, all gold cases were made by Gruen; they went to others for gold filled. Most of the gold filled cases were made by Wadsworth, across the river. Then Gruen began making both gold and gold filled. Gold filled really came in strong in the '30s. Some of the *Curvex* cases were made by Wadsworth and Gruen. Star Watch Case Company made the lower price wristwatch cases. The lady's wristwatches in 14k gold, 18k gold and platinum were made by Katz & Ogush in New York. They made a lot of the cases." And it is from Katz & Ogush that Gruen's new president, Benjamin Katz, would come.

GRUEN, ca 1940. The 10k yellow gold filled case of this Gruen has an engraved dial and sculpted lugs. The enamel painted dial is two-toned. It has a 370 grade, 17-jeweled Precision movement

BULOVA, 1930s. The elongated curved, die-struck case of this wristwatch is 10k gold filled and is embossed. The dial is matte silver enamel painted with gold numerals and hands. There is a subsidiary seconds chapter at 6:00. 21-jeweled Swiss movement.

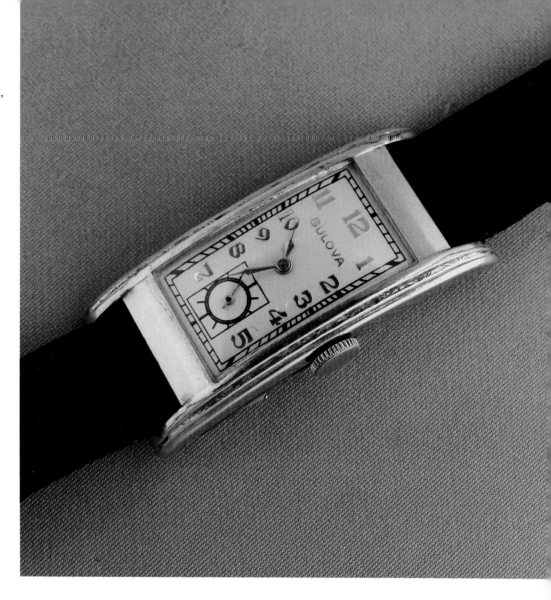

GRUEN, 1940s. The original crystal of this wristwatch was faceted and would have added considerable value to the collector. This is an extremely curved case and dial with a beveled articulated bezel and ridged lug. It is 14k white gold and has a black enamel painted dial with white applied markers. The wristwatch was also available in 14k white and yellow gold filled and 14k yellow gold. The Precision Gruen Swiss movement has 17 jewels.

Right in the middle of all this *Curvex* innovation, Gruen was going through another financial crunch. The banks, says Robert Gruen, put Katz into the company as president in May of 1935. "They wanted newer and younger management." While Katz was president, Fred Gruen stayed on in the position of chairman of the Board of Directors from 1935 until 1940. In an article that appeared in the *Buckeye Horology* in 1940, Frederick Gruen wrote, "[Mr. Thiebaud] has done a very good job for Mr. Katz who came into the picture in 1935, and I will give him credit for pushing and getting behind the thing and carrying on the old traditions and standard of quality and getting Mr. Thiebaud to be a real producer."

The quality of the Gruen wristwatch was undisputed. Eugene Fuller takes pains to point out that "Gruen in those years was what Rolex is today." Indeed, Rolex in those years sometimes beat with the very heart of Gruen. The Gruen and Rolex factories were located just a couple of hundred yards apart in Bienne, Switzerland, and were the best of neighbors. But they had more than just a geographical closeness. Gruen was commissioned by Rolex's founder, Hans Wilsdorf, to make certain movements for Rolex, including the famous Rolex *Prince*, according to Ken Specht, a long-time watch dealer specializing in Rolex. "Rolex took these movements," Specht relates, "and by making very slight refinements, was able to get them chronometer rated." The Gruen movements were so well regarded, Specht adds, "Wilsdorf took 500 of them, had them chronometer rated in the *Prince* model, and gave them serial numbers 501-1000. This was the first time they were mass produced. It was for the 25th anniversary celebration of King George V." It is a tribute to the skills of Gruen's watchmakers that the movements were regarded worthy of this very special use. Gruen's Swiss plant was the most modern of its day, well

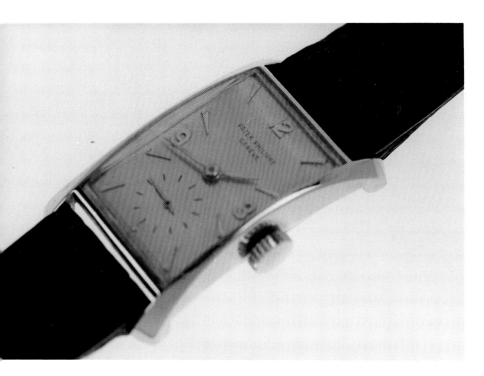

BULOVA, 1930s. This classic example of the period has an 10k gold filled, elongated curved case. The dial features embossed Arabic numerals and a slightly exaggerated subsidiary seconds chapter. 17-jeweled Swiss Bulova model Swiss #7AP movement.

PATEK PHILIPPE, 1934-50 and 1947-67. This *Geneve* model #140 was made in two series. Series A had serial numbers from 830,000-839,999, and series B had numbers 970,000-977889. It was a very successful design for Patek Philippe. The case is 18k gold with an enamel painted dial. It was made in both large and medium versions. This example is 18 x 25.6 mm and 3.65 mm high. Swiss movement, 18 jewels.

advanced over those of the other Swiss firms. Irvin Gruen Bieser, a grandson of founder Dietrich Gruen, says, "The Gruen plant was the most up-to-date. At one time, Rolex and Gruen had an agreement for a combined distribution of their watches in Europe under the name "Rolex/Gruen". Rolex's distribution was very valuable to Gruen, and Gruen's factory was very valuable to Rolex."

Robert Gruen, reflecting on this relationship, describes how very close the two families were: "In 1926 my sister Emily, and my mother and dad went to Europe and stayed in the home of Hermann Aegler, the managing director of the Rolex plant. His house was on the grounds of the factory. There was a movement to merge the two companies but it didn't go ahead because of the depression." Instead, Gruen continued to make its reputation in the United States while Rolex was directed toward the English market, including Canada. Robert Gruen, who worked for Gruen in Toronto, says, "Rolex was not a big entity in the U.S. at that time. In 1936, when I moved to Canada, I became aware of it. It was an English oriented company."

Just as Rolex saw the quality of the Gruen movement, other watch companies were quick to pick up on the popularity of the *Curvex* which captured trade attention as well as that of the public. Versions of the elongated, curved profile were made by virtually all the companies that had survived the depression. Most borrowed the idea of the curve without the innovative and complementary movements. They simply adapted existing movements and fitted them into curved cases. Some also carelessly or intentionally "borrowed" the term *Curvex* as a generic description of the shape, but only Gruen owned, and still owns, the trademark.

OMEGA, 1930s. Cased in the U.S., the gold filled case is of American manufacture. It is an elongated, slightly curved rectangle. The dial is also rectangular but the hours chapter is round with markers for the hour positions. The subsidiary seconds chapter repeats the rectangular shape again. 17-jeweled Swiss movement.

BULOVA, 1930s. One of Bulova's elongated curved wristwatches, this 10k gold filled case is die-stamped. The white enamel painted dial has raised stylized Arabic numerals. 17 jewel Swiss model #7 AP Bulova movement.

BENRUS, 1930s. The curved American case of this wristwatch has a rolled gold plate bezel and steel back. The rectangular enamel painted dial has full Arabic numerals and a minutes chapter. Swiss movement, 15 jewels.

WALTHAM, ca 1942. The *Premier* has a curved pink gold filled case with a matching pink painted dial. The curves are on all sides of the case and house a well-defined dial with Arabic numerals and a subsidiary seconds chapter.

BULOVA, 1930s. One of Bulova's elongated curved wristwatches, this wristwatch has a stepped, embossed bezel and lugs. The 10k gold filled case holds a white enamel painted dial with Arabic numerals. Swiss, 17 jewels.

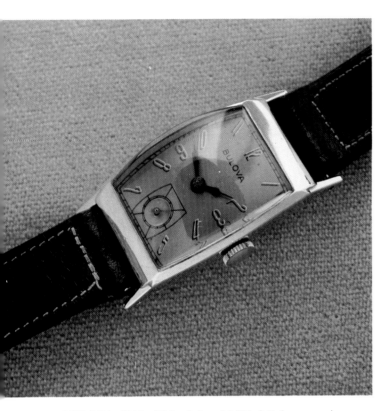

BULOVA, 1940s. This pink gold-filled Bulova case is an elongated curve. The shape is repeated on the sides of the bezel. The dial is painted pink and has stylized Arabic numerals. 17-jeweled Bulova model 7AP Swiss movement.

Hamilton marketed its own curved wristwatch in the very year the first Gruen model was introduced. The catalogue copy describes it: "At last complete harmony between style and mechanical perfection has been achieved and Hamilton is indeed proud of this new series of watches curved to fit the wrist." Its contour model was introduced in 1938, the wearer choosing how to position the wristwatch: "For the side or top of the wrist. Here at last is a perfected side-of-the-wrist watch (an allusion to Gruen's version, also introduced in 1938). Unlike ordinary models of this type, its use is not confined to the side of the wrist alone...flexible lugs permit a close, natural fit on the top or beneath the wrist as well." By 1938, Hamilton had brought its curved wristwatch down to everyone's price. For $37.50, one could purchase the Dodson model in 10k gold filled with black enamel numbers. For $40, the same model could be had with 18k applied gold numeral dial.

HAMILTON, 1940s. Shown in pink gold, this wristwatch begins to show the transition into the Retro-Modern period. The unusual pink dial has diamond-set numerals and hour markers. The slightly curved case was available in 14k white and yellow gold, and platinum, as well as in the 14k pink gold of this example. It is uncommon for an American wristwatch of this period to have a diamond dial. 19 jewels.

In wristwatch design, rectangles captured the streamlined feeling of the decade. This tank shape, as it came to be known, reflected the modern, clean '30s idea of design. According to Robert Gruen, informal historian for the Gruen Company, the *tank* name and design were the mark and patent of Gruen which featured the new model in a November, 1923, National Geographic advertisement. A lawsuit between Gruen and Cartier was brought over the ownership of the *tank* name and Cartier prevailed. Cartier appears to have brought out the tank during the First World War in France. Whether they protected their idea and name in the United States is open to question. Other American manufacturers including Hamilton, Elgin, Waltham and Bulova created tank-shaped wristwatches with movements that related to the rectangular cases. The movement that provided the base for Gruen's rectangle was the *Quadron* which it introduced in 1925. Bulova had a semi-barrel, tonneau-shaped rectangular movement. Waltham offered its 7¾ line and Hamilton was making the 980 and 982 movements which are close to rectangular. Elgin, too, had a movement which employed a rectangular type of construction.

GRUEN, ca 1930. An unusual two-toned rectangular case of 18k gold features yellow band at the top and bottom, and lugs with yellow gold center pieces. The dial has silvered matte finish, with applied Arabic numerals, subsidiary seconds chapter and white gold moon styled hands. 17-jeweled Swiss, Gruen Precision movement.

GRUEN, 1930s. The beautifully rounded edges and rectangular case of this *Curvex* exemplify the streamlined look. It is 10k gold filled and the simplicity is carried onto the dial with its well defined hours, minutes, and subsidiary seconds chapters. 17-jeweled Swiss movement.

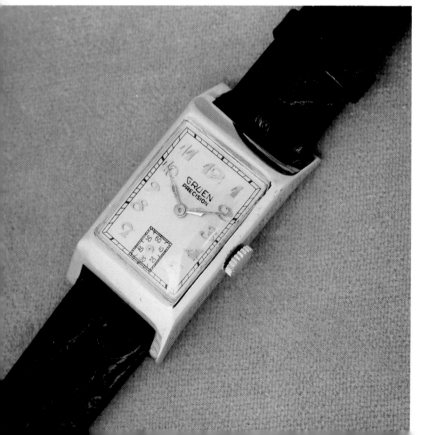

GRUEN, 1930s. A nicely designed 14k gold case reflects the elegance of the streamlined period. The case, minutes chapter and seconds chapter all reflect the rectangular design. The white enamel painted dial has applied Arabic numerals. 15-jeweled Swiss Precision movement.

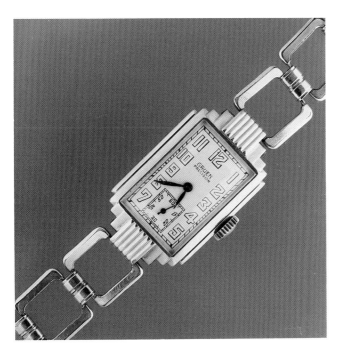

GRUEN, ca 1933. The *Varsity* was available in 14k white gold, shown here, and in yellow gold with a white dial. The stepped ridge forms a pleasing geometrical design. The stylized black dial has gold painted chapters. The 12 is the only numeral, the other hours and seconds being represented by markers. The hours and seconds chapters overlap. The Precision Swiss movement has 17 jewels.

GRUEN, 1920s-30s. The 14k gold filled die-struck case has stepped sides and ribbing over the lugs. The case reads, "Reinforced with extra gold." The enamel painted dial features silhouetted Arabic numbers, blued steel hands, and a subsidiary seconds chapter. The Swiss movement has 17 jewels.

GRUEN, ca 1935. This 14k yellow gold Gruen is a disciplined example of simple streamlined design, utilizing the successful Precision movement, Swiss, 17 jewels.

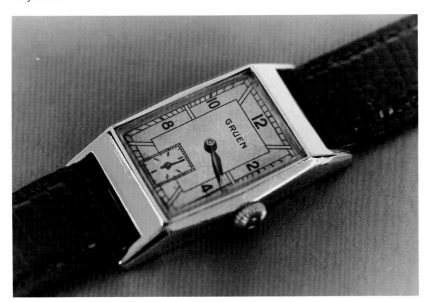

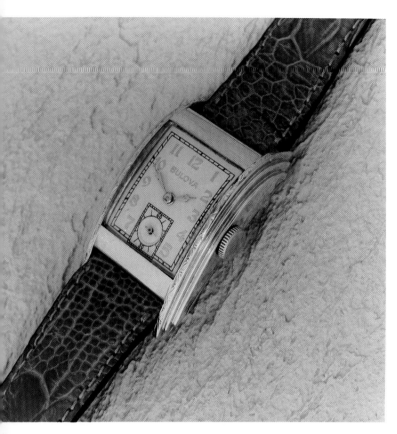

BULOVA, 1930s. A simple elegance marks this stepped 10k gold-filled case. White enamel painted dial. 17-jeweled, Bulova model 7AK Swiss movement.

BULOVA, 1930s. The case of this "right angle" wristwatch is thicker at 12:00 than at 6:00, angling it on the wrist for easier reading of the time. Several manufacturers used similar designs, including both European and American companies such as Rolex, Omega, Patek Philippe, and Hamilton. The case is gold filled with die struck embossing on the stepped bezel and lugs. 15-jeweled Swiss movement.

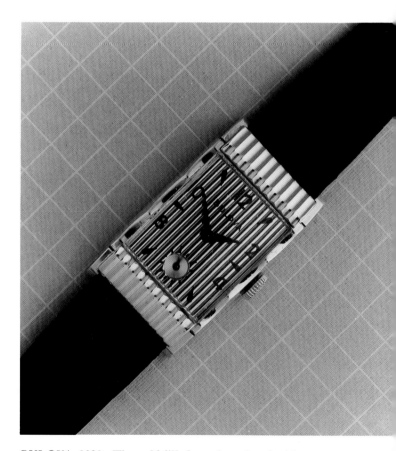

BULOVA, ca 1936. The stepped case of the *Ambassador* is of 10k rolled gold plate. The enamel painted dial has markers for the hours and a subsidiary seconds chapter. The *Ambassador* came with a 15- or 17-jeweled Swiss movement.

BULOVA, 1930s. The gold filled case is sculpted with fluting on the covered lug and scalloping along the sides of the dial. The dial is painted to reflect the fluting on the bezel and alternates Arabic numerals and diamond-shaped markers to denote the hours. Swiss, Bulova Model #7AK movement, 17 jewels.

BULOVA, 1930s. A very good example of the Bulova curved watch, this elongated rectangular 10k gold filled case incorporates a number of fine design elements. The die stamped case compliments the stylized Arabic numerals. 15-jeweled Swiss movement.

BULOVA, ca 1948. The *Excellency* carries the streamlined look well into the '40s. The elegant sculpted case is 14k gold. The enamel painted dial is white with stylized Arabic numerals. Also available in 14k yellow gold filled. 21-jeweled Swiss movement.

Courtesy: the Bulova Watch Company

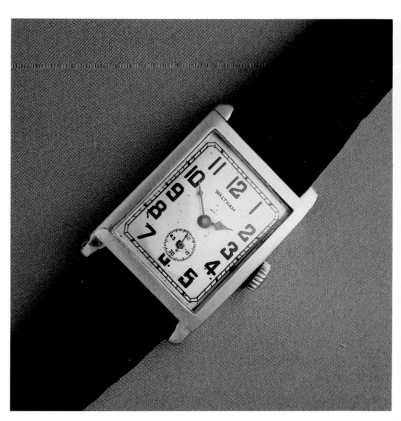

WALTHAM, 1930s. This gold filled rectangular wristwatch has an enamel painted dial with Arabic numerals and a subsidiary seconds hand. 17-jeweled Waltham movement.

HAMILTON, ca 1935. This *Rutledge* has a signed case made of platinum (alloyed with 10% iridium). Signed cases of platinum or 18k gold are extremely rare in American wristwatches. Fewer than 10 examples exist of different models by Hamilton, Elgin, Gruen and Waltham. The enamel painted dial of this wristwatch has 18k white gold applied numerals and hands. 19 jewels, grade 982 Hamilton movement.

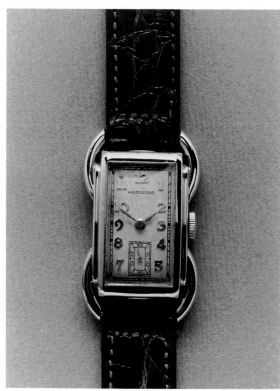

HAMILTON, 1937. The 14k gold case of this Hamilton *Bentley*, features highly stylized horn type lugs. An unusual design for Hamilton in the '30s. During this period most of the production was of classic wristwatches. This *Bentley* has a painted silver dial with applied 18k gold numbers. The movement has 19 jewels. Rare. (Courtesy Time Will Tell)

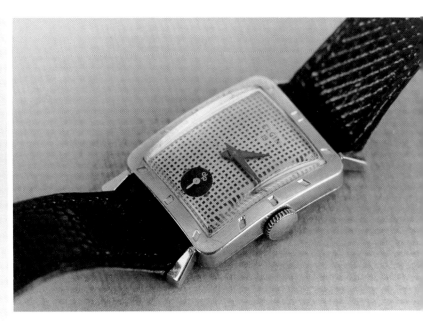

ELGIN, 1930s. A handsome wristwatch, this Elgin features a gold filled case with the hours markers stamped into the bezel. The dial is painted in a grid pattern with black subsidiary seconds chapter at 6:00. 17-jeweled Elgin movement.

ELGIN, 1930s. A rare and distinctive wristwatch, this Lord Elgin digital features a raised lion on the case with a red gemstone in its mouth. The window in the gold filled rectangular case reveals hours and minutes discs as they rotate. 19-jeweled Elgin movement.

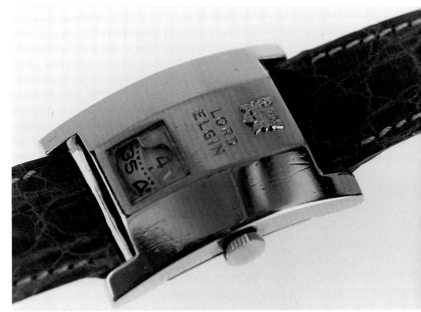

ELGIN, 1930s. The case is 14k white gold filled with a 22k yellow gold bezel overlay. It surrounds a rectangular dial with Egyptian Revival-style Arabic numerals. There is a subsidiary seconds chapter at 6:00. Elgin movement, 15 jewels.

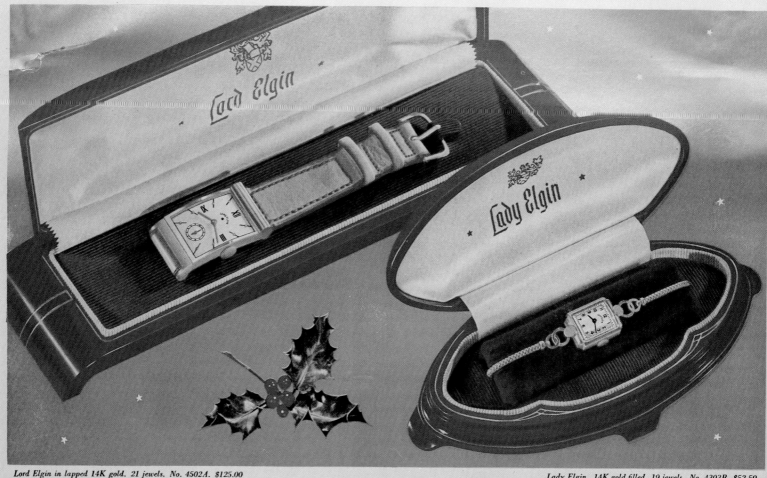

Lord Elgin in lapped 14K gold. 21 jewels. No. 4502A. $125.00

Lady Elgin. 14K gold filled. 19 jewels. No. 4303B. $52.50

Adding a golden glow to Christmas giving—

★ Lord Elgin ★ ★ Lady Elgin ★
21 JEWELS   19 JEWELS

Holly, candlelight, carols . . . and a Lord or Lady Elgin from you . . . It's the traditional way to say "Merry Christmas." And it's the smart, modern way as well. For these Lord and Lady Elgins achieve new heights in artistry and accuracy.

There's real character in every one of these expertly adjusted timepieces. Leading American designers have chosen new materials, conceived new styling in tune with the times. There are smart models in rosé, natural, and white gold, and in platinum-diamond combinations of breath-taking beauty. Lady Elgins appear in the brand new "Demi" size—distinctive smaller timepieces of rare charm.

And such amazing accuracy! Only the Lord and Lady Elgins may bear the Observatory Certificate, awarded for ability proved right in a great observatory. Two ELGIN advances protect that accuracy—the Elginium hairspring* and the Beryl-X balance. Both are rustproof, non-magnetic, unaffected by temperature and climatic changes. And every watch is produced from finest materials by skilled American craftsmen—completely created in the world's largest fine-watch factory. See your jeweler's Lord and Lady Elgins. Prices start at $50.00. Other ELGINS from $24.75. Slightly higher in Canada.

*Patents No. 1,974,695 and 2,072,489
Copr. 1940 by Elgin National Watch Company
Elgin, Ill.

Lady Elgin in lapped 14K gold with black overlay on ends. 19 jewels. No. 4201A.
$70.00

Lady Elgin. 14K rosé gold filled with high curved crystal. 19 jewels. No. 4302E.
$50.00

Lord Elgin. Extremely thin lapped 14K gold case. 21 jewels. No. 4506A.
$85.00

Lord Elgin. Lapped 14K rosé gold filled. 21 jewels.

Give them time and they'll win success!

REMEMBER YOUR OWN GRADUATION?
Ruffles and Sunday bests ... valedictory ... dreams ... a little gulp of uncertainty. And then somewhere afar off someone reading out your name ...

REMEMBER THE BIGGEST THRILL OF ALL?
Remember the moment dad and mother gave you your ELGIN watch? What a glow of confidence it brought! You knew then you'd win success. For "the folks" believed in you ... and you could never let them down.

THEN DON'T DISAPPOINT YOUR GRADUATE!
Make certain your boy or girl will know that same thrill. Plan now to give an ELGIN! Your own jeweler is showing the newest models.

CHOOSE AN ELGIN FOR YOUR GRADUATE

FINEST GRADUATION ELGINS EVER CREATED!
There is such a modern lilt and swing ... such loveliness in the newest ELGINS for girls that you'll almost wish graduation came oftener. The models for men are handsome, sturdy, competent-looking. You sense at once their honest value and workmanship . . . their extreme dependability.

Each ELGIN is produced by master craftsmen and scientists working in perfect partnership. Each is timed for accuracy to the absolute standard of the stars. The quality of every case is plainly marked. ELGINS of 15 jewels or more: $25 to $500. Other models from $17.50. Slightly higher in Canada.

☆ ELGIN ☆
CHOICE OF AMERICAN GRADUATES SINCE 1865

$125.00 $37.50 $45.00 $39.75 $45.00 $39.75 $47.50 $37.50 $55.00

$85.00 $35.00 $37.50 $47.50 $39.75 $37.50 $90.00

ELGIN, ca 1939. The unusual and attractive dial layout of this wristwatch places the numbers 12 and 6 outside the minutes chapter, while the other numbers remain inside. All the numerals and the minutes chapter are raised. The gold filled case has a steel back. 15-jeweled Elgin movement.

ELGIN, 1935. The white gold filled case frames the rectangular dial of this Elgin, creating a very clean, strong look. The sapphire crown is a replacement. 15-jeweled Elgin movement.

ELGIN, 1930s. The simple case is typical of the streamlined period, with a touch of the decorative era in its stylized Arabic numerals. The rectangular case is gold filled. 15-jeweled Elgin movement.

ELGIN, 1930s. The dial and stepped case show the influence of the Deco period, but the placement of the steps over the movable lugs belongs to the age of streamlining. The tonneau enamel painted dial uses an unusual configuration for the ten, juxtaposing the one on top of the zero. The case is white gold filled, and the Elgin movement has 15 jewels.

ELGIN, 1930s. The 14k gold filled case surrounds a strikingly designed dial. The Arabic numerals of the hours chapter are within the minutes chapter. In the center is the seconds chapter with Arabic numerals marking the 10 second positions. A short red and black sweep seconds hand brings a spot of color to the white and black dial. 15-jeweled Elgin movement.

ELGIN, 1940s. This diamond-dial Elgin is a rare wristwatch for the firm. The case is 14k gold and the rectangular black enamel painted dial has diamonds inset in the numerals at 12, 3, and 9 and as markers at the other hour positions. The hooded lugs contrast with the other design elements. 17-jeweled Elgin movement.

ELGIN, ca 1931. The two-toned case of the *Clubman 903* is very unusual for the '30s. The yellow gold filled lugs on the white gold filled case create a pleasing contrast. The dial is painted silver and features stylized Arabic numerals and lance-shaped hands. Size 18/0, grade 488 Elgin movement, 17 jewels.

ELGIN, 1930s. The dial of this curved rectangular wristwatch is unusual for its center seconds chapter and red-tipped sweep seconds hand. It makes for an outstanding looking wristwatch and is quite rare. In addition to the center seconds chapter the enamel painted dial has stylized Arabic numerals with triangular indicators at the 3 and 9 o'clock positions. The case is gold filled. Elgin 15-jeweled movement.

PAUL BREGUETTE, 1930s. The chrome-plated steel case of this Swiss wristwatch has applied batons on the sides of the case. The enamel painted dial has stylized outline Roman numerals at 12:00 and 6:00 and unusual hour markings at the other positions. A date window below the 12:00 and a subsidiary seconds chapter at 6:00 are also present. Swiss movement, 17 jewels.

Wristwatch designers experimented with the rectangle in an ongoing desire to keep new shapes and models before the public. With a rectangular movement, they were free to change the shape of the case in many directions. By rounding the sides, a gentle tonneau is created. From there it is a step to classic tonneaus, finally culminating in bulbous tonneaus, quite different in feeling from the very refined rectangles. These presage the exaggerations of the Retro '40s period, just over the horizon. Moving in another direction, the rectangle is shortened to become a square.

The subtle sophistication of the modified tonneau takes shape. The restraint of these wristwatches is remarkable and completely at one with the look of architecture and graphic design of the Thirties. Subsidiary seconds chapters on the dial often repeat the exact curve of the tonneau. Even within the more restricted space available they add their own design statement.

OMEGA, 1930s. Simplicity in style marks this streamlined Omega. It has a steel case and white enamel painted dial with black painted Arabic numerals. The case is manufactured in the U.S. and the movement is Swiss, 15 jewels.

WESTFIELD, 1930s. Bulova manufactured Westfield wristwatches as a less expensive line in the '20s using fewer jewels. The first wristwatches usually had 7 jewels. Gradually, however, the Westfield began to compete with Bulova's own brand and the jeweling was increased to 15 or more jewels. The rolled gold plated case shown here has some wear on the bezel. 15-jeweled Swiss movement.

OMEGA, ca 1931. This straightforward curved 14k gold filled wristwatch was cased and timed in the U.S. with a Swiss, 15-jeweled movement. The dial is painted pink with Arabic numerals.

PATEK PHILIPPE, 1930s-40s. An unusual combination of stainless steel and pink gold form this case. The body of the case is of stainless steel while 18k pink gold is used for the lug hoods. A large subsidiary seconds chapter distinguishes this enamel painted dial. Patek Philippe manufactured this wristwatch for Brock & Co., a California retailer, whose name appears above the subsidiary seconds chapter. Swiss movement, 18 jewels and 8 adjustments.

LONGINES, 1930s. Longine's versions of the elongated curved case, such as this one, were not as dramatically curved as the *Curvex*. Constructed of 10k gold filled, this wristwatch has a white enamel painted dial with embossed Arabic numerals. 17-jeweled Swiss movement.

WITTNAUER, 1940s. A typical wristwatch of the period, the 14k gold case is rectangular with a horizontal tonneau shape to the bezel and dial. The enamel painted dial uses Roman numerals at 12, 3, and 9 and markers as the other hours indicators. 17-jeweled Swiss movement.

PATEK PHILIPPE, 1940s. A fine example of the classic streamlined look, this 18k gold wristwatch has an enamel painted dial with applied Arabic numerals and a subsidiary seconds chapter at 6:00. Swiss movement, 18 jewels and 8 adjustments.

WALTHAM, 1930s. Interestingly, this case is designed so that the strap passes through, an unusual feature for a U.S. manufactured wristwatch. The case is gold filled, with a white enamel painted dial and a full set of Arabic numerals. 17 jewels. (Courtesy Time Will Tell)

WESTFIELD, 1930s. Westfield, a division of Bulova, created this long rectangular wristwatch. The bezel is rolled gold plate. The enamel painted dial has slash markers for the hours. 15-jeweled Swiss movement.

GRUEN, ca 1935. The stylized tonneau-shaped case leads to
teardrop lugs. The simple design is characteristic of the
streamlined period. The two-toned dial has applied numerals.
15-jeweled Precision Swiss movement.

WALTHAM, 1930s. The curved elongated case is
gold filled and has a white enamel painted dial
with applied Arabic numerals. Waltham
movement, 15 jewels.

WALTHAM, 1930s. The *Premier* has a gold filled
case with a sealing gasket under the bezel which is
somewhat unusual. The enamel painted dial has
applied Arabic numerals. The subsidiary seconds
chapter has numerals at 10 second intervals and a
center portion which is counter sunk for the
seconds hand. 17-jeweled Waltham movement.

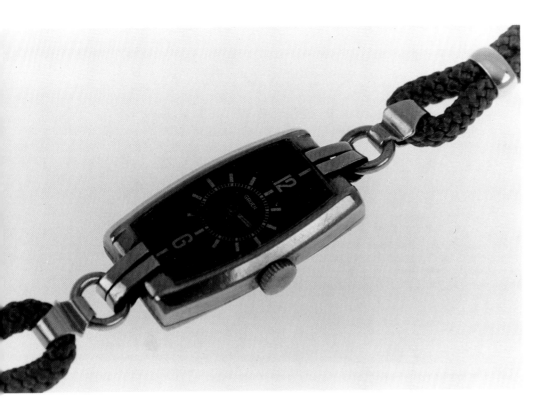

GRUEN, ca 1930. The elegant, clean lines of this case identify it as a wristwatch of the streamlined era. An elongated tonneau, it has single center post lugs which attach to a cord band. 17 jewel, Precision Swiss movement.

ILLINOIS, 1930s. This tonneau-shaped 14k white gold wristwatch has a black enamel painted dial with stylized Arabic numerals. 17 jewels.

WALTHAM, ca 1930. This gold filled Waltham mechanical digital is rare. The hours and minutes are painted on separate discs and appear in the curved windows. The name Waltham is prominently embossed on the cover/bezel. 17 jewels.(Courtesy Time Will Tell)

BULOVA, 1930s. The stepped curve case of the *Fifth Avenue* is extreme enough to challenge the Gruen *Curvex*. The enamel painted dial has applied Arabic numerals and a subsidiary seconds chapter. Swiss movement, 15 jewels.

BULOVA, 1930s. This is one of the finest looking wristwatches manufactured by Bulova. The 10k yellow gold filled cushion case is embossed on the lug ends of the bezel and has deeply sculpted and offset stepped lugs. The pink enamel painted dial hasraised Arabic numerals. 17-jeweled Swiss movement.

LONGINES, 1930s. The elongated curved case of this streamlined Longines ends in crescent styled lugs and bezel. The 10k gold filled case is American-made. The enamel painted dial has full Arabic numerals. Swiss movement, 17 jewels.

HAMILTON, 1930s. The 14k gold filled case of the *Brooke* is designed with a wedge-profile so that the dial is higher off the wrist at 12:00 than at 6:00, to make the time easier to read. The case is wider at the bottom than the top. The dial is two-toned and has raised 18k gold numerals wichapter. The patented design of the *Brooke* was unusual in the wristwatch industry. This very rare wristwatch is the essence of streamlined design. Its asymmetrical trapezoidal shape makes it highly desirable. 17 jewels. Issue price: $52.50.

Courtesy: the Bulova Watch Company

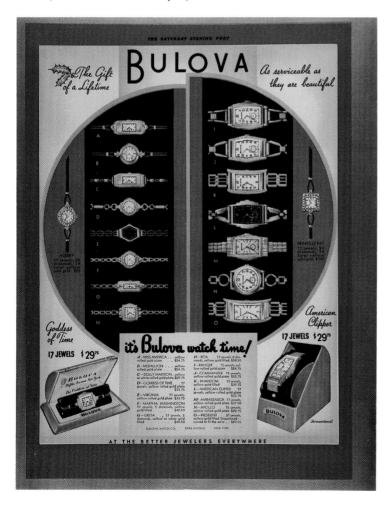

HAMILTON, ca 1940. The *Bagley* fits the streamline category with its square tonneau shape and gracefully shaped lugs. It is a clean, elegant wristwatch with a 10k gold filled case and silver dial with applied gold numerals. 17-jeweled Hamilton movement.

WALTHAM, 1920s-30s. The tonneau-shaped case is gold filled. It houses an enamel painted dial with stylized Arabic numerals. The bulbous crown recalls an earlier period. 15 jewels, American movement.

HAMILTON, 1930s. This stepped, tonneau-shaped wristwatch is 14k gold filled. It has a 17-jeweled Hamilton movement and an enamel painted dial which features luminous Arabic numbers and hands and a subsidiary seconds chapter.

BENRUS, ca 1937. The 14k rolled gold plate case is American and features a wide tonneau shape with hooded lugs. The dial has Arabic numerals and a subsidiary seconds chapter. Swiss, 15-jeweled movement.

GRUEN, ca 1926. An early example of the Gruen *Quadron*, the tonneau-shaped case was designed to fit the elongated tonneau movement introduced by Gruen in 1925. The stepped case is of reinforced 14k white gold with an engraved outer edge. The dial is silver matte with gold painted numbers and luminous skeleton hands. 17-jeweled Swiss Gruen Precision movement.

ILLINOIS, 1930s. The 14k gold filled tonneau case of this Illinois is devoid of decorative work, unlike its Deco predecessors. The dial reflects an earlier era with the subsidiary seconds chapter at 9:00 and the style of numerals and Mercedes skeleton hands that are used. 17-jeweled Illinois movement. (Courtesy Dr. Jerry Solin)

ILLINOIS,ca 1930. The smooth lines of *The Ritz* distinguish it from its Deco predecessors. The offset stepped case is two-toned, 14k gold filled. The dial is white with very unusual, angled Arabic numerals. This is an exquisite, rare wristwatch. 17-jeweled Illinois movement.

GRUEN, 1930s. This Gruen Precision has a 14k gold case made by Wadsworth Watch Case Company. The dial is enamel painted and features a subsidiary seconds chapter. It has an automatic Swiss movement with 17 jewels.

GRUEN, ca 1938. This Gruen Veri-Thin has 14k gold filled square stepped case. The dial has 24 hour inner chapter in addition to an outer minutes chapter and gold numerals and markers in the hours chapter. The solid lugs are shaped as inverted "C's". 17-jeweled Swiss Gruen Precision movement.

GRUEN, 1940s. The case of this Veri-Thin is 14k gold filled with a slight curve to its body. Articulated U-shaped flexible lugs are attached to the square case by a central tube. The dial is two-toned with applied numerals. A Swiss Gruen Precision movement, 17 jewels.

BULOVA, ca 1940. The *Corrigam* has a 10k rolled gold plate case, sculpted and stepped at the extended lugs. The enamel painted dial has stylized raised numerals. 17-jeweled, Swiss 7 AK Bulova movement.

BULOVA, 1930s. This 10k rolled gold plate case is nicely sculpted with scalloped work at the lug ends of the bezel. The enamel painted dial incorporates alternating Arabic numerals and triangular stick markers. 17-jeweled Swiss movement.

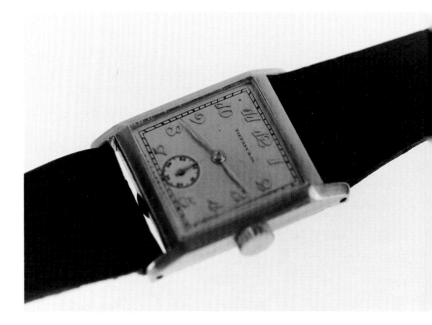

BULOVA, 1930s. The square case of this 10k gold filled Bulova has pyramid-like steps in all directions. The subsidiary seconds chapter is at 6:00 on the enamel painted dial. The alligator strap is original. Swiss movement, 17 jewels.

PATEK PHILIPPE, 1930s. The name "Tiffany & Co." appears on the dial of this platinum hinged case wristwatch, made by Patek Philippe as indicated inside the back of the case and on the movement. The square, enamel painted dial displays Arabic numerals and has a subsidiary seconds chapter. The Swiss movement has 18 jewels and 8 adjustments.

ELGIN, 1920s-30s. The square gold filled case of this Elgin features three piece case construction. The enamel painted dial has squared Arabic numerals and a subsidiary seconds chapter at 6:00. 15-jeweled Elgin movement.

ELGIN, 1930s. With its "Universal" logo on the dial this may have been a promotional wristwatch manufactured by Elgin for use as advertising or as a premium for a company named "Universal". This Lord Elgin is 14k gold with an hourglass type case design, curved lugs continuing the line of the case and bezel. The enamel painted dial uses Arabic numerals and there is a subsidiary seconds chapter. Elgin movement.

GRUEN, ca 1938. The 14k gold filled, die-struck case has a long tonneau shape with a ridged, embossed bezel. The enamel painted dial has Arabic figures and a subsidiary seconds chapter at 6:00. 15-jeweled Swiss movement.

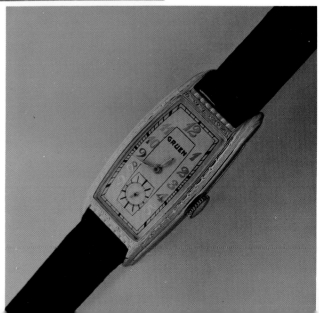

HAMILTON, ca 1936. A classic example of the tank style of the 1930s, the *Clark* was manufactured in yellow gold filled. It had a sterling silver dial with applied gold numerals, and was available with a black painted dial. The Hamilton movement was 14/0 size, grade 980 with 17 jewels. It sold originally for $52.50 with the silvered dial and $50 with the black.

HAMILTON, ca 1937. The curved case of the *Morley* is an example of Hamilton's challenge to the successful Gruen *Curvex*. The case is 10k gold filled. The enamel painted dial has black numerals but was available with applied gold numerals. The 17-jeweled grade 987 Hamilton movement had nickel plates and bridge, steel escape and an *Elinvar* hairspring.

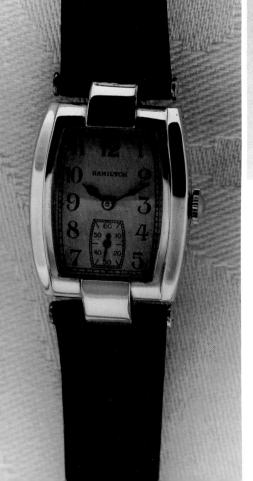

HAMILTON, ca 1935. The streamlined look of the *Mt. Vernon* is emphasized by the stepped tonneau bezel supported by the wide central lugs. The case is 14k yellow gold filled and was also available in white gold filled. The enamel painted dial has stylized Arabic numerals in black. 17-jeweled Hamilton movement.

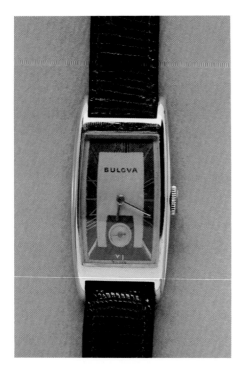

BULOVA, 1930s. This curved, long
tonneau-shaped 10k rolled gold plate case
holds a two-toned enamel painted dial.
The dial is in pink and yellow gold with
a subsidiary seconds chapter at 6:00. 17-
jeweled Swiss movement.

BULOVA, 1930s. The elongated curved case of this Bulova is 10k gold filled. The
two-toned white dial has outlined Arabic numerals in black. Swiss 17-jeweled,
Bulova model 7 AP movement.

HAMILTON, ca 1946.
The *Donald* features a
14k tonneau case with a
silver enamel painted
dial and applied 18k
gold numerals. 19
jewels.

HAMILTON, ca 1936. A typical streamlined tank shape, the proportions of the *Clark* are elegant and stylish on the wrist. The case is 14k gold-filled and the dial is enamel painted on silver with 18k gold applied numerals. A 14/0 size, grade 980 movement with 17 jewels. This *Clark* is illustrated with a typical strap of the period made of pigskin.

The round wristwatches made during the Thirties share the same design characters of the rectangular groups of designs, a clean, modern look that sets them apart from earlier round styles. Sometimes the round dial is set within a tonneau- or cushion-shaped case.

The opulent decoration of the Twenties gives way to more subtle touches, just a bit of engraving on the bezel. Minutes chapters follow the shape of the rectangle, with plain open squares broken at each five minute mark with a simple black square. Simple, easy to read Arabic numbers are almost universal, but stick markers as hour indicators are often combined with numerals. Roman numbers are rarely used. The subsidiary second at 6:00 takes the same shape as the wristwatch dial. And where architectural details are echoed on the cases, the motifs are restrained and understated.

Dials move away from porcelain toward painted or plated surfaces. Hamilton begins to use raised 18k gold figures applied to sterling silver dials which give the dial more dimension and definition. The hands are slim and modern, much simpler and straight forward in keeping with the overall look of the wristwatches. Coordination of all elements of the dial is a hallmark of the decade. This is a defined, refined classic dial.

BALL, 1930s. The window below the 12 indicates the number of hours left in the wind of this automatic wristwatch. The painted enamel dial has outlined Arabic numerals and a sweep seconds hand. 17-jeweled Swiss movement.

SWISS, 1930s. The *Uptodate* uses various devices to give the wearer the date, day and month. In each lug is a cutout, one of which reveals the day of the week and the other the month. These are manually changed by turning a tooth wheel on the edge of each lug. A red sweep hand indicates the date on an outer date chapter, also in red. The case is chrome-plated steel with an enamel painted dial and luminous numerals and hands. 15-jeweled Swiss movement.

GRUEN, 1930s. This *Chronatimer* is a single button chronograph. The round gold filled case frames a black enamel painted dial. The sweep seconds hand records up to one minute on the chronograph. Also available in gold with a waterproof type screw back. 17-jeweled Swiss movement.

SWISS, 1930s. Abercrombie & Fitch, the American sporting goods and adventurer's store, contracted for the manufacture of the *Shipmate* with a Swiss manufacturer. The steel case houses a two-toned, round, enamel painted dial. The black minutes/seconds chapter surrounds a light hours chapter, with luminous Arabic numerals at 12, 3, 6, and 9 and luminous hands. There is a sweep seconds hand. Swiss movement, 17 jewels.

ELGIN, 1930s-40s. Production was limited on this Lord Elgin, owing in part to the public uneasiness with the digital readout concept. None of the companies that experimented with this form of wristwatch were able to capture the consumer's interest and create a niche in the market place. The gold filled case has an embossed chevron and a triangular window which reveal the hours and minutes as they passed by on enamel painted discs. 19-jeweled Elgin movement. A highly unusual and rare design.

ELGIN, 1930s. Often called the "Golf Ball" wristwatch after the dimpled pattern on its case, this digital Elgin is quite different in design. The case is gold filled and the enamel painted discs which carry the hours and minutes chapters. The time appears digitally through a triangular window at the 6:00 position. 17-jeweled Elgin movement.

ELGIN, 1930s. This gold-filled wristwatch has unusual T-shaped, hooded lugs. The enamel painted dial has a subsidiary seconds chapter. 17 jewels.

HAMILTON, ca 1940. The clean, elegant, easy to read dial of the *Lexington* typifies the Hamilton wristwatches of the streamlined period. The case is stainless steel. The enamel painted dial is white, though it was also available in black with white numerals. 17-jeweled Hamilton movement.

GENEVE, 1930s. The bezel of this wristwatch extends under the crystal in the form of skeletonized numerals, giving the wristwatch a dramatic look. The American case is rolled gold plated with a stainless steel back, and has an embossed chain around the edge. It has a black enamel painted dial, gold hands and a subsidiary seconds chapter at 6:00. Swiss movement, 7 jewels.

ROLEX, 1930s. This *Oyster* is unusual in that it is designed more like a dress model, while keeping the screw-on back and crown that give the *Oyster* its waterproof character. The case is 18k gold and has shaped hooded lugs. The dial is painted in a gold color and has Arabic numerals around an inner hours chapter. It has an outer minutes chapter and a subsidiary seconds chapter at 6:00. Swiss movement, 15 jewels.

WALTHAM, 1940s. The *Premier* is a round doctor's
wristwatch with an outer chapter that instructs "Count 30
Pulsations" and has a scale for calculating a patient's pulse
rate. It has a gold filled bezel with a stainless steel back,
and a white enamel painted dial. 17 jewels.

WALTHAM, 1930s. The *Premier* lady's wristwatch has a
round 14k gold case. The dial uses precious stones for the
hours markers. In this example the stones are sapphires,
but the wristwatch also came with rubies or emeralds. 17-
jeweled.

ILLINOIS, 1930s. This *Tivoli* model has a round porcelain dial within a cushion-shaped yellow gold filled case made by the Elgin Watch Case Company. The dial has a digital seconds window. 17-jeweled Illinois movement.

ILLINOIS, 1930s. The case of this Illinois wristwatch has a gold filled bezel and stainless steel back. A subsidiary seconds chapter with blued steel hands is at 9:00. 15 jewels.

HAMILTON, ca 1934. Streamlining is incorporated into this *Cushion Strap Watch* with its clean, simple lines. The case is 14k gold filled and was available in 14k gold or silver. The aviation styled painted silver dial has luminous numerals and hands. 6/0 size, grade Hamilton 979 movement, 19 jewels.

ELGIN, ca 1931. The *Avigo 426* has a unique dial design, placing the six over the seconds chapter. The cushion-shaped case is chromium plated nickel. The dial is enamel painted with bold Arabic numerals and a winged "Avigo". Elgin movement, 7 jewels.

ELGIN, ca 1931. The *Clubman 1001* features a 14k white gold filled case with yellow gold filled lugs extending onto the bezel. The case is nearly square with a round two-toned enamel painted dial. 17-jeweled Elgin movement.

ELGIN, 1930s. The gold filled American case is square with a round dial. The enamel painted dial has outlined Arabic numerals and blue-steeled hands. 15-jeweled Elgin movement.

WALTHAM, 1920s. This very rare case is designed for left-handed people with the crown at 9:00 and a subsidiary seconds chapter at 3:00. The case is gold filled and the dial is porcelain with Arabic numerals. 15-jeweled Waltham movement.

WALTHAM, 1930s. The *Pilot* is a chrome-plated, cushion-shaped wristwatch with an enamel painted dial. It has full Arabic numerals, with the 12, 3, 6, and 9 and the pierced hands painted to be luminous. The insignia is of a propeller and wings. With its seconds read digitally in a window above the 6:00 position, this is an unusual wristwatch. 15 jewels.

HAMILTON, ca 1934. This stepped 14k gold filled case is similar to the Hamilton *Putnam* with the exception of the hours chapter. 17-jeweled, 6/0 sized Hamilton movement.

LA SALLE, 1930s. This wristwatch offers an early use of the digital date chapter. It combines with a digital seconds chapter to create a rare watch, especially in as fine a condition as this. The gold plated case is stepped. 15-jeweled Swiss movement.

ILLINOIS, ca 1930. The enamel painted dial has a subsidiary seconds chapter at 9:00, a common design for Illinois. It is housed in a cut-corner rectangular case. 15 jewels.

Besides this seeming imitation of the Gruen *Curvex* design, Hamilton scored some successes of its own during the depths of the depression. Hamilton's company publication notes that the firm enjoyed steady sales volume increases up to 1929's $5,769,000. The low point was reached just three years later with a volume of just $1,558,000. Yet in 1928/29, Hamilton introduced three enamel bezel designs, the *Coronado*, the *Piping Rock*, and the *Spur*, that are among today's most desirable collector's models. These three stand out in the firm's 1931 catalog which otherwise is still wedded to the feeling of the '20s.

In a 1929 ad, Elgin features a similar wristwatch, but with Roman numbers, in its *Legionnaire* series. This Elgin design is described as "A brilliant new touch—numerals on the outside of the case upon a band of bright black enamel...$24.00." With both wristwatches coming out virtually at the same time, one can only speculate as to whether this was an instance of the same idea striking two designers at once—which often happens—or an example of industrial espionage. And if it was the latter, who was the thief and who the victim?

HAMILTON, Ca. 1928. The Hamilton *Coronado* has a tonneau shape with stylized Arabic numerals set into the enameled bezel. It came in 14k yellow gold and white gold. The minutes chapter is on the dial, and there is a subsidiary seconds chapter at 6:00. 17 jewels.

HAMILTON, ca 1929. This Hamilton *Spur* has an unusual sculpted, asymmetrical stepped case in 14k yellow gold, with a matte silver dial. It was also made in white gold. The case was manufactured by the Wadsworth Watch Case Company and has a black enameled bezel containing the hours chapter in Roman numerals. The Spur was produced for only one year and there were probably only 1000 made, making this a very rare model. #979 movement, Hamilton, 19 jewels. (Courtesy Aaron Faber Gallery)

HAMILTON, 1920s (First edition), 1940s (Second edition). The black enameled round bezel of this 14k gold *Piping Rock* is framed in a tonneau case. The bezel displays the hours chapter with Roman numerals while the dial has the minutes track and a subsidiary seconds chapter. It features moveable lugs and blued steel hands. The Hamilton movement has 17 jewels.

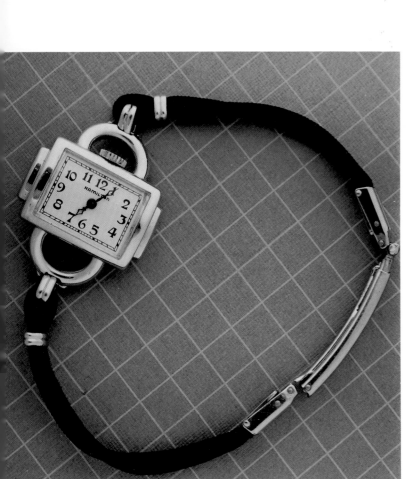

HAMILTON, ca 1938. This unusual woman's wristwatch was designed to be worn on the top or side of the wrist. The 14k yellow gold stepped case has exaggerated hooped lugs. The horizontal position of the rectangular case called for the return to the 12:00 crown position. Like the other edge-of-wristwatches, the style did not catch on, making this a highly prized and rare wristwatch. 17 jewels.

ELGIN, ca 1929. The triangular shapes that make up the bezel of this lady's Elgin are beveled away from the diamond-shaped dial, making this a very dramatic watch. The case is 14k gold filled with an enamel painted dial. Very rare and collectible because of its extreme geometry. Elgin movement, 21 jewels.

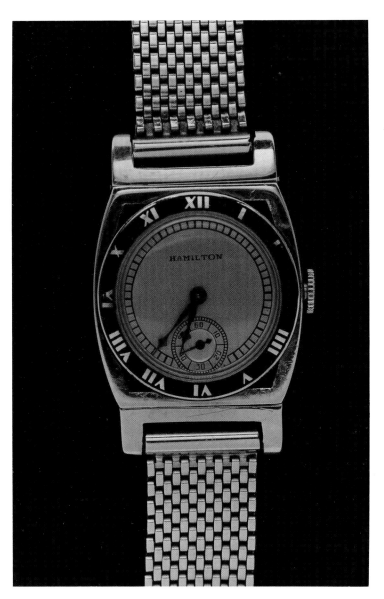

Same as Hamilton, 1920s watch shown on left.

ELGIN, Ca. 1928. This *Presentation* model 212 is extremely rare. It combines a square case with a round bezel and a stretched hexagonal dial. The bezel has an enameled hours chapter with Roman numerals. The case material is 14k white gold. The enamel painted dial has a minutes chapter. The case has hinged lugs. A more common variety of this wristwatch came in 14k yellow gold with a round dial. 17 jewels. (Courtesy Aaron Faber Galleries)

GRUEN DOCTOR'S WATCHES. In the streamlined period, Gruen produced a series of wristwatches which came to be called doctor's wristwatches. These wristwatches featured the striking duo-dial and were manufactured from 1929 through the 1940s. The independent subsidiary seconds chapter was enlarged and controlled by a larger gear train. The wristwatches came in lengths from 41mm to 48mm and widths from 20-21mm. They were available in 14k white and yellow gold filled as well as white and yellow gold, with Roman or Arabic numerals and black or white dials. In addition there was a jump hour variation made. The movements and cases were also modified for use in the Rolex doctor's wristwatch series, with the Rolex name on the movement. These wristwatches are valued by collectors, particularly when the dials are in their original condition. The more unusual and elaborate the case designs, the higher the value.

Ca. 1930. This watch shows the famous Gruen *Alpina* dial. *Alpina* designates the Gruen doctor's watch. The hours chapter uses Roman numerals and the seconds chapter is divided into 10 second intervals.

The introduction of the *Flintridge*, Hamilton's covered wristwatch design with a spring released cover, evoked the old hunting case watch. The design was heralded as "A New Sports Watch. Here it is—the out-of-doors watch with a cover! This cover is operated by a spring in the upper right hand lug. It serves as a protection against dust and dampness, jolts and jars, and broken crystals!" This "sportsman's" wristwatch was available only in 14k gold.

Doctor's wristwatches captured the fancy of many who were entranced with the idea of seeing the seconds tick away as clearly as the minutes and hours. The divided dial on these rectangular cases offered the hours/minutes chapter in the upper half, the seconds chapter in the lower half. The seconds chapter was not subsidiary but a co-equal to the hours/minutes chapter. Gruen's (#877) *Techni-Quadron* made its appearance in a *Saturday Evening Post* advertisement of September 7, 1929. Building on its rectangular *Quadron* movement, introduced in 1925, the *Techni-Quadron* case featured two dials within a rectangular case. It was not called a doctor's wristwatch by Gruen but the audience to which it was directed is evident:"Technicians, doctors, and men in other professions who desire accurate time in seconds, will welcome this newest addition to the famous group of *Quadron* wristwatches for men—the *Techni-Quadron*."

"To permit quick, accurate reading, the *Techni-Quadron* movement is specially constructed for an extra-large seconds dial, free from interference by minute and hour hands."

Hamilton's doctor's wristwatch appears in its 1935 catalogue, along with another "innovation". Hamilton calls its split-dial wristwatch, the *Seckron*, "A new Hamilton for doctors, nurses, and others requiring split-minute precision." This two-dial wristwatch in a rectangular case bears a remarkable resemblance to Gruen's in both name and actual appearance.

Ca. 1930. A 14k yellow gold-filled doctor's wristwatch with a white dial and a red hour wheel with the hour appearing in a window at 12:00. The top dial has a minutes chapter and hand with numerals at five minutes intervals, and the lower dial is the seconds chapter. The articulated step case has side batons. Swiss movement with jump hour, 15 jewels.

Ca 1929. A 14k yellow gold filled case has a "crown guard" indentation on the side. The Arabic numerals on the hours chapter are plain but attractive. 41mm x 21mm. 15-jeweled Swiss movement.

This unusual doctor's wristwatch has a railroad style stepped ridge 14k white gold filled case. The sharply defined stepped case makes this a desirable streamlined watch. The dial is a fine example of the original Arabic numerals and art.

1930s. This jump hour version of the doctor's wristwatch has a steel case with pink gold batons on the edges. The black enamel painted dial has an hour window at 12 o'clock with painted pink minutes and seconds chapters and pink gold hands.

Ca 1930. Advertised "for Doctors and other professional people who require dependable, split-second timekeeping accuracy," the *Olympiad* has a 14k gold filled case and white duo-dial. Swiss movement, 17 jewels.

HAMILTON, ca 1936. Hamilton's version of the doctor's wristwatch was called the *Seckron* and is much sought after by collectors. Less streamlined than other wristwatches of the period, the case is more a classically elongated stepped tank. The case is 14k gold-filled and framing a black or white dial. Rare in good condition, it is a "must have" for wristwatch collectors. 17-jeweled Hamilton movement. Originally priced at $55.

A wristwatch that manages to be totally in the streamlined spirit of the Thirties yet looks back to the hunting case watch of the transitional period is the *Reverso*, introduced in 1931. It was first made by Tavannes for the Swiss company LeCoultre and a few years later was made by LeCoultre itself.

The movement and case are fixed on a grooved hinge enabling the wristwatch to flip over into its own jacket, which is often engraved and gives some protection to the crystal. The *Reverso* evokes the hunting case watch, yet with its elegant black enamel and metal cover, it clearly has the look of the streamlined era.

The idea of this wristwatch was copied by other firms, just as the Gruen *Curvex* was copied. Hamilton had a version of this idea which it introduced in 1938. The model name was *Otis*. The black or silver dial wristwatch was unusual in that it was offered only in a gold filled case but had 18k applied gold numerals. Ignoring LeCoultre's 1935 introduction of its *Reverso*, Hamilton's catalogue description reads, "Exclusively Hamilton, this smartly designed strap wristwatch ingeniously fulfills its double duty in a practical, foolproof manner. Slight pressure from the side, a flip of the finger—and the watch locks firmly into reversed position."

At the end of the 1920s, a quiet innovation brought the wristwatch to a new level of convenience. This was the removable pin or spring bar which makes it possible to change a wristwatch band at will. Two methods are used. In one, the spring bar was made with pins (male) that fit into holes (female) on the sides of the lugs. In the other, pins projected from inside the lugs and fit into holes in the ends of the bar. Before, the solid lug restricted

SWISS, 1930s. An exotic reversible, it pivots to turn the dial so it rests either upward for reading or downward for protection. 17-jeweled Swiss movement.

BULOVA, ca 1930. A Bulova doctor's wristwatch is extremely rare. The hours/minutes chapters are separate from the seconds chapter on this enamel painted two-toned dial. The dials have distinctively designed chapters. The hands are gun metal. The stepped metal case is chrome plated. Swiss movement, 15 jewels.

HAMILTON, ca 1938. The *Otis* imitates the appearance of the LeCoultre *Reverso* style exactly, though the mechanics are somewhat different. Hamilton lost a patent fight with LeCoultre, and the *Otis* was dropped from the line after only three years of production. The case is 14k "extra heavy natural gold filled," and was typically engraved on the closed cover as in this example. The dial is sterling silver with a black or silver finish, with applied 18k gold numerals. 19 jewels, grade 982 movement. The *Otis* belongs in any serious American wristwatch collection. (Courtesy: Aaron Faber Gallery)

ELGIN, ca 1941. A rare duo-dial wristwatch, the hours and seconds chapters overlap to give it an extra-ordinary look. The American-made case is 10k gold-filled. The black enamel painted dial has white numbers and figures. 17-jeweled Elgin movement.

the type of band that could be put on. The removable spring bar permitted an easy and quick change of straps, whether they were worn out or simply for a change of mood. No longer did straps have to be sewn or glued on. This change brought about a whole new industry. Exotic animal skins played their part in the look of the Thirties wristwatch: alligator, elephant, buffalo, crocodile, ostrich, all were used for wristwatch straps. This was before the public became aware of endangered species.

The metal band took on a Thirties look, and more important, a Thirties feel. The metal band of the 1920s had a tendency to grab the hair on the skin; the wristwatch bands of the '30s were coiled differently and overcame this painful problem both in karat gold and in gold filled and rolled gold plate.

Leading the way in the American watch band industry were the innovative designs of Hadley Kalbe. It created a variety of linkage bands, some with springs, in the effort to overcome pulling of the hair. As men finally accepted the wristwatch in greater numbers, the metal band bows to their special needs. Because the leather strap doesn't allow the skin to breathe, sweat collects underneath. The metal band solved this problem.

The streamlined look of Gruen's *Curvex* and its many competitors was right in tune with the look of the entire period. Streamlining captured the American imagination; it summed up our presence as the forward-thinking, forward-acting, forward-looking nation—one that had so little history to look back on when compared with our European forbearers. The commercial airliner as well as the transatlantic oceanliner and all that was streamlined and modern would be encapsulated in the World's Fair of 1939-1940 in New York. At the culmination of the decade, in the moments before America was forced into the Second World War, the design of the period was made manifest in the Fair. Significantly, the look was the work of a team of industrial designers headed by Walter Dorwin Teague. The curve of the Gruen *Curvex* cases would be echoed in the soaring cantilevered walkways of the World's Fair. The fair marks not only the end of the decade, it was also the end of the peace that we in the United States had known since the First World War. It also brought an end, finally to the depression.

The coming war in Europe would bring these glory years of America's watch companies to a deadening halt, whether their movements were made in this country or abroad. Although Elgin had started to think in terms of war production as early as 1937, the entry of the United States into the war following the bombing of Pearl Harbor on December 7, 1941, put the design of consumer products on hold. For the next half decade, watch manufacturers would devote their design, engineering and manufacturing skills to the war effort. Another chapter in American watchmaking had come to a close.

BULOVA, ca. 1938. Curved tank with extended "saddle" lug. (Courtesy of Harry Stecker)

LORD ELGIN, ca. 1938. Curved tank with applied numbers. A classic example of the American tank, exhibiting strong European influence. 14k gold, 21 jewels. (Courtesy of Time Will Tell)

Chapter Four
The Novelty Wristwatch
1933-The present

It's been sixty years since Mickey Mouse first appeared as a cartoon character, and fifty years since Superman first streaked his way across the sky, fighting for truth, justice and the American Way. What could be more American than turning those symbols into salable, tangible products such as wristwatches? Novelty watches express the best and the worst about us; they're brash and colorful and none too subtle. They're fun and disposable; they're trendy and right this minute. If ever a manufactured item was created that said, "I'm an American", the novelty wristwatch is it. Unlike the fine, jeweled movements used in the period watches detailed in this book, novelty wristwatches owe their success to inexpensive pin-lever movements of little intrinsic value. They do work and often work very well for a very long time, but they are no competition for a well-made jeweled movement. The contemporary value attached to these wristwatches is a function of fashion and nostalgia, not horology.

There was no watch manufacturer more ideally suited to making this brash, trendy, inexpensive watch than Ingersoll. This company devoted itself to getting the price of a watch down to where it equalled a day's pay at the turn of the century—the $1.00 watch. By 1905, Ingersoll was selling millions of watches. By the end of the First World War, Ingersoll's various factories had made more than 50 million watches. Ingersoll was purchased by the Waterbury Clock Co. in 1922, but the Ingersoll trademark continued. By 1928, its total production soared to more than 90 million watches.

Scarcely had the watch manufacturers worked out the basic problems of the wristwatch than the novelty watch companies were at hand to put a new face on this new-fangled timepiece. In 1933, shortly after wristwatches surpassed pocket watches in sales, the first novelty wristwatch made its appearance. On its dial was that lovable rodent, Mickey Mouse. His yellow-gloved hands first told the time on a wristwatch by Ingersoll that was introduced to the public at the Chicago World's Fair in 1933. Ingersoll's exhibit at the Century of Progress Exposition, as the Fair was officially known, included a miniature factory where people could see their Mickey Mouse wristwatch being made and take delivery on the spot. Mickey outsold the World's Fair commemorative wristwatch three to one, even though it sold for $2.95 at a time when pocket watches that were guaranteed for a year could be had for $1.00. He has remained the most popular cartoon wristwatch of all time. By August of that year, a contemporary magazine story reported that Ingersoll was making more than 500 pieces a day but that production was "considerably behind orders".

Although it might seem extravagant to buy such a frivolous wristwatch in the depth of the depression, the Ingersoll comic wristwatch was in the tradition of the $1 watch. It was made to be bought by adults for children,

EXACTA TIME, 1949. This stainless steel watch came in a plastic baseball shaped case which read "Official Babe Ruth Wristwatch—Sports-watch of Champions". Swiss movement.

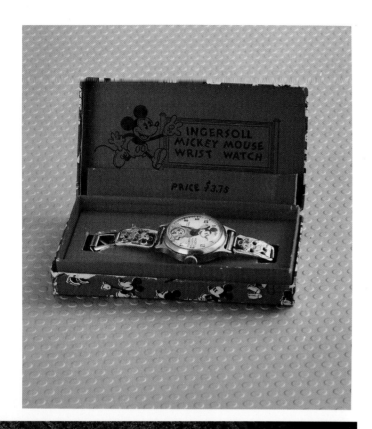

INGERSOLL, ca 1933. This Mickey Mouse watch, known as "Mickey One" is the first and most important collectible character watch. Introduced to the public in 1934 it was available with pierced cut-out Mickey Mouse figures, on an attached metal or Mickey printed on a leather strap. The case was chromium-plated base metal and had a coated paperboard polychrome painted dial with matching cut-out hands. The subsidiary seconds chapter was a revolving disc with three small Mickey Mouse images and an arrow indicating the seconds. The wristwatch was a great success with two million pieces being sold by 1936.

INGERSOLL, 1947. A very rare example of the Mickey Mouse wristwatch in the original four-color paper box with original price labels ($6.95). This 1947 version has a tonneau-shaped chromium-plated base metal case. The dial features red minutes and hours. The wristwatch also has its original red patent leather strap. Pin ever movement. (Courtesy of the S. Manolis Collection)

INGERSOLL, ca 1937. This Mickey Mouse wristwatch has a chromium-plated tonneau case with a coated paperboard dial. Mickey's cut-out hands serve as hours and minutes hands. The patent numbers on the movement are dated 1935 and 1937. There were two or three variations using the same movement and dial. The earliest models are marked "W.D.Ent." (Walt Disney Enterprises) on the dial. Later, after 1944, that was changed to W.D.P. (Walt Disney Productions). This wristwatch has a pin lever movement. Its serial number is F1699463. It may have come in this happy birthday wristwatch box.

but often the adults bought it for themselves. Though they contained only pin-lever movements, the wristwatches were remarkably accurate and a very good value.

Production of the Mickey Mouse wristwatch, like other non-essential products, stopped during the Second World War. However, as the nation went to war, so did Mickey Mouse. It was worn on the wrists of many American soldiers, spreading the popularity of the wristwatch across the ocean. Phenomenal prices were reportedly received by many GIs who sold their Mickeys before returning home.

After the war, production resumed under the banner of U.S. Time Corporation which had bought the Ingersoll-Waterbury Clock Co. in 1944. This switch of brands easily dates Mickeys: pre-war wristwatches carry the name Ingersoll, post-war the U.S. Time brand. Production continued apace. During the post-war consumer fever, one million were made in 1948 alone. By 1957, the 25 millionth Mickey Mouse wristwatch was sold. Eventually, U.S. Time became Timex, and continued to produce the contemporary equivalent of the dollar watch. By 1968, the 40th anniversary of Mickey's first appearance in a cartoon, a whole new generation was ready to wear the mouse. Millions more were sold leading up to the electric Mickey.

INGERSOLL (U.S. TIME), 1955. The popularity of the
television show, *The Mickey Mouse Club* and the
Mouseketeers endeared Mickey Mouse to yet another
generation of young people. This wristwatch was marketed
particularly to this new audience. The figure of Mickey is on
the dial with his oversized hands pointing out the hours and
minutes. The wristwatches here have their original bands and
are in their original packaging. Pin lever movement.
(Courtesy: Jack Feldman).

U.S. TIME, ca 1950. Exaggerated cut-out hands mark the time in this Mickey Mouse wristwatch. The round, polychrome painted metal dial has black script style numerals on a beige background. Pin lever, tonneau-shaped movement.

INGERSOLL, ca 1949. This Mickey Mouse wristwatch, marked U.S. Time on the case, is tonneau-shaped and has a chromium plated base metal case. The pin lever movement turns Mickey's yellow-gloved hands to tell the time. Produced in conjunction with Mickey's 20th birthday.

INGERSOLL. This Mickey Mouse wristwatch has a chromium plated bezel with a stainless steel back. There is a possibility that it was manufactured for Ingersoll in Japan, though it may be a Japanese imitation of an Ingersoll Mickey Mouse watch. The red patent leather strap is original.

TIMEX, 1960s to the present. In the '60s and 70s' Timex continued to produce variations on the Mickey Mouse wristwatch with imported movements including electric versions. The venerable cartoon figure wristwatch resurfaces in the 80s in plastic variations. A quartz 18k gold Mickey Mouse wristwatch is currently available with a gold bracelet for $12,000.

SWISS, 1976. This American flag wristwatch commemorates the nation's 200th birthday. The legend at the top says "1776 Bicentennial 1976". It has an all plastic case in the shape of a waving revolutionary period flag. The wristwatch dial is in the blue field and has thirteen stars. Political and patriotic examples of wristwatches are unusual and have become collectible because of their rarity. Although of late vintage, this wristwatch is desirable to the wristwatch collector. 17-jeweled Swiss movement.

HONEST TIME COMPANY, 1970s. Another example of the political cartoon on the dial of the wristwatch is this one growing out of the Watergate scandal in American politics. It features Senator Sam Irwin, chair of the Senate Watergate Committee, clinging to the top of the Capitol Dome. The U.S. Constitution is in his back pocket and his fingers point to the names of the principal Watergate figures. 17-jeweled Swiss movement.

In a prescient article in *Playthings* magazine, dated August 1933, the introduction of Mickey Mouse wristwatches was described as a sell-out even before the Christmas selling season.

"Already many of the leading department stores are displaying full lines and have found it necessary to re-order not once, but several times. Already there is a forecast of really important volume." The article goes on to pinpoint a telling dilemma: "Arguments between toy buyers and jewelry buyers as to which department this merchandise rightfully belongs are already on the horizon." The solution, it notes, is to stock them in both departments.

Novelty wristwatches do tell the time—after a fashion. Usually mounted with pin lever movements, and costing a couple of dollars, they never purported to be anything but a way to wear your heart on your wrist. Although pin lever watches do run faithfully for many years, what they really have to tell is information about the wearer rather than the watch company. wristwatches proclaim our admiration for characters from comic strips and fables, for film stars, for political figures—those we admire and those we mock—even for the products we consume. Status, at least in the American versions, is a peculiar beast. The novelty wristwatch is intended not to set us above others, but to indicate membership in a club, an informal club with no dues, no meetings, no obligations at all. It's a way of identifying like-minded individuals in our supremely mobile, largely classless society. For the person who chooses it, the Mickey Mouse wristwatch carries the same message as the Rolex *Oyster* or the old school tie—it's an instantly recognizable form of identification with an idea, a social grouping.

AGON CHROMATIC WATCH COMPANY, 1970s. This wristwatch bears the caricature of Spiro Agnew, the Vice President under Richard Nixon. The bezel is gold plated. The movement is 1-jeweled Swiss and is engraved "EB".

UNKNOWN, 1970. Novelty wristwatches often took on political overtones. At times they were designed to satirize a political figure and at other times they were used for self-aggrandizement, as here. The copyright "L.M." probably means that Mr. Maddox owns the rights to this caricature. The case is chromium-plated stainless steel. The polychrome painted metal dial features Mr. Maddox on his bicycle with his infamous baseball bats as minutes and hours hands. Similar items form an interesting subgroup of collectibles occurring, generally, after 1960. 17-jeweled Swiss movement.

A look at the wristwatches we have worn through the decades tells us where America has been politically and morally. When we admire the virtues of Roy Rogers and his faithful horse Trigger, or when we strap Pinocchio to our wrists, or when we mock our own government with the Watergate wristwatch, we're telling everyone exactly how we feel.

The whole notion of character wristwatches, what they mean, and why people wear them, is summed up in a joke printed in *Time* magazine July 6, 1970: Q: Have you heard what Mickey Mouse is wearing these days? A. A Spiro Agnew watch." After one person stopped laughing at the joke, he realized the sales potential and so began the Dirty Time, Inc.'s Spiro Agnew wristwatch. Novelty wristwatches are pedestrians' bumper stickers. Freedom of speech comes in many forms. Comic, character, symbolic, and advertising wristwatches add up to one of the very American ways of letting freedom ring.

Robert Lesser's *A Celebration of Comic Art and Memorabilia* follows the companies that took advantage of the enormous interest in the comic characters and turned them into wristwatches. Ingersoll was the novelty wristwatch specialist. Whatever the group or event, Ingersoll had a wristwatch to match. Like Hallmark, the great American card company, Ingersoll had a wristwatch for every sentiment or occasion, with comparable prices. $2.98 bought a New Deal wristwatch, complete with the Capitol dome on the dial and President Roosevelt on the band. The Three Little Pigs, Donald Duck, Pluto, Snow White and Tom Mix wristwatches all were made by Ingersoll.

The second most popular cartoon wristwatch, Popeye, was the 1934 creation of the New Haven Clock Co. Since Ingersoll worked hand-in-glove with the Disney organization, New Haven Clock Co. turned to the King Features syndicate which owned Popeye and his friends. The third comic wristwatch producer was Ingraham which came out with the Roy Rogers wristwatch.

NEW HAVEN WATCH AND CLOCK COMPANY, 1948. The round, chrome-plated base metal case of this Popeye wristwatch has exaggerated lugs. The polychrome painted metal dial has Olive Oyl, Swee' Pea, and Wimpy at 3, 6 and 9 o'clock respectively. Cut-out hands point to the hours and minutes. Originally this wristwatch had a blue patent leather strap. This model and its tonneau-shaped predecessor from the '30s are considered extremely rare and collectible. Pin lever movement.

UNKNOWN, 1970s. The King Features Syndicate character, Popeye, is featured on this watch. The case is base metal with a stainless back and is designed to be dustproof. The movement is Swiss with one jewel. Popeye's arms, one holding a can of spinach, make up the hands of the watch. There is also a sweep seconds hand.

NEW HAVEN CLOCK & WATCH CO., ca 1936. This, the earliest model of the Popeye wristwatch, is considered extremely rare and highly collectible. The base metal tonneau-shaped case is chromium-plated. The polychrome painted image of Popeye has cut-out arms which act as hours and minutes hands. Popeye is surrounded by pictures of nine of his cartoon friends. Popeye et al are copyrighted by King Features Syndicate. Pin lever movement. (Courtesy of the Stanley Marx collection)

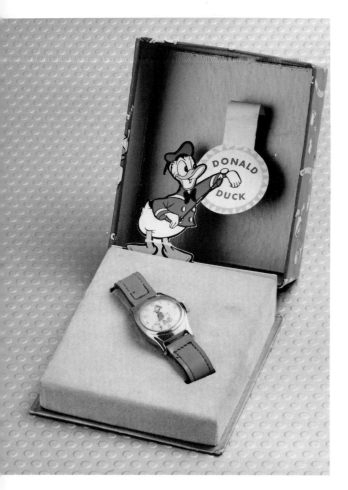

U.S. TIME, 1955. This Donald Duck wristwatch came in a cardboard box with a stand-up figure of Donald inside the lid. The wristwatch is chromium-plated base metal with a stainless steel back. This example has its original patent leather strap. Patented by Walt Disney Productions, this wristwatch is rare. Pin lever movement. (Courtesy: Jack Feldman)

INGERSOLL (U.S. TIME), 1950s. Mickey Mouse's girlfriend, Minnie Mouse, had her own wristwatch. It is shown here in its original box with a bas relief stand-up of Minnie. The chromium-plated base metal case had a stainless steel back. The metal dial was polychrome screened and had cut-out hands. Pin lever movement. (Courtesy: Jack Feldman)

HELBROS, ca 1972. This Goofy wristwatch lives up to its name. The numbers and movement run backwards, going counter-clockwise. This wristwatch had a short run and is rare. It is also unusual for its fine 17-jeweled movement. The Goofy character is copyrighted by Walt Disney Productions.

BRADLEY, 1960s. Though Bradley made hundreds of examples of analog character and comic wristwatches in the '60s and '70s, the digital character wristwatch is rare. This has the polychrome image of Winnie the Pooh, a Walt Disney Productions' character A 17-jeweled Swiss movement moves discs which reveal hours and minutes through cut-outs in the bezel.

U.S. TIME, 1950s. This Pluto wristwatch features a black enameled dial with Pluto's face encircled in the center. There are full hours and minutes chapters, with luminous hands and the words "Made in U.S.A." on the dial. The gray plastic band, made to emulate patent leather, is original. Pin lever movement.

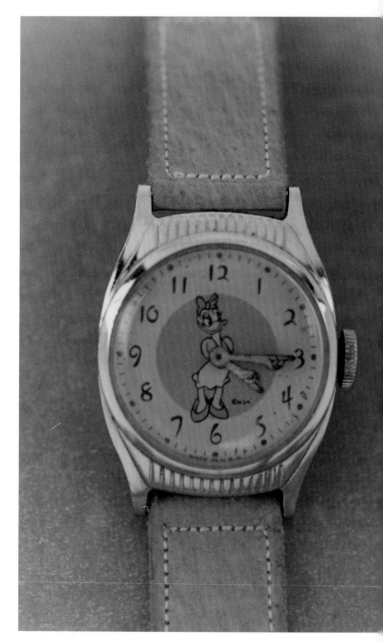

U.S. TIME, ca 1950. The figure of Daisy Duck is another of Walt Disney Production's copyrighted characters. Her cut-out hands serve to mark the hours and minutes. The tonneau-shaped case is chrome-plated base metal with a polychrome painted metal dial. Made in the U.S.A. Pin lever, tonneau-shaped movement.

U.S. TIME, ca 1949. This Bambi wristwatch is one of a series of Disney wristwatches that U.S. Time (Ingersoll) produced to commemorate Mickey Mouse's 20th birthday. The case is base metal, the movement one-jeweled pin lever. The hour hands, though somewhat awkwardly placed, represent the ears of Bambi. Pin lever movement.

Several of the comic wristwatches including Dick Tracy, Annie Oakley and Gene Autry, feature automata—repeater motions that "fire" 120 shots a minute from a moving gun. Not all automata involved guns, though this was a popular rendition.

NEW HAVEN CLOCK AND WATCH COMPANY, ca 1951. The Annie Oakley and Dick Tracy wristwatches are two of a series of wristwatches with automata. Li'l Abner and Gene Autry were also included. Their guns, attached at the 6:00 position, moved back and forth 120 times per minute. The moving character wristwatches are considered highly collectible when in good working condition. Chromium-plated base metal bezels, pin lever movements.

NEW HAVEN, 1950s. This Li'l Abner wristwatch has a plated base metal case and a 1-jeweled pin lever movement. The dial bears the character of Li'l Abner and a mule which is an automaton at the 7:00 position. The hands are luminous.

CHANCELLOR WATCH COMPANY, 1960s. This Swiss wristwatch features an all-American image: the quarterback. The case is base metal, the dial enamel painted. The quarterback's throwing arm is an automaton seconds hand. Note the stem and crown at 4:00.

NEW HAVEN, ca 1948. This Gene Autry wristwatch has a plated base metal case and a one jewel movement. The dial features Gene Autry and a pistol that serves as a seconds automaton. The legends read "Gene Autry Watch" and "Always Your Pal Gene Autry." The wristwatch bears the original imitation ponyskin strap with stamped western-style hardware.

Western heroes hold a special place in the American legend. This was especially true when these characters first appeared, as the nation was struggling to find its way again after the shock of the First World War. There had been a dramatic loss of innocence in the trauma of that struggle. Subconsciously the American psyche turned back the clock in search of a more innocent time. It came to focus on the "Old West". The belief in the purity and essential goodness of the cowboy captured in this group of character wristwatches, epitomized that struggle to go backward in time, to ignore the technological advances which had only led to more efficient methods of killing one's enemies. The cowboy was the simple, pure man and the wristwatches that depict cowboys are straight forward, straight shooters all, with simple round dials, Arabic numbers, and brightly depicted characters.

E. INGRAHAM CO., ca 1950. Roy Rogers and Trigger adorn the round dial within this chrome-plated tonneau case. Pin lever movement. Model # 58L.

E. INGRAHAM, ca 1950. The tonneau-shaped chromium-plated case hold a metal dial painted with the image of Roy Rogers and his horse Trigger. Pin lever movement.

INGRAHAM, ca 1951. Roy Rogers upon a rearing Trigger adorns the dial of this tonneau-shaped watch. The case is base metal and the movement is one-jeweled pin-lever. This wristwatch has its original stamped western-style strap with silvertone engraved buckle and keeper.

E. INGRAHAM & CO., ca 1950. Dale Evans and her horse, Buttermilk, surrounded by a horseshoe are portrayed on this round dial. The case is tonneau-shaped. Pin lever movement.

NEW HAVEN, ca 1948. Same as previous watch on page 136 except with different band. Shown with original paper box.

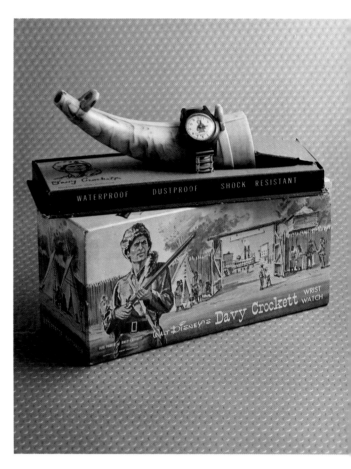

BRADLEY, ca 1954. The character of Davy Crockett caught the American imagination when Disney brought his story to the screen. Every boy wanted a coon-skin hat. The Davy Crockett wristwatch had a plastic case and was advertised as waterproof, dustproof, and shock resistant. It was packaged with a plastic powderhorn, in a polychrome paper box. Pin lever movement. (Courtesy: Jack Feldman)

U.S. TIME, 1957. Zorro, another Disney creation, enjoyed great popularity in the late 1950s. This wristwatch has a chromium-plated bezel and stainless steel back with a matte black painted metal dial. It came on a black sombrero in a red box featuring Zorro on a rearing horse. Pin lever movement. (Courtesy: Jack Feldman)

U.S. TIME, ca 1951. This Hopalong Cassidy wristwatch has a tonneau-shaped case with a round dial. The case is chromium plated base metal with a stainless steel back. The dial features a picture of "Hoppy" and the legend "Hopalong Cassidy". On thback of the wristwatch is engraved: "Good luck from Hoppy" and "U.S. Time". Pin lever movement.

U.S. TIME, ca 1950. This Hopalong Cassidy wristwatch is shown in its original paper box with its original patterned, printed leather strap, silver buckle and silver keeper. The chromium-plated case is 30mm X 33mm, though it was available in a smaller size. Pin lever movement. (Courtesy: Jack Feldman)

U.S. TIME, ca 1951. This Hopalong Cassidy wristwatch is identical to the Gene Autry watch on page 136 except that it is housed in a round case.

U.S. TIME, 1950. This 27mm X 24mm Hopalong Cassidy wristwatch came in a cardboard saddle display case. It had a chromium-plated case with a stainless steel back. Its dial was engraved "Good luck from Hoppy," and had red hands. The strap featured a silvertone buckle and keeper. Pin lever movement. (Courtesy: Jack Feldman)

NEW HAVEN, ca 1940s-50s. This wristwatch is very similar in shape and movement to the watch shown bottom left of this page. The only significant difference is in the decorative lug treatment.

NEW HAVEN, 1940s. This tonneau-shaped Lone Ranger wristwatch has a stainless steel case and a pin lever movement. On the dial is written "The Lone Ranger" and "Made in the U.S.A.", as well as the ballooned caption "Hi-Yo Silver." The dial is enamel painted.

UNKNOWN, 1950s. Double images on a micro-faceted dial gives the illusion of three dimensions, with the cowboy in motion. The dial has a red outer hours chapter with reversed Arabic numerals, and cut-out red hours and minutes hands. The case is chromium plated base metal and houses a Swiss movement.

E. INGRAHAM CO., 1949. In its original display box, the Porky Pig wristwatch is 25mm X 30mm. The case is chromium-plated. Copyrighted by Warner Bros. Cartoons, it has a pin lever movement. (Courtesy: Jack Feldman)

INGRAHAM CO., ca 1949. Porky Pig, a Warner Brothers Cartoon creation, is at the center of this wristwatch, his arms indicating the hours and minutes. The base metal case houses a 1-jeweled pin lever movement. This wristwatch has its original patent leather band.

It's not coincidental that during the same period in which the public was looking back to the innocence of the cowboy, Americans were also captivated by the comic strip which was a standard feature of newspapers in the 1920s. Tens of millions of readers followed the doings of Blondie and Dagwood, Little Orphan Annie and Daddy Warbucks, Mutt and Jeff.

Through the thirties, mythical figures such as Superman and Snow White belied the reality of the evil that was afoot, both at home and in Europe where the seeds of the Second World War had already been sown. Some of the heroic figures are square jawed, incorruptible crime fighters: Dick Tracy, Superman, Batman, Wonder Woman. Some are innocent of the outside world entirely: Li'l Abner, Howdy Doody, and the whole beloved range of fairytale characters, many of them from the prolific Walt Disney Studios. Still others encounter their own brand of evil but in a storybook world: Pinocchio, The Big Bad Wolf and the cast of the Wizard of Oz.

The cartoon wristwatch designers didn't restrict themselves to the past. Long before there was a man on the moon or a space program of any sort, there was Space Ranger Rocky Jones, a heroic figure created in the late 1940's, looking bravely into the future. Ingraham created a Tom Corbett Space Cadet wristwatch, and, although it has never been found, there is said to have been a Buck Rogers wristwatch, based on the 1929 comic strip, *Buck Rogers in the 25th Century*. An example of a Buck Rogers pocket watch does exist.

INGRAHAM, 1950. While the Woody Woodpecker wristwatch is not nearly as popular as the Mickey Mouse watch, it is becoming increasingly valuable to collectors. It is hard to find in the original, early version. The tonneau-shaped case is chromium-plated base metal with a polychrome painted metal dial. The minutes chapter is red. Woody Woodpecker is copyrighted by Walter Lantz Productions. Pin lever movement.

INGERSOLL (U.S. Time), ca. 1953. Joe Carioca adorns this polychrome painted dial, his cut-out hands serving as wristwatch hands. The case is chromium-plated base metal. There is a sweep seconds hand. This is one of the more obscure, hard to find character watches. The figure of Carioca is a variation of the 1948 original. Swiss pin-lever movement.

SHEFFIELD WATCH CO., 1970s. The character of Merlin the Magic Mouse is a Warner Brothers creation, and the copyright on the dial reads "W7". The gold plated case holds a one-jeweled Swiss movement. The dial features Merlin and has a sweep seconds hand.

NEW HAVEN, ca 1935. This tonneau-shaped wristwatch features the character of Smitty on the dial. The dial is signed "Bernd". Pin lever movement.

NEW HAVEN WATCH AND CLOCK COMPANY, ca 1947. Joe Palooka was a popular comic character for many years. Sporting figures from the '30s and '40s, fictional and real, have become highly collectible and are sought after by collectors. The case of this wristwatch is chromium-plated base metal in a tonneau shape. The dial is polychrome painted enamel. Fake wristwatches are now entering the market using sophisticated four-color photocopying techniques to reproduce the older dials. A fake dial severely compromises the value of the wristwatch to the collector, so a careful examination is important. Pin lever movement.

NEW HAVEN WATCH CLOCK CO., ca 1948. The Orphan Annie wristwatch was available in this size (20mm X 26mm) and in a larger size as early as 1937. The tonneau case is stainless steel with a painted metal dial. Pin lever movement. Copyrighted by Harold Gray. Shown in its original box. (Courtesy: Jack Feldman)

NEW HAVEN, 1940s. Dick Tracy is the hero of this tonneau-shaped watch. The case is of stainless steel and is stamped "X-S" inside. The band may be original. Pin lever movement.

MARVEL IMPORTING CORPORATION, ca 1948. Mary Marvel, whose flying figure adorns the dial of this watch, was copyrighted by Fawcett Publications in 1948. The case is of base metal and the enamel painted dial has luminous hands. The Swiss movement has no jewels.

NEW HAVEN WATCH & CLOCK CO., ca 1948. A Dick Tracy wristwatch in its original box, this has a chromium plated case with a painted metal dial. The tonneau case is 30mm X 25mm. Dick Tracy and Smitty are pictured on the box. Copyrighted by Chester Gould. (Courtesy: Jack Feldman)

DABS & CO., ca 1977. TIMEX, 1960s-'70s. CLINTON WATCH CO., 1970s. During the late '60s and '70s D.C. Comics aggressively promoted their comic characters by issuing a series of wristwatches. They all had 17-jeweled Swiss movements with hours, minutes, and sweep seconds hands, housed in chromium- or gold-plated stainless steel cases. The polychrome painted dials featured dramatic stylized superhero images. They included Batman, Robin, Superman, Wonder Woman, and other heros, as well as a few villains such as the Joker. The '70s series in original boxes are generally available for under $200 each.

TIMEX, ca 1976. One of the most venerable comic characters, Superman, now over 50 years old, continues to be a true collectible in many variations of the wristwatch. This one is in stainless steel with a polychrome painted metal dial. It has a sweep seconds hand and 17 jewels. Superman is copyrighted by D.C. Comics, Inc.

SWISS, 1960s. Superman is printed on a clear, rotating plastic disc so that his arm serves as the hour hand as he flies through the sky. The case is gold plated base metal with a stainless steel back. Superman is copyrighted by D.C. Comics. 17-jeweled Swiss movement.

U.S. TIME, 1950s. This Snow White wristwatch has a base metal case and an enamel painted dial featuring the popular Disney character. It has a one-jeweled, pin lever movement. The band is grosgrain leather and is original.

U.S. TIME, ca 1951. Disney's Cinderella is on this round, enamel painted dial. The case is chromium-plated base metal with a stainless steel back. On the back is engraved U.S. Time. Pin lever movement.

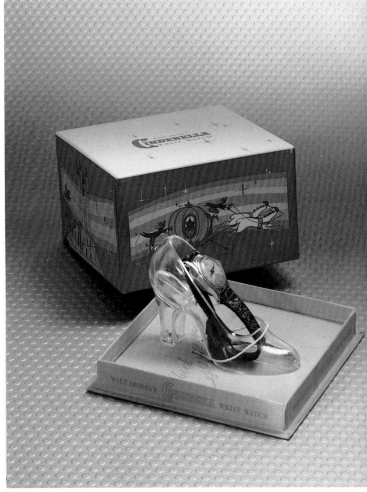

TIMEX, ca 1950. The Cinderella was packaged in a "glass" slipper within a decorated box. The chromium-plated case has a stainless steel back and is 24mm x 27mm. The band is decorated with the gold imprint of a coach and horses. The pin lever movement is promoted as "shock resistant." Cinderella is another of Disney's copyrighted creations. (Courtesy: Jack Feldman)

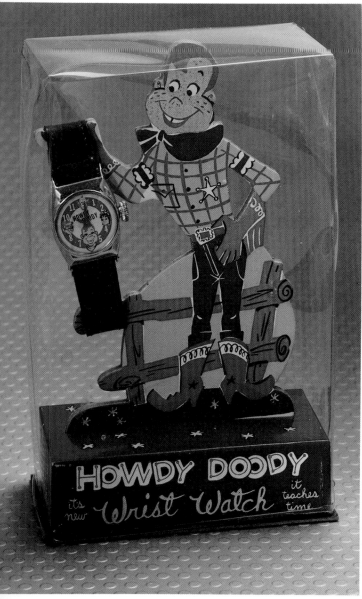

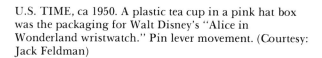

PATENT WATCH CO., ca 1954. The popular puppet character of Howdy Doody is at the center of this wristwatch. In the hours chapter his name is spelled out. Howdy's eyes are cutout automata. The character of Howdy Doody was copyrighted by ("Buffalo") Bob Smith. 1 jewel, unadjusted Swiss pin lever movement.

INGRAHAM, ca 1954. A cut-out figure of Howdy Doody holds the wristwatch in this original box. The round, polychrome painted dial of the wristwatch is decorated with Howdy's face as well as those of three of his friends. The wristwatch has its original blue patent leather band. (Courtesy: Jack Feldman)

U.S. TIME, ca 1950. A plastic tea cup in a pink hat box was the packaging for Walt Disney's "Alice in Wonderland wristwatch." Pin lever movement. (Courtesy: Jack Feldman)

U.S. TIME, 1950. Jiminy Cricket, a character from Disney's classic animated film "Pinocchio," is at the center of this wristwatch. His cut-out exaggerated hands rotate to indicate the hours and minutes. The case is chrome-plated base metal and the dial is polychrome painted metal. This is part of the Disney series and is rare and hard to find.

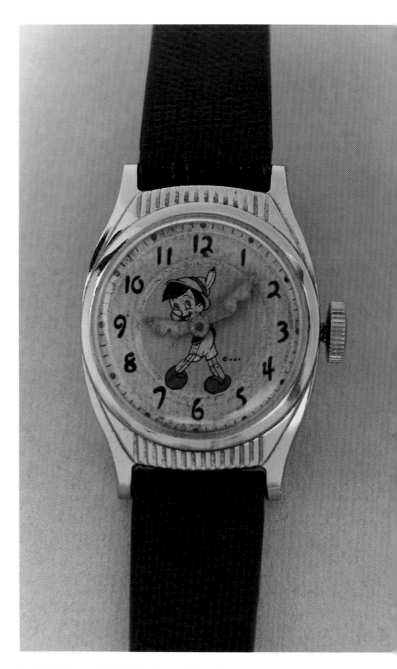

UNKNOWN, ca 1970. Novelty wristwatches have often been used as promotional vehicles by film studios for original or reissued pictures. This Wizard of Oz wristwatch dates from the early 1970s.

U.S. TIME, ca 1951. This Pinocchio wristwatch is among the rarest of the Disney collectible character watches. The ribbed tonneau-shaped case is chromium-plated base metal and measures 38mm X 28mm. Pinocchio is copyrighted by Walt Disney Productions. Pin lever, tonneau-shaped movement.

SWISS, ca 1938. No manufacturer's name appears on this Robin Hood wristwatch. The dial features the name and full body likeness of Robin Hood. There are luminous hands and a red sweep seconds. This is probably the original band. Pin lever movement.

UNKNOWN, ca 1960. Wristwatches such as this Lassie wristwatch were often used to promote the introduction of a new television series, movie, or book. Stainless steel case with chromium-plated bezel. Pin lever movement.

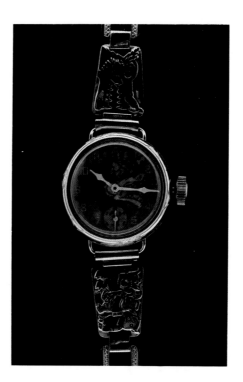

INGERSOLL (U.S. TIME), ca 1947. The polychrome painted metal dial features the Little Pig, a character created and copyrighted by Walt Disney Productions (W.D.P.). The chromium plated base metal case is tonneau-shaped, with a pin lever tonneau-shaped movement. The minutes and hours hands are red.

INGERSOLL, 1934. The Big Bad Wolf and his prey, the Three Little Pigs, decorate the polychrome painted metal dial of this novelty wristwatch. The chromium-plated case is attached to a bracelet with cut-outs of the Big Bad Wolf on one side of the case and the Three Little Pigs on the other. These Disney copyrighted characters were popular. This 1934 version is extremely rare. Pin lever movement.

Whether noble or base, since the 1930s Americans have worn wristwatches proclaiming their affiliations. Some of these, chiefly the Masonic and Boy Scout wristwatches, signified actual membership in an organization. Some were more generic, indicating a passion for golf, or basketball, and some made a political statement.

With the national passion for wearing brand names and mass marketed logos, there came inevitably the advertising wristwatch, with a faithful recreation of a product name and logotype on the dial. With inexpensive, four-color printing, these short-lived items could be created quickly, and at a very reasonable cost. More discreet than a T-shirt, they offered the added advantage of giving the correct time in exchange for carrying around an advertising message. It's the American way: I'll wear your message but I'll get something out of it too. But the advertising wristwatches are meant for the short term. They'll never have the staying power, the incredible numbers of the very first novelty wristwatch, the one and only Mickey Mouse.

INGRAHAM, 1954. The Space Ranger Rocky Jones wristwatch has a chromium-plated base metal case with a polychrome painted metal dial. The hours chapter uses red numerals and markers. Pin lever movement.

E. INGRAHAM & CO., ca 1951. This Tom Corbett wristwatch is rarely seen with its original rocket display. The wristwatch is chromium-plated with a polychrome painted metal dial and is 25mm X 30mm. The original leather strap has rockets and the rings of Saturn stamped into it and an elaborate silver keeper. Pin lever movement. (Courtesy: Jack Feldman)

INGRAHAM COMPANY, ca 1951. This model #53 Tom Corbett Space Cadet wristwatch features a round dial in a tonneau case. Tom Corbett, his space ship and name are featured on the enamel painted dial. The hands are shaped as lightning bolts. The movement is Swiss, 1-jeweled pin lever. The original band, stamped with images of Saturn and of Tom's space ship is attached.

ABRA, 1920s. This handsome wristwatch has a gold plated case with a die-struck embossed bezel. At the four corners gold-plated and enamel Masonic symbols are applied. The tonneau-shaped case houses a round dial with luminous Arabic numerals. 7-jeweled Swiss movement.

ILLINOIS, ca 1925. This early Masonic wristwatch has a subsidiary seconds chapter at 9:00. The other hour positions on the dial are marked by painted Masonic symbols. The engraved case is silver. 15-jeweled Illinois movement.

NEW HAVEN WATCH AND CLOCK COMPANY, ca 1938. The tonneau-shaped case of this Boy Scout wristwatch is chromium-plated base metal. The painted metal dial has full luminous numerals and hands, and carries the Boy Scouts logo in the center.

NEW HAVEN CLOCK AND WATCH COMPANY, ca 1934. The polychrome painted metal dial of this Boy Scout wristwatch is tonneau-shaped and has around the outer edge key words from the Boy Scout pledge: Trustworthy, loyal, helpful, friendly, courteous, etc. The legend on the minutes hand is the beginning of that pledge: "A Scout Is". On the hours hand is another slogan from scouting: "Be Prepared." The subsidiary seconds chapter has a rotating Scouting symbol. The chromium-plated base metal case is in a stepped tonneau shape. This earliest model is extremely rare. Pin lever movement

ELGIN, 1950. This example of a sports award wristwatch was used to commemorate a championship in the Metropolitan Bowling Association. The tonneau-shaped case is 14k yellow gold and has an enamel painted dial with a subsidiary seconds chapter at 6:00. 17-jeweled tonneau-shaped Elgin movement.

SWISS, ca 1965. The shooting arm with the basketball is an automata and moves back and forth. Many novelty wristwatches with sports formats were introduced to the U.S. market in the late '60s and the '70s. Despite their novelty they do not carry much value in the collectibles market. The bezel of this wristwatch is gold plated and it has a stainless steel back. Swiss pin lever movement.

SWISS. Novelty and character wristwatches often expressed sporting interests. Here is a golfer's wristwatch portraying a golfer in a swinging position. The minutes hand is the golf club. The hours hand consists of a clear plastic disc with a golf ball painted on it, which revolves to indicate the hour. The tonneau-shaped case is gold plated base metal. 17-jeweled Swiss movement.

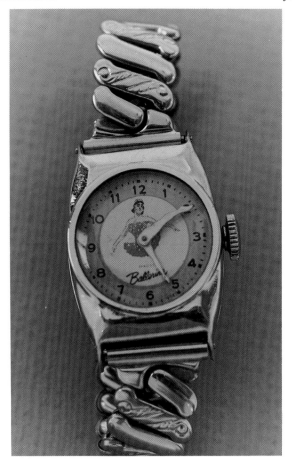

U.S. TIME, ca 1951. The *Ballerina* has a full figure of a ballerina centered on its polychrome painted metal dial. Her cut-out legs rotate to serve as hour and minute hands. This wristwatch is shown with its original stretch metal band typical of '50s bands. Pin lever movement.

UNKNOWN, 1927. Chevrolet presented these wristwatches to salespeople as a sales achievement reward. The wristwatches are inscribed "For Meeting the Quota, 1927." The plated steel case is in the shape of the Chevrolet car grille, the crown being the radiator cap. The Chevrolet logo is in blue enamel. This is a very rare watch. 7-jeweled Swiss movement, American case.

ROYAL ROULETTE, 1960s. A Swiss wristwatch manufactured for the American market, the bezel has a glass cover and contains a loose steel ball which can be spun around as in a roulette wheel until it comes to rest on one of the concave numerals. 17 jewels.

HONG KONG, 1971. This example of an advertising novelty wristwatch features Charlie the Tuna, a creation of Star Kist Foods and used in their animated commercials. The case is gold plated, and was available in stainless steel. Severely limited in availability. 17-jeweled Swiss movement.

SWISS. Promotional and advertising wristwatches often become "pop" culture symbols. This one for Ritz Crackers is, stylistically, one of the most extraordinary dials ever achieved in a promotional watch. Because of the vivid polychrome design it is one of the more recognizable examples. This is a very special and very rare wristwatch. It has an American case and a 1-jewel pin-lever Swiss movement.

CUSTOMTIME CORPORATION, 1960s. This mechanical digital wristwatch is an advertising piece featuring the logo of the Planters Peanuts Company, Mr. Peanut. It has a base metal case and an enamel painted dial. The movement is 1-jeweled Swiss. The hours and minutes appear in windows to the left of Mr. Peanut.

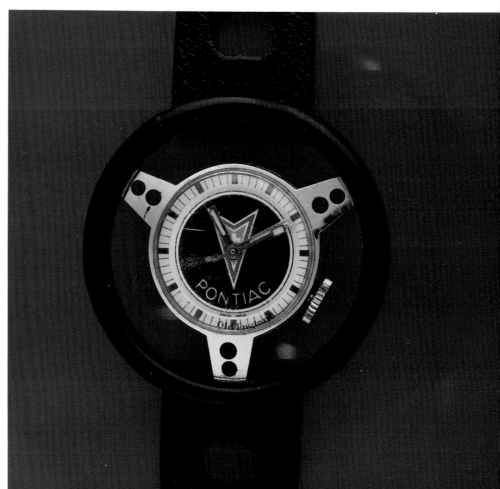

OLD ENGLAND WATCHES LIMITED, 1960s. This steering wheel-shaped wristwatch features the Pontiac automobile logo at the center. A one-jeweled Swiss movement drives the wristwatch with its sweep seconds hand. "Old England" is printed on the crystal.

Chapter Five
The Military Watch
World War I to Viet Nam: 1914-1972

From the First World War, where the wristwatch firmly established its worth, through the Second World War, and conflicts in Korea and Vietnam, watch companies have played an ongoing and crucial role. Watch manufacturers were so intimately involved in the various war efforts that in many cases the war itself determined whether a firm would continue in business or go bankrupt. Waltham, for example, was rescued by the timing and timely demands of the Second World War. The firm would surely have closed much earlier than it did were it not for the business given it by the U.S. government on behalf of the military.

The First World War proved the importance of timing to the movement of ships. Before the development of Long-Range Navigation Systems (LORAN) about 1932, only the precise time allowed naval officers to determine their position at sea. The British admiralty was obsessed with accurate time.

Because of the pressing need for the watch companies' expertise, the soaring, streamlined Thirties era in wristwatches came to a crashing end with the onset of the Second World War. While America didn't officially enter the war until after the bombing of Pearl Harbor, the watch industry was already retooling to meet the government's demand for precision timing devices. Since everything from the movements of troops and materials to the targeting of projectiles is coordinated by time, the demands of the military for precise timing devices were far greater than that of the civilian world. Consequently the industry was called upon by the war effort to make technological improvements and advances.

The First World War saw the introduction of the waterproof watch case. By using a screw-type back instead of a hinged case a much tighter fit was accomplished and water was kept from the movement. This was a Swiss development as were most of the military advances in watchmaking in the 20th century. Americans did contribute the hack feature which aided soldiers in coordinating their activities. By putting a damper on the balance, the sweep seconds hand can be stopped and then restarted to achieve synchronization that is precise to the second.

By 1945, the War Department's technical manual for ordnance maintenance noted in passing that all wristwatches supplied to the department were of American make and all were issued in waterproof cases.

Of course the soldier's wristwatch was always important and placed clear-cut demands on the watch manufacturer: time had to be told at a glance. It had to be as accurate as contemporary technology could make it. Time had to be synchronized to the second, leading to the hack feature. It had to be read in the dark, leading to the luminous markers, numerals and hands on the dial.

INGERSOLL, ca 1917. This fourteen ligne wristwatch from the First World War has a pierced shrapnel cover over its porcelain dial. The dial is black with gold numerals and a subsidiary seconds chapter. Pin lever Ingersoll movement.

DEPOLLIER, ca 1919. This American watch is a precursor to the Oyster/Rolex waterproof, dustproof wristwatch. J. Depollier & Son manufactured the watch in Brooklyn, NY, using a Waltham movement. The watch was patented on June 11, 1916 as the D & D Field and Marine Watch and was used in the military. A civilian version was introduced in 1919. The case is nickel with a 15 jeweled movement. (Courtesy: Kurt Rothner)

BENRUS, 1950s. The American case of this soldier's wristwatch is steel and waterproof. The dial has an inner hours chapter which reads from 13 to 24:00, and a sweep seconds hand. The uncirculated example shown here has its original canvas strap with an attached compass. Swiss movement, 15 jewels.

BENRUS, 1950s. The anodized steel case of this soldier's wristwatch is of American manufacture. The black enamel painted dial has full Arabic numerals from 1 to 24 in a two concentric hours chapters. It has a sweep seconds hand and a minutes/seconds chapter with triangular markers at five seconds intervals. 17-jeweled Swiss movement.

H. MOSER & CO., ca 1917-20. This is a very fine surviving example of a Swiss wristwatch manufactured expressly for the U.S. Signal Corps in the First World War. H. Moser also supplied wristwatches to Russia and other countries during the war. The case is sterling silver with a white porcelain dial. The hours chapter has luminous Arabic numerals and there is an inner chapter with the hours from 13 to 24. A subsidiary seconds chapter is at 6:00 and a red numeral 12 tops the watch. This pin set wristwatch has a Swiss 17-jeweled movement. It is highly collectible, especially prized by military collectors. (Courtesy: Michael Schub)

SWISS, ca 1920. The pierced-cover, hinged-back, sterling case of this Swiss military wristwatch reveals the hours indicators and hands beneath. The dial is porcelain with a concentric 24 hour configuration. The Arabic numerals are luminous from 1 to 11 with a red 12 and red inner hours chapter from 13 to 24. The outlined hands are also luminous. This is a very rare pierced-case watch. 15-jeweled Swiss movement.

BENRUS, 1960s. The anodized steel case has military specifications etched into its back, including the manufacturer and date of production. The black enamel painted dial is marked for 24 hours with white Arabic numerals. Sweep seconds hand. 17-jeweled Swiss movement.

ELGIN "U.S.A." ca 1930. Nickel case made for the U.S. Army. Star minute track. Subsidiary second. 15 jewels. (Courtesy of Time Will Tell)

BENRUS, 1960s-70s. This plastic-cased military wristwatch is of water resistant construction and has solid lugs. The black enamel painted dial has 24 hour indicators. In order to repair the movement in this one-piece case, the crystal and crown must be removed. On the back of the case are the military specifications molded into the surface. Plastic military cases are very rare. The production appears to have concentrated between 1967 and 1976. 17-jeweled Swiss movement.

LONGINES, 1940s. Charles Lindbergh was a navigational student of Lt. Commander P.V.H. Weems, and took the principle of the *Weems* navigational wristwatch a step further in the *Hour Angle* watch. By adding various other navigational information, the wristwatch enables the wearer to quickly calculate the hour angles of the sun or stars, and use that information to determine location. This small version of the *Hour Angle* wristwatch is in a stainless steel case with a sterling silver movable bezel, but was also manufactured in gold filled. The grey enamel painted dial has Roman numerals in the hours chapter and a movable disc at the center that is controlled by the crown at 2:00. 17-jeweled Swiss movement. Very rare.

LONGINES, ca 1940. The *Weems* bears the name of its inventor, Lt. Commander P.V.H. Weems, U.S. Navy (retired) and is an unusual and somewhat rare wristwatch. Weems had taught navigation at the Naval Academy in Annapolis and devised this wristwatch as a fast way to adjust for chronometer error. In a time of air travel and its faster speeds, this was important for the safety of the crew. Greenwich Civil Time is broadcast by a radio signal every minute. To set this wristwatch to the proper seconds configuration, the wearer would rotate the movable bezel, keeping the 60-second mark over the sweep seconds hand until the minute tone was broadcast. He would stop turning the bezel at that point and lock it into place with the crown at two o'clock. On the larger version of this wristwatch, the seconds are on a disc in the center which is rotated by turning the crown. Hours and minutes are set in the traditional manner. The case is gold filled and has a white enamel painted dial. 17-jeweled Swiss movement.

For the wristwatch to truly take its place in the military arsenal, it needed to offer protection from the thousand and one shocks that it would be subject to during the course of its everyday wear. The *Incabloc* shock absorber offered the durability that protected the balance. Given the ability to vibrate so that it didn't snap off the pivots, the *Incabloc* system would be used for decades, continuing up to the present. Although invented in 1935, the system didn't come into widespread civilian use until after the war. The role of the watch manufacturer in modern warfare cannot be overstated. Modern warfare is directly involved with and related to time.

In addition, the extreme tolerances needed to produce precision time-pieces put the horological industry in position to be commandeered to make a wide variety of defense items. In the Second World War they produced marine chronometers, mechanical time fuses, altimeters, rocket fuses, drift sights, aircraft clocks, speedometers, tachometers, gun camera timers and magnetic compasses, in addition to the soldier's wristwatch.

ELGIN, 1920s. The Army Air Corps used this steel cased wristwatch. The enamel painted dial is black with luminous hands and dots at the hours. Stylized solid lugs hold the canvas strap. 17 jewels. The bulbous crown is typical of the transitional period.

ELGIN, 1917-19. This Navy diver's wristwatch is among the earliest waterproof the authors have seen. The case is of U.S. manufacture, using nickel painted in black enamel. The black dial is porcelain with white Arabic numerals, red hours and minutes hands and a subsidiary seconds chapter. The bezel, crown and back of this wristwatch screwed off, giving it its waterproof quality. The patents for this case were Swiss, and the cases were manufactured for both European and American divers. It is a precursor to the Rolex Oyster. The movement is Elgin, 15 or 17 jewels.

ELGIN

Exemplifying the American watch manufacturers' ability to provide the armed services with these precision items was Elgin National Watch Company of Elgin, Illinois. Elgin was a mass producer of timepieces that started out in Chicago in 1864 as the National Watch Company. By 1903, the company had made one million pocket watches and had a factory operation employing 3300 people. By 1931, it had moved into wristwatch production with enthusiasm. 90% of its production was devoted to wristwatches, only 10% to pocket watches, although the demand for all watches was down during these post-crash years.

Scarcely had Elgin recovered from the depression when its president, T. Albert Potter, foresaw the coming war. According to James Shennan who succeeded Potter as president in the late 1940s, "The management of Elgin was quite astute." Many Elgin workers were taken off the regular production and set to work at tasks related to the military. "Mr. Potter was particularly astute; there was no question in his mind the war was going to happen." That foresight saw Elgin hard at work on time fuses a year before Pearl Harbor. Two days after Pearl Harbor, the first pilot lot of time fuses was ready for testing. This American watch company had shifted to war production before President Roosevelt declared that America was in the war.

For companies such as Elgin that had finally recovered from the devastating effects of the depression, the war meant another wrenching change. All thoughts of civilian products were put on the shelf. From 1940-1945 the only customer was the military. Half a decade that would have been devoted to style in peacetime went instead to substance: how to make a timing fuse more accurate to give our side an edge in the fighting.

ELGIN, ca 1915. This early example of an American military wristwatch has a silver case with a porcelain dial. This is protected by a removable pierced shrapnel cover held in place by the strap. 17-jeweled Elgin movement.

ELGIN, 1930s. Made for the U.S. Navy, this steel-cased wristwatch is in the shape of a canteen. More than decorative, the screw-on cover which fits over the crown and is attached to the case, was an attempt at dustproofing and waterproofing the wristwatch. The dial is black enamel painted with white Arabic numerals and a sweep seconds hand. This example has its original khaki strap. 17 jewels. Elgin movement.

ELGIN, ca 1931. The die-struck embossed case is gold filled and cushion-shaped. It has a black porcelain dial with painted stars to mark the minutes and white Arabic numerals in the hours chapter. Elgin movement, 7 jewels.

ELGIN, 1941. A typical U.S. military wristwatch, this Elgin has a 10k rolled gold plate and steel waterproofed case and bears its original canvas strap. The white enamel painted dial has painted Arabic numerals. 15 jewels.

Elgin's war production included wrist, pocket, hack and navigation watches for the armed services. They also designed and produced a torque control device, a 30-minute timing device for Naval ordnance, and an 8-day timing device. The watch factory made several thousand engine speed indicator parts for the British in 1941. Other products included altimeter parts and elapsed time clocks for aircraft as well as a more effective means of controlling the timing of fuses used in naval anti-aircraft guns.

The War Department manual lists three Elgin wristwatches with 7, 15, and 16 jewels. "The 16-jewel (Hack) type A-11 differs from the standard Elgin wristwatch in that it is equipped with a waterproof case, a sweep seconds hand, and a black dial. Although they are normally issued to the Air Corps as a navigation wristwatch, some have been issued, however, to ground troops." Hands and numbers were coated with radium for night use.

This devotion to war production would leave Elgin in no condition to take advantage of the post-war boom. It took the company three years to return to pre-war civilian production levels. The advertisements of the day tell the whole story. In the December 5, 1942 issue of the *Saturday Evening Post*, Elgin shows two soldiers "in the islands of the Pacific" opening a box from home containing "an Elgin from the folks!" But after suggesting that the Elgin is the perfect remembrance of home, the copy reminds the reader, "Of course, fewer of these watches are available this year, due to Elgin's war effort. Long before Pearl Harbor even, the government requested Elgin to produce special military devices and precision instruments. And these today are Elgin's first concern. Fighting planes, tanks and guns must be equipped."

In fact, according to the company's house publication, "From 1942 through 1945 Elgin manufactured no watches for the civilian market but devoted itself exclusively to the production of war materials." Their reward: the Army-Navy "E" award, the highest honor the government had to offer. Elgin won ten of them during the war. While the men were off fighting on the front line, women took their place on the production line.

By 1945, seeing an end to wartime production, Elgin ran an advertisement headlined "Hold fast to your desire...there will be more Elgins." Reminding the public of its service in war time, the copy reads, "Before Pearl harbor and steadily until VJ Day, Elgin craftsmen were busy making precision instruments and timing devices for our fighting men on the land, the sea and in the air. Now that those special tasks are finished, new Elgins are coming your way!"

At the end of 1949, Elgin's production received a boost from military orders for the Korean war, but by 1950, Elgin had laid off 300 workers and slowed to a four-day week. The firm announced the first American-made self-winding wristwatch in 1950 but production was soon abandoned. A battery-powered wristwatch was developed in 1952 but never made it to the production stage. Perhaps Elgin's last moment in the sun was the production of its 50 millionth timepiece in 1951.

HAMILTON

In 1917, Hamilton produced navigation watches for use on United States Navy torpedo boats, destroyers, and submarines in the First World War. The company was also asked to produce a ship's chronometer. They developed a working model, but the war ended before tooling was completed for production.

In the Second World War, however, Hamilton successfully produced marine chronometers, an item that had not even been within the purview of the American watch manufacturer before the war. Starting in 1942, and continuing through 1948, Hamilton produced more than ten thousand marine chronometers; 25,000 chronographs with navigation time and stop watch feature, as well as myriad other military-related items.

The War Department's maintenance manual lists only one Hamilton wristwatch as regular issue, the 987A, 6/0 size, 17-jeweled model. "This movement was originally issued in a cup-type case but is now issued in the waterproof type." Like the Elgin models, it features radium coated numbers and hands for night use.

In 1945, Hamilton reissued its 1940 catalog with a notice attached. In it Hamilton advised, "This catalog was the last to be issued before Hamilton's factory was converted to 100% war production.

HAMILTON, 1940s. The anodized steel case has waterproof-type construction. The enamel painted dial has outlined luminous hands and Arabic numerals, with a subsidiary seconds chapter at 6:00. This wristwatch has its original khaki strap. 17-jeweled Hamilton movement.

HAMILTON, 1930s. This military wristwatch has a steel case of water-resistant construction. The white enamel painted dial has black outlined luminous hands with Arabic numerals and a subsidiary seconds chapter. It is equipped with a hack feature. When the crown is in the setting position, the sweep seconds hand does not advance. The movement is a Hamilton model 987A, 6/0 size with 17 jewels.

BULOVA, 1940s. This military wristwatch has a waterproof steel case. The black enamel painted dial has full Arabic numerals with a sweep seconds hand. The name Bulova does not appear on all examples of this wristwatch. Often the names on military wristwatches are omitted both from the dial and from the embossed legend on the back of the watch. 15-jeweled Swiss movement. Original khaki strap.

"Many of the watches shown in it will be among those released first as reconversion to civilian production proceeds. Until Hamilton is fully reconverted, however (it takes at least six months to make a fine watch), not enough of any one model can be distributed to assure availability through all Hamilton Distributors. For that reason, no new catalog can be issued immediately.

"Although reconversion is proceeding steadily, shortages will continue to be acute throughout the remainder of 1945—easing considerably after the first of the year."

That 1940-41 catalog opened with a discussion of "Hamilton and the nation's defense program". After making note of the role its craftsmen played in "producing vital equipment for the army, the navy, and the air service", Hamilton went on to say that while the firm was proud to do its part it had other obligations. "Today fine watches rank high on the list of essential commodities in civilian life, too!" This essential role included "watches needed to time America's teeming industries, in factories, and offices throughout the land. Watches are needed to coordinate fast moving transportation. Watches will be needed in civilian defense maneuvers when radios are silenced, electric current cut off, and blackouts simulate air raid conditions. Watches—fine watches, accurate watches—must be produced for all these vital civilian defense needs." Despite their fine intentions, they produced very few civilian wristwatches during the war years. That was left to the likes of Bulova and others.

BULOVA

This firm occupies an unique category. Although it was undoubtedly a significant part of the war effort, Bulova also had a Swiss factory that merrily continued to produce for the civilian market during the war. This would certainly have eased its way back into normal production when the war ended. But Bulova did everything on a big scale and was a major supplier to the military, and its reconversion would likewise be a tremendous effort.

It was designated an "A" company, according to Haskell Titchell, Bulova's public relations executive for many years. "There were three categories of manufacturers. Those designated in the "C" category could do what they wanted during the war years; they were free to make anything. The "B" companies were told, you will have to convert to war production in six months. The "A" companies had no choice: you have to do

BULOVA, 1930s. This steel cased soldier's wristwatch has an enamel painted dial with Arabic numerals and a subsidiary seconds chapter at 6:00. It still bears its military canvas strap. Swiss movement, 15 jewels. Note that this example does bear the Bulova name on the dial.

BULOVA, ca 1950s. The black enamel painted dial of this soldier's wristwatch has white Arabic numerals in the hours chapter as well as at 10 minute intervals on the outer minutes chapter. The subsidiary seconds chapter is at 6:00. The anodized steel case is attached to an authentic military canvas strap. Swiss movement, 15 jewels.

WALTHAM, ca 1938. The model 1061f soldier's wristwatch has a round white dial with luminous hands and a subsidiary seconds hand at 6:00. The case is steel and is water resistant as is the crown. The canvas strap completes the military look. 17 jewels.

government work." This was the War Production Board at work, an agency created on January 16, 1942, that controlled what had to be produced for the war effort; production of products deemed to be non-essential was prohibited. "Bulova was prohibited from making civilian products during the war although it made many, many wristwatches. These were for the military, according to military specifications."

Bulova's wristwatch was described in the War Department manual as a 10 AK, 10½ ligne size, 15-jeweled movement that "may be identified by a black dial with the manufacturer's name on it. The bezel is formed as an integral part of the case ring and is equipped with an unbreakable crystal. The movement is secured with a case ring and is not held in the case with screws." Many times the Bulova name did not appear on the dial, despite the War Department's description.

WALTHAM

In one of the most successful episodes of its precarious existence, Waltham coasted through the war years on a production level it had rarely seen before. Thanks to government orders, the firm had plenty of work and no concerns about selling the product. Waltham supplied two wristwatches as service timepieces: the 6/0 size, 9-jeweled movement and the 6/0 size, 17-jeweled movement which was issued to the Air Corps. In both instances, the wristwatch was identified by the Waltham name on the dial.

Just as the company reached the very peak of its production, Waltham's president Dumaine sold his shares and left the company's finances tottering once again. Whether Waltham, with its antiquated equipment, would have successfully reconverted to civilian production if he had stayed is questionable. In any case it found itself instead sputtering through its latest financial reorganization after the war. In 1948, the firm laid off its 2300 workers. It went into receivership in 1949, reorganized and was bankrupt again the next year. The firm spun from one management to another until, in 1957, the watch company had been reduced to nothing more than a name.

WALTHAM, 1917-18. This First World War pierced case wristwatch is of anodized base metal. The bezel is friction-fitted to the case. The enamel painted dial has a subsidiary seconds chapter at 9:00. This example has its original adjustable woven khaki strap. Very rare. 7-jeweled Waltham movement.

GRUEN, 1940s. The enamel painted dial has 24 hour markings using Arabic numerals reflecting the military mode of timekeeping. It also has a red sweep seconds hand. The case has a gold-plated bezel and stainless steel back. 17-jeweled Precision movement.

THE SWISS

While American firms were commandeered to turn their civilian watch production over to the needs of the military, Switzerland geared up to fill the gap. The Swiss had been providing the movements for many of the wristwatches sold in the United States before the war, including those of Gruen and Benrus, and a good part of Bulova's production. Now, they would sell the entire wristwatch. During the five years that America was actively engaged in the war effort, Swiss watches took over the civilian wristwatch market here. From 1941-45, more than 30 million jeweled lever movements entered the United States from Switzerland. Imports of jeweled watches averaged 7.4 million per year in the following five year period, from 1946-50, 75% of total domestic consumption.

In some respects, that was the watershed in American wristwatch production. Although the great eccentric wristwatches of the Fifties, notably by Hamilton, and the *Accutron*, Bulova's stunning technical achievement in the Sixties, were yet to come, the assumption that the watch industry was an indispensable part of the American landscape proved to be more wishing and hoping than the facts would bear out.

Chapter Six
Retro Modern:
The Decade After the War
1945-1955

For half the decade, civilian needs took a distant back seat to the production demands of war materiel. When the war was over, designers returned to their drawing boards and to the happy task of satisfying the pent up demand for consumer products.

But getting back was "a terror", according to James Shennan who became president of Elgin in the late 1940's, after the sudden death of T. Albert Potter. Two thirds of Elgin's war production was in ordnance work; it had nothing to do with watches at all. The other third was military wristwatches which at least were cousins to the movements of civilian wristwatches.

For the companies that had made it through the war, all energy had to be devoted simply to getting back into production and taking advantage of the tremendous post-war demand for consumer products. Just as the factories were re-converting to civilian demands, the soldiers were re-converting themselves into civilians. The men had returned from the war, the women had left the factories, everyone was trying to put their lives back together, and the baby boom was about to happen. The country was at peace and the manufacturers were on their own again. There was no longer a government agency directing product lines and the loosening of the restraints resulted in a certain sense of chaos. It was a time of "anything goes" and the results, not surprisingly, were confused and lively.

The consuming public was eager for anything, it seemed, anything that is but the understated streamlined look of the Thirties. These consumers were ready for glitz, for excess, for flamboyance; the giddy wristwatches of the late forties answered their needs.

They were the antithesis of the streamlined wristwatches that dominated the marketplace in the period just before the war. The cool, lean, stripped-down *Curvex* and its cousins were too close in mood to the no-nonsense designs demanded by the military. It was only logical that post-war design would reflect the craving for the human touch, the rounded, warm look utterly unlike that of the war years. The designers, who along with the factories, had been commandeered for war work, once more could cater to the dreams and desires of civilians and they piled on the details with abandon. Warmth and curves were back. The serious mode necessary for war production gave way to the voluptuously rounded curve.

Some designers did return to the quiet subtlety of the thirties, but more typically the period is symbolized by the flashy, jewel-encrusted, highly ornamented style that has come to be called Retro-Modern. The hyphenated name itself is an indication of the "looking backward, looking forward" design confusion of the period. These wristwatches are striving to make an effect; unlike the sleek wristwatches that preceded them in the Thirties, or

WITTNAUER, 1940s. This highly sculpted gold filled case has a swirl bezel design. The movement is Swiss but the case is American. It has an enamel painted dial with subsidiary seconds chapter. (Courtesy: Time Will Tell)

HAMILTON, ca. 1940s. 14k solid gold tank case, 19 jewels. (Courtesy of Harry Stecker)

HAMILTON, Late '40s. This Hamilton *Vincent* has a distinctive 14k gold filled case with a swirled bezel that flows into the lugs. The raised numerals are 18k gold. There is a subsidiary seconds chapter at 6:00. The *Vincent* is powered by Hamilton's 17 jewel #980 movement.

BULOVA, 1930s. Though dating from the Thirties, the highly sculpted scrolled lugs on this Bulova wristwatch foreshadow the post-war Retro look. The wristwatch case is of rolled gold plate. The enamel painted dial has gold Arabic numbers and hands, a minutes chapter and a subsidiary seconds chapter. It has a fifteen-jeweled Swiss movement. (Courtesy: Time Will Tell)

WITTNAUER, 1940s. This Wittnauer *Revue* has a gold filled, American rectangular case with highly sculpted lugs. The enamel painted dial has a subsidiary seconds chapter. The movement is Swiss, 17 jewels.

BULOVA, 1940s. Unusual overlapping, curved, winged lug covers, give a dramatic look to this 14k gold case. The white enamel painted dial has slashes for the hour indicators and stick hands. 17-jeweled Swiss movement.

WALTHAM,1950s. The Masonic wristwatch incorporates the symbols of the Masonic movement. From the triangle of the bezel to the hour markers, the symbols have significance in the Mason's ritual. There is a sweep seconds hand and the minutes hand is a triangular skeleton. The bezel is yellow gold plated with a steel back. Swiss movement, 17 jewels. This wristwatch is highly sought after and collectible when found in original condition.

ELGIN, 1930s. This 24 hour wristwatch was probably made for the Bureau of Ships (Buships). The case has a 10k yellow gold bezel with a stainless steel back. The tear drop lugs are quite dramatic. There is a sweep seconds hand. 17-jeweled American movement.

the ornamented wristwatches of the Twenties, the wristwatches of the late-Forties are self-consciously cheerful. They appeared at a time when the demand for consumer goods exceeded the supply.

Elgin's move back into the civilian marketplace depended on a sales force that brought back a lot of style and trend ideas, and a well-directed design team. The merchandizing manager, Alex Fekula, worked hand-in-hand with Elgin's chief case and dial designer, Emory Lee, and Charles Hennix, an Elgin stylist, to create a line that would put all thoughts of the war behind them. According to *The Watch Word*, the Elgin company magazine, these three rode herd on a flock of freelance designers who submitted ideas. They also coordinated the efforts of watch case-makers, in particular Wadsworth, the principal case-maker for the firm and in 1951, a wholly-owned subsidiary of Elgin.

And all of them kept a close eye on what everyone else in the industry was doing. The retail stores that stocked Elgin watches told the sales force, some 50 or 60 of them, what their customers wanted. This became part of the feedback to the design team. Designs, sometimes generated at Wadsworth and sometimes at Elgin, went back and forth until agreement was reached. Then these designs were made into case prototypes to see if the artist's vision was a practical one.

The technical end was not neglected either. In 1947, Elgin announced its *Durapower* mainspring, guaranteed never to break in service. It was made from an alloy dubbed "Elgiloy", and was non-magnetic and rustproof, too.

ELGIN, ca 1951-53. The Lord Elgin *Mansfield* has a case of 14k gold. The enamel painted dial is black with Arabic numerals and triangular markers for the hours indicators. The case is curved and the lugs are offset from the sides of the case. There is a diamond-shaped subsidiary seconds chapter at 6:00. 21 jewels.

ELGIN, 1940s. Overlapping lug covers mark this Lord Elgin's bezel. The tonneau-shaped, 14k gold case holds an enamel painted dial with alternating Arabic numerals and star-shaped markers. It has a subsidiary seconds chapter at 6:00. Elgin movement, 21 jewels.

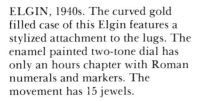

ELGIN, 1940s. The curved gold filled case of this Elgin features a stylized attachment to the lugs. The enamel painted two-tone dial has only an hours chapter with Roman numerals and markers. The movement has 15 jewels.

ELGIN, 1940s. This Lord Elgin's case has concave sides and well-sculpted lugs. The dial is enamel painted black with gold numerals and a subsidiary seconds chapter. The movement has 21 jewels.

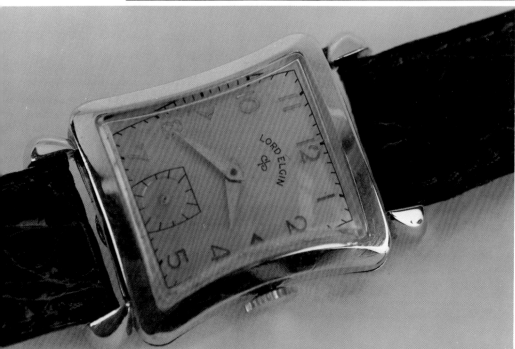

ELGIN, 1950s. A special 24-hour black enamel painted dial marks this dial. All 24 hours are included in one revolution of the hours hand. The hours are marked with alternating Arabic numerals and dots. The case has a gold-plated bezel and a stainless steel back. 17 jewels.

ELGIN, 1940s. This Lord Elgin has a 21-jeweled movement housed in an inverted tonneau gold filled case. There is a minutes chapter and a subsidiary seconds chapter on the enamel painted dial.

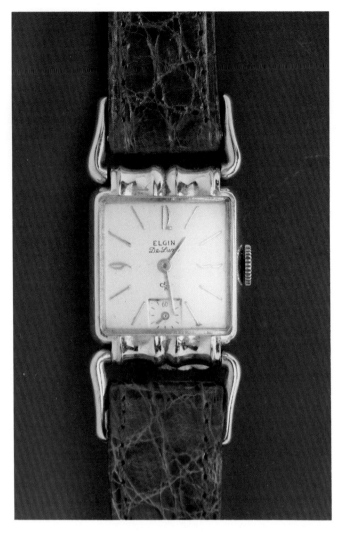

BULOVA, ca. 1940s. Gold-filled tank with T-bar lug. 17 jewels. (Courtesy of Harry Stecker)

ELGIN, 1940s. This 19-jeweled Elgin *DeLuxe* has a gold filled case with unusual U-shaped movable lugs. The enamel painted dial has highly stylized Arabic numerals at 12, 3, and 9, markers at the other positions, and a subsidiary seconds chapter at 6 o'clock.

ELGIN, 1940s. The bezel of this Lord Elgin is embossed with a basketweave pattern, and the lugs are scalloped. The enamel painted dial has raised gold markers instead of numerals, and there is a subsidiary seconds chapter. The movement has 21 jewels.

ELGIN, 1940s. This gold filled Lord Elgin integrates the lugs with the two-tone dial to create an interesting design. The wristwatch has 19 jewels and a subsidiary seconds chapter at 6:00. Markers are used instead of numerals on the hours chapter.

ELGIN, 1940s. The rounded, bold bezel of this Lord Elgin frames a black enamel painted dial. The dial is painted with gold ridges and radii going out from the center to the hours positions. Applied triangular and dot markers indicate the hours, and there is a subsidiary seconds chapter. A 21-jeweled "Shock Master" Elgin movement.

ELGIN, 1950s. Of special interest in this Elgin is the fan-shaped lugs and the way the motif is carried onto the dial. The case is gold filled with a stainless steel back and the Elgin movement has 17 jewels.

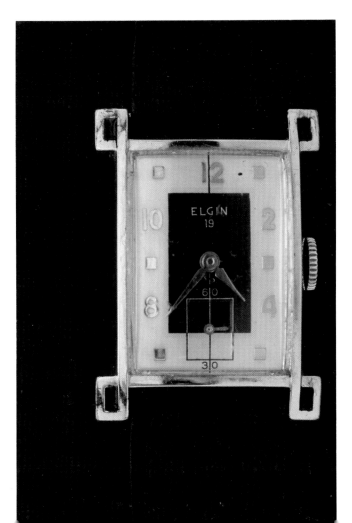

ELGIN, 1940s. This striking rectangular wristwatch has extended corners in an overlapping design, and a black enamel painted center. The two-tone enamel painted dial has raised Arabic numerals and square markers in the hours chapter. The case is 14k gold filled and the Elgin movement has 17 jewels.

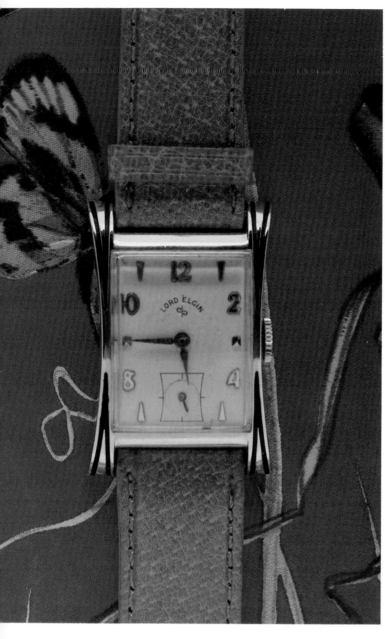

ELGIN, 1940s. 17-jeweled manual Elgin movement in a gold-filled case with an enamel painted dial. Subsidiary seconds chapter.

ELGIN, 1950s-'60s. The concave cushion-shaped case of this Shockmaster is 10k gold filled. The waffle patterned dial is enamel painted with Arabic numerals at 3, 9, and 12 and a subsidiary seconds chapter at 6:00. It has its original gold filled band. 17 jewels.

ELGIN, 1940s. A gold filled rectangular case houses a 17-jeweled movement in this Lord Elgin wristwatch.

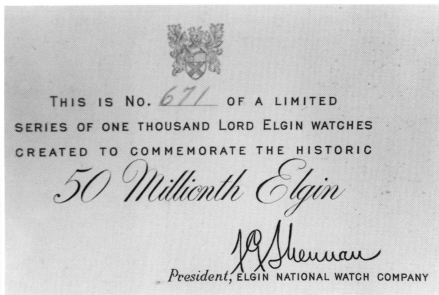

THIS IS NO. *671* OF A LIMITED SERIES OF ONE THOUSAND LORD ELGIN WATCHES CREATED TO COMMEMORATE THE HISTORIC *50 Millionth Elgin*

President, ELGIN NATIONAL WATCH COMPANY

ELGIN, Ca. 1953. This Lord Elgin was created to commemorate the 50 millionth Elgin watch. The case is 18k gold with large hooded and movable lugs. The Elgin movement is gold plated and has 21 jewels. The enamel painted dial has a subsidiary seconds chapter.

ELGIN, 1940s-50s. This gold filled square case has raised markers on its stylized embossed bezel. The hours chapter on the dial is a combination of Arabic numerals and gold markers at the 1, 5, 7, and 11 o'clock positions that carry the bezel design onto the dial. There is a "markless" subsidiary seconds chapter at 6:00. Elgin movement, 15 jewels.

ELGIN, 1940s. This Elgin Shockmaster has a gold filled bezel with architectural lugs. The back is steel. It has an unusual diamond pattern in the background of the hours chapter on the enamel painted dial. The numbers and hour markers are raised gold. 17-jeweled movement with a subsidiary seconds chapter. (Courtesy: Time Will Tell)

ELGIN, 1940s. The case of this Elgin Shockmaster is ridged between the lugs and flared at the sides, making a convex shape. It is of 14k gold and houses a 19-jeweled Elgin movement.

ELGIN, 1940s. This gold filled case houses a 15-jeweled Elgin movement. The dial bears Arabic numerals at 2, 4, 8, and 10 and alternating gold stick markers and triangles at the other positions. The pyramid-shaped lugs are unusual.

GRUEN, 1940s. The 14k yellow gold case of this *Curvex* is massive with the clustered ring designs at 10, 2, 4, and 6:00 dramatizing the high-Retro style. The original black dial emphasizes the powerful case design. This is a highly prized late example of a *Curvex*, rare and desirable to collectors. 17-jeweled, Gruen Precision Swiss movement.

GRUEN, 1940s. This tonneau-shaped Gruen Veri-Thin has a black enamel painted dial with a subsidiary seconds chapter reflecting the overall shape of the watch. It is marked with Arabic numerals at 9, 12 and 3:00 and slash markers at the other hours. It has a Swiss 17-jeweled manual movement and the bezel is ribbed.

GRUEN, 1940s. This Gruen Precision is a single button chronograph. It has a subsidiary seconds chapter at 9:00 and a sweep recording hand. The 17-jeweled Swiss movement is encased in a gold filled case, and has an enamel painted dial.

Gruen, that '30s master of streamlining, jumped into the '40s mood with enthusiasm. Its black dial wristwatches with their scrolled lugs, ruffled bezels, and gem markers show how far the firm had traveled in just one decade. Gruen was in the last phase of its life as an independent watch company. It continued to make the *Curvex*, adding a new model in 1948, the *Curvametric*. The *Curvex* wristwatch was made at least until 1950. Although it had built an addition to its Cincinnati facility in 1953, two years later the Gruen heirs sold their interest and the firm became Gruen Industries Inc. When it was moved to New York in 1958, their archives were thrown away and generations of history were discarded.

The curved wristwatches that so captivated the Thirties found expression in the Forties, but with a decidedly Retro-Modern touch. The curved sides were notched, or engraved, or exaggerated beyond the profile of the original models. These wristwatches were convex on all four sides, their bezels wider and more aggressive in appearance.

GRUEN, 1940s. The 14k gold case has hours markers on the bezel and unusual keystone-shaped lugs attaching the wristwatch to a metal bracelet. The white enamel painted dial has stylized Arabic numerals at the 12, 3, 6, and 9 o'clock positions. There is a sweep seconds hand. 17-jeweled Swiss movement.

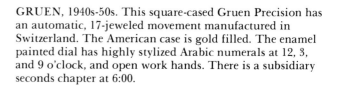

GRUEN, 1940s. An example of Gruen's entry into the highly stylized Retro-Modern period, this rectangular 14k gold filled case has exaggerated braided lug covers. The white enamel painted dial has Arabic numerals at 12, 3, and 9 and markers at all other hour positions. 21-jeweled Swiss movement.

GRUEN, 1940s-50s. This square-cased Gruen Precision has an automatic, 17-jeweled movement manufactured in Switzerland. The American case is gold filled. The enamel painted dial has highly stylized Arabic numerals at 12, 3, and 9 o'clock, and open work hands. There is a subsidiary seconds chapter at 6:00.

GRUEN, 1940s. This Gruen "Precision" has a signed gold-filled case and a Swiss 21-jewelled movement. The retro-modern feeling is evident in the spider-angled lugs and the stylized framework around the bezel. Subsecond dial has applied gold batons. (Courtesy of Harry Stecker)

GRUEN, 1950s. The black enameled dial of this Gruen Precision has diamonds to mark the 12, 3, and 9 hours and a subsidiary seconds chapter. The case is gold filled and has the extended lugs characteristic of this period. The movement is Swiss and has 15 jewels.

GRUEN, 1940s. The gold filled Veri-Thin case has roped embossing at the lugs. The dial is unusual in that it has a military-style double hours chapters, 1-12 and 13-24. 15-jeweled Precision movement.

GRUEN, 1950s. This simple round wristwatch has extended lugs. The enamel painted dial is fluted and uses Arabic numerals at 3, 6, 9, and 12, and slash markers at the other hour positions. Swiss, 17-jeweled movement.

GRUEN, 1940s. An oval-shaped dial in a tonneau case marks this wristwatch. The case is gold filled with a stainless steel back. The movement is Swiss with 15 jewels.

GRUEN, 1930s. This Gruen Veri-Thin has a 15-jeweled Swiss movement in an American made gold filled case with a steel back. The enamel painted dial has raised Arabic numerals and a subsidiary seconds chapter.

GRUEN, 1940s. Highly unusual sculpted spiraled lugs mark this 14k gold case. The enamel painted dial uses no numerals. It is marked "Gruen 21, Precision." The movement is Swiss, 21 jewels.

HAMILTON, 1940s. The gold filled case of this Hamilton extends to cover the lugs. The dial design draws diagonal lines to the corners of the square dial. There is a subsidiary seconds chapter at 6:00. The case is American-made. 17-jeweled Hamilton movement.

SIMMONS, 1940s. The rolled gold plate wristwatch has raised pediment-shaped lugs. The enamel painted dial has Roman numerals in the hours chapter. 15-jeweled Swiss movement.

LE COULTRE, ca 1952. The bezel seems to run through the slotted lugs in the unusual design of the *Coronet*. The 14k gold filled case is round. The enamel painted dial and the crystal make way for the intrusion of the lugs. Painted Arabic numerals mark the 12, 3, 6, and 9:00 positions while applied dots are used at the others. A subsidiary seconds hand is above the 6. This American made case is also available in yellow gold filled. 17-jeweled Swiss movement.

If one idea can be said to sum up an entire period of design, in the late Forties the idea was exaggeration. Like tropical plants that flourish to excess, the bezel and lugs seemed to just grow and take exotic shape. The expansive growth began with simple extensions from the watch case to the band. Then it started to curve upward, away from the case; it curled around the band at the corners of the case, it swooped, it flew, it was no longer earthbound. The bezel seemed to have a life of its own as it made its way farther and farther away from the timepiece itself. Lugs became flexible and elaborately decorated, echoing and enhancing the decoration of the lavish bezel and the dial.

The look began its gymnastics on the rectangle where the strap attachments leapt across an open space. The case was somewhat detached from these extensions, the design more forcefully growing along the band. The more restrained bezel extensions appeared as rods or bars attached to the band.

Exaggeration being the leitmotif of the forties, it's logical that the bezel/lug extensions should continue to grow until they threatened to take over the entire case. In the more exuberant of these designs, the lugs had the broad-shouldered look of Joan Crawford in her classic film roles.

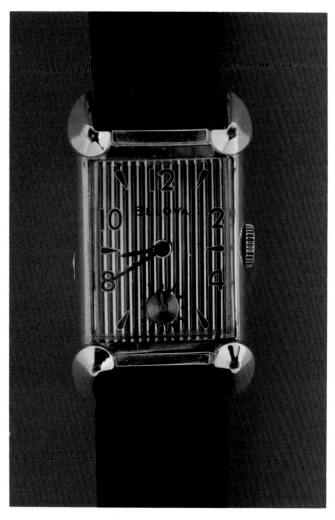

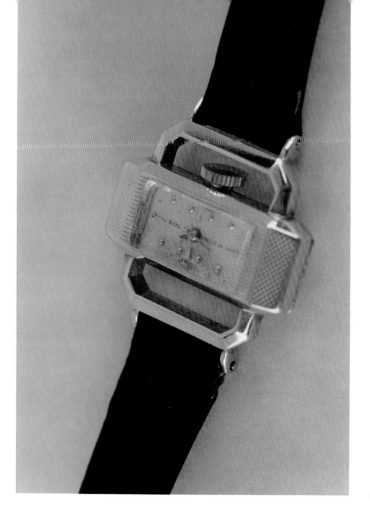

LE COULTRE, 1940s. Extended stirrup-styled open lugs mark this 14k wristwatch. Between the lugs is an elongated tank-shaped case set vertically. The enamel painted dial has applied hours markers. Swiss movement, 17 jewels.

BULOVA, 1940s. The 10k gold filled rectangular case has sculpted cone-shaped decorations on each corner. The dial is die-stamped in a ribbed pattern, with alternating Arabic numerals and triangular markers. The Bulova model 7AK Swiss movement has 17 jewels.

HELBROS, 1940s. The gold filled American case of this wristwatch has unusual triangular-shaped lugs and bezel. The white enamel painted dial has diamonds at 12, 3, and 9 o'clock, and Arabic numerals and markers at the other positions. Swiss movement, 15 jewels.

HAMILTON, 1940s. This *Emerson* model has a 10k gold filled case in a modified tonneau shape, with ribbed lugs. The dial is painted with enamel over silver and has 18k gold numerals. There are 17 jewels and a subsidiary seconds chapter.

LONGINES, 1940s. The 14k pink gold filled American case incorporates the covered barrel lugs into the overall Retro design. The two-tone pink dial has Roman numerals at 12, 3, and 9, and bar markers at the other positions. Swiss movement, 17 jewels.

HAMILTON, 1950s. This wristwatch takes a basic man's style and reduces it to a woman's size. The round case is 14k gold filled with sculpted lugs. The white enamel painted dial has full Arabic numerals with a sweep seconds hand. The minutes/seconds chapter is numbered at five minute intervals. 17 jewels.

Arbib rendering. Courtesy: Jeff Hess

HAMILTON, 1940s. The 14k gold square case is suspended between the lugs by a "V" of gold, giving the wristwatch the feel of lightness. The sterling silver dial has applied 18k gold markers and a subsidiary seconds chapter. 17-jeweled Hamilton movement.

VACHERON & CONSTANTIN, ca 1955. The 14k gold case for this Swiss wristwatch was manufactured by Cress Arrow, and the wristwatch was cased and timed in the United States. The split barrel-shaped hooded lugs decorate the case. The dial has Arabic numerals at 12, 3 and 9 and applied markers at the other positions. This is a very good example of the company's work. 17 jewels.

WITTNAUER, 1940s. This gold filled wristwatch is unusual for the date chapter and day window. A sweep center hand points to the date on this chapter while the day of the week appears in the cutout. The movement is 17-jeweled Swiss and the case is American. (Courtesy: Time Will Tell)

HAMILTON, ca 1938. The *Contour*, an edge-of-the-wrist driver's wristwatch, has the look of the Retro period though it is earlier. The large lugs suspend the 14k gold filled case. The rectangular dial is painted sterling silver with 18k gold applied Arabic numerals. The crown is situated at the 12:00 position. This is a very unusual and extremely rare wristwatch. 17 jewels.

BULOVA, 1940s. The enamel painted dial on this gold filled rectangular wristwatch has diamonds at the 3, 9, and 12 o'clock positions and raised gold markers at the others. It has a 17-jeweled Swiss movement with a subsidiary seconds chapter.

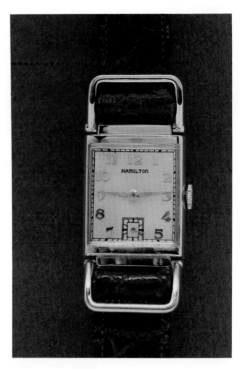

BULOVA, 1940s. This gold filled rectangular wristwatch
has an enamel painted dial with stylized Arabic numerals.
It has a 15-jeweled Swiss movement, with a subsidiary
seconds chapter. The curved lugs are somewhat unusual in
that they are movable. (Courtesy: Time Will Tell)

HAMILTON, 1940s. This Hamilton
Tuxedo has a 14k gold filled case with
large movable lugs which allow the strap
to be attached over or under the lugs. It
has a painted silver dial with raised 18k
gold Arabic numerals. There is a
subsidiary seconds chapter at 6:00.
17-jewels.

ELGIN, 1940s. The heavily
sculpted lugs and bezel of this Lord
Elgin are typical of the Retro-
Modern period in wristwatches.
The case is gold filled and houses a
21-jeweled Elgin movement. The
enamel painted dial has raised
numeral 12 and raised markers.
There is a subsidiary seconds
chapter.

EBERHARD, 1940s. Sculpted winged lugs bring the Retro look to this 14k yellow gold wristwatch. The white enamel painted dial has painted Arabic numerals at 12, 3, and 9 o'clock, a subsidiary seconds chapter at 6:00, and raised dot markers at the other hours positions. Swiss movement, 17 jewels.

WITTNAUER, 1930s. The 10k gold filled case is distinguished by its flexible, extended stirrup lugs. The enamel painted dial has alternating Arabic numerals and markers, with a subsidiary seconds chapter at 6:00. 17-jeweled Swiss movement.

HELBROS, 1940s. A 17-jeweled Swiss movement in a gold-filled die-struck American case. Subsidiary seconds chapter at 6:00. Dramatic extension of the lugs from the case.

HAMILTON, 1940s. The 18k gold case of this rectangular wristwatch features flexible lugs with hidden hinges. The black enamel painted dial has Arabic numerals alternating with markers in the hours chapter and a subsidiary seconds chapter. 19-jeweled Hamilton movement.

HAMILTON, 1940s. The 14k gold filled case has horned type lugs which are unusual for Hamilton. The dial is painted silver with raised 18k gold Arabic numerals. 17-jeweled Hamilton movement with a subsidiary seconds chapter.

WITTNAUER, 1940s. The angled split-hooded lugs make a strong Retro-Modern design statement. The case is 14k gold and has a white enamel painted dial with Arabic numerals and slash markers in the hours chapter. 17-jeweled Swiss movement.

BULOVA, 1940s. This gold filled case has shield shapes on the bezel which cover the lugs. The painted dial has Arabic numerals and markers with a minutes chapter and a subsidiary seconds chapter. The movement is 15-jeweled Swiss.

ELGIN, ca 1950. The Lord Elgin was the top of the Elgin line. The exaggerated curved lugs and the unusual patterned honeycomb dial are key elements in this dramatic design. The case is 14k gold filled and the enamel painted dial has dauphin hands and stick markers in raised gold. Arabic numerals are used at 12, 3 and 9 and there is a subsidiary seconds chapter at 6:00. This wristwatch came with a black dial, and was marketed as the "Black Knight." 21 jewels. Rare.

HAMILTON, 1940s. The *Emerson* is a tonneau-shaped wristwatch with fluted hooded lugs. The white enamel painted sterling silver dial has applied 18k gold numerals and a subsidiary seconds chapter. 17 jewels.

WITTNAUER, 1950s. The 14k gold American stepped case has
architectural lugs. Dramatic triangular cut-out gold hands grace the
black enamel painted dial. It has double raised triangular markers at
12, 3, 6, and 9:00 and indented marks at the other positions in the outer
gold hours chapter. The minutes chapter uses gold-plated dots on the
dial. 17-jeweled Swiss movement.

GUBELIN, 1960s. This wristwatch
features an unusual elliptical concentric design in a massive 18k yellow
gold case. The fabulous '50s look is
emphasized by the black dial and
gold hands. It has a 19-jeweled Swiss
movement with 3 position adjustments and was marketed by the
famous Genevan retailer Gübelin.

NORMAN, 1940s. Marketed under the name Norman, this
is essentially a generic Swiss wristwatch in an American-
made gold filled case. The square case has a sculpted bezel
and is attached to an integrated bracelet. The enamel
painted dial has Arabic numerals and a subsidiary seconds
chapter. 17-jeweled Swiss movement.

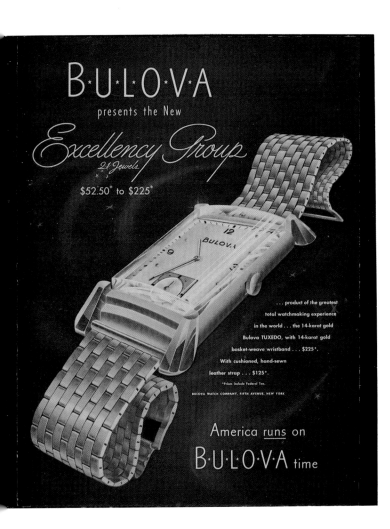

HAMILTON, 1930s-40s. It is unusual to see the name Hamilton and Illinois together on a watch, particularly this late. After Hamilton bought Illinois they continued to use the name for many years, but usually by itself. The case is gold filled with an enamel painted dial, and has the name Hamilton/Illinois stamped inside the back of the case. Hamilton movement, 17 jewels.

BULOVA, 1940s. The motif of the ridged and fluted 10k rolled gold plate case is carried into the gold enamel painted dial. Black numerals at 12, 3, and 9 are outlined in gold, while the square markers at the other positions are outlined in black. A nice coordinated Retro design. 17-jeweled, Bulova model 7AK Swiss movement.

BENRUS, 1940s. Made of 14k gold, this American-cased Benrus *Shockresist* has a heavily sculpted bezel and lugs. Its enamel painted dial has applied markers for the hours. The subsidiary seconds chapter is at 6:00. Swiss movement, 15 jewels.

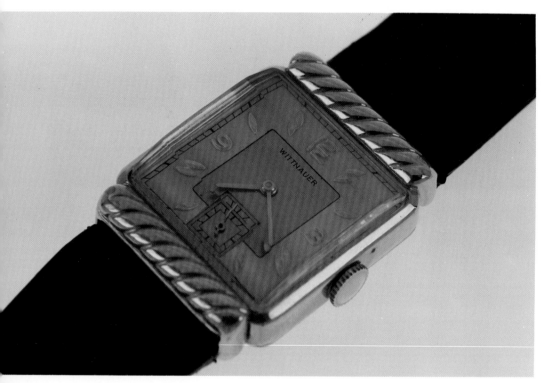

WITTNAUER, 1940s. Beautifully scrolled lugs mark this American case of 14k gold. The enamel painted dial is two-toned with Arabic numerals and slash markers. (The crystal gives some distortion to the shape of the dial figures.) The movement is 17-jeweled Swiss and there is a subsidiary seconds chapter.

LEE, 1940s. The bezel and back of this wristwatch are glass, giving a dramatic look from the front and a view of the movement from the back. The bezel is framed in a rolled gold plate case and surrounds a white enamel painted dial. Slash marks are used in the hours chapter and are carried into the bezel design. 17-jeweled Swiss movement.

GRUEN, 1945-55. 17-jeweled Swiss movement in a 14k white gold case, highly stylized with a nuts and bolts motif around a wide bezel. The black enamel painted dial has diamonds for five-minute markers. Subsidiary seconds chapter at 6:00.

GRUEN, 1940s. The sculpted case of this wristwatch uses gems and raised markers on the bezel for the hours chapter. The minutes chapter is on the black enamel painted dial. The Swiss movement has 17 jewels.

BULOVA, 1940s. This nicely sculpted stepped case is reminiscent of an earlier period. The rectangular case holds a white enamel painted dial with alternating Arabic numerals and hour markers. 15-jeweled Swiss movement.

BULOVA, 1940s.

BUREN, 1940s. This rare hunting case was manufactured in the U.S. by
the ID Watch Case Company. It is rolled gold plate, with an enamel
painted dial and Arabic numerals at 12, 2, 4, 8, and 10 and has a
subsidiary seconds chapter. The movement is 17-jeweled Swiss.

BENRUS, 1940s. The red-tipped sweep hand
points to the inner date chapter on this calendar
wristwatch while the day appears in the cut out
window. The date advances automatically at
midnight or one day for each depression of the
crown. The outer, white portion of this two-toned
dial has raised Arabic numerals and markers for
the hours chapter. The rolled gold plate case
features highly sculpted lugs. Swiss movement, 17
jewels.

GENEVA, 1940s. The bezel of this rolled gold plate case has a raised hours chapter using Arabic numerals and triangular markers. The white enamel painted dial has the minutes chapter and a subsidiary seconds chapter. Swiss movement, 17 jewels.

BENRUS, 1940s. The case is American and is gold-filled. It has a ribbed construction on the outer perimeter. The enamel painted dial has gold Arabic figures and markers and embossed leaf cluster below the Benrus name. Swiss 15 jewels. (Courtesy Time Will Tell)

BENRUS, 1930s-40s. While this wristwatch is difficult to date precisely, it has the hallmarks of the Retro-Modern period. The decorated lugs and the black enamel bezel with Roman numeral hours chapter give it the dramatic feel of the era. The black enamel painted dial is divided into quadrants and has a subsidiary seconds chapter at 6:00. The movement is Swiss and has 15 jewels.

GUBELIN, 1945-50. A massive stepped cushion-shaped case of 14k yellow gold marks this Ipsomatic as part of the Retro-Modern period. The two-toned, silver and cream dial has an Arabic numeral 12 and raised markers. This triple-signed wristwatch has a 25-jeweled automatic Swiss movement.

LE COULTRE, 1950s. The 14k gold case of the *Beau Brummel* has a conical bezel rising to a flat plateau around the crystal. On the plateau are embossed raised hours markers. Except for the name, the white enamel painted dial is without markings. American case; 17-jeweled Swiss movement.

BULOVA, 1940s. The gold-filled case is deeply fluted and the dial has raised gold Arabic numbers, and a subsidiary seconds chapter. The movement has 17 jewels and is a model 7AK Bulova movement from Switzerland.

LONGINES, 1940s-50s. This 10k gold filled American case has unusual engravings on the bezel. The enamel painted dial has a subsidiary seconds chapter, and uses markers for the hours chapter instead of numerals. 17-jeweled Swiss movement.

BULOVA, 1940s. This tonneau-shaped, gold filled case has a highly embossed bezel. The dial is painted and has a subsidiary seconds chapter. 17-jeweled Swiss movement.

HAMILTON, ca. 1940s. "Piping Rock" with round black enamel bezel on a two-piece case. Similar to the 1920s design (see page 114), but the lugs are restricted on this model and the back is not removable. (Courtesy of Harry Stecker)

BULOVA, 1940s. The sculpted gold filled stepped case frames a fluted enamel painted metal dial. Applied black Arabic numerals and teardrop markers make up the hours chapter. A subsidiary seconds chapter is at 6:00. 17-jeweled Swiss movement.

LONGINES, 1940s. This 14k gold case has a very unusual bezel. Diamonds are used at the 12, 3, 6, and 9 o'clock positions and raised relief markers indicate the other points in the hours chapter. The enamel painted dial has a subsidiary seconds chapter. The case is American, the movement Swiss.

LONGINES, 1940s. This classic, bold looking wristwatch has a 14k gold filled case with a black enamel painted dial with applied slash markers in the hours chapter. Swiss movement, 17 jewels.

The numbers and markers were exaggerated as well, leaping onto the bezel in a more prominent role. Numbering systems were as varied as the colors and shapes of the wristwatches: Arabic numbers prevailed, but Roman numbers were very popular as well. Markers of all sorts were also used. Sticks, dots, slashes, and sometimes round or baguette gems were used to indicate hours.

Real wristwatches with fake gems form their own sub-category of Forties design. Although genuine stone-set wristwatches had already appeared, the stones of the Forties were usually glass. They appeared on the bezel, on the cover of a closed watch, and in place of hour indicators. To use a phrase that had not yet come into the language, they were "frankly fake".

Many of these same design notions were employed on round wristwatches of the decade giving them a curiously split personality. The round wristwatch has the familiar old dial that takes us back to the pocket watch, but the bezel attachments on the more flamboyant of these styles are decidedly part of the new wave.

BULOVA, 1940s. This self-winding, 17-jeweled wristwatch has a gold filled case with scrolled lugs, typical of this era. There is a sweep seconds hand.

BULOVA, Early '50s. Reminiscent of Longine's *Weems* wristwatch of an earlier era, this self-winding wristwatch has a rotating dial which is used to measure elapsed time. The outer chapter is rotated with the crown at 2:00, while the crown at 4:00 sets and winds the watch. The case is steel and waterproof. The black enamel painted dial has luminescent numerals and hands. Swiss movement, 17 jewels.

BULOVA, 1940s. The case is 14k white gold with movable lugs. The square dial is two-toned enamel painted with Roman numerals and a subsidiary seconds chapter. Swiss movement, 17 jewels.

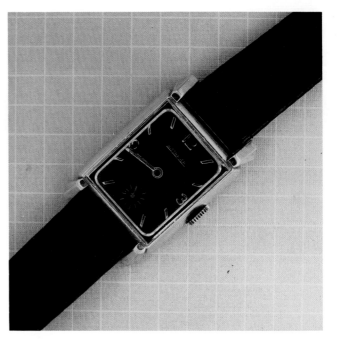

WITTNAUER, 1940s. The case is of 14k gold and has decorative lugs. The dial is enamel painted with a subsidiary seconds chapter. The movement is 17-jeweled Swiss.

BENRUS, 1930s-40s. This round wristwatch has an unusual enameled bezel with a Roman numbered hours chapter. It is attached to the strap with movable lugs. The case material is rolled gold plate. The dial has an unusual waffle pattern. There is a subsidiary seconds chapter. 17-jeweled Swiss movement.

CORT, 1940s. This is an American-cased, Swiss movement wristwatch. The case is gold filled with an interesting bezel treatment. The hours are marked on the bezel with raised geometrical symbols, diamonds, triangles, and circles, reminiscent of the Deco style. 17 jewels, subsidiary seconds chapter.

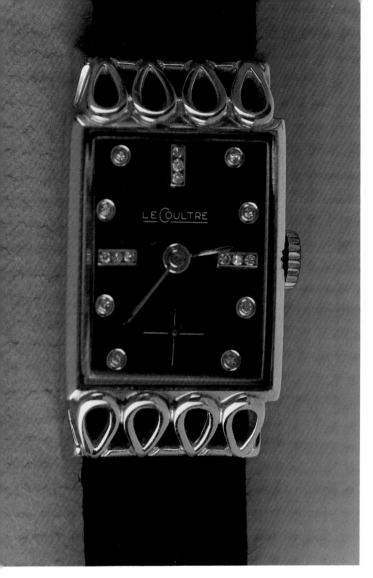

LE COULTRE, 1940s. This Swiss 17-jeweled movement was cased in the U.S. in an American case. It is 14k gold and has unusual and rare lattice work at the top and bottom of the bezel, over the lugs. The enamel painted dial is black with diamonds to mark the hours. There is a subsidiary seconds chapter at 6:00.

BULOVA, Ca.1945-55. This gold filled case is highly unusual in its treatment of the bezel: raised Arabic numerals alternate with markers. The enamel painted dial has a subsidiary seconds chapter. Swiss movement, 15 jewels.

GENEVA, 1940s. This man's wristwatch is unusual for its use of glass gems on the bezel and dial. These clear and red glass gems are set into a gold plated case with a steel back. The enamel painted dial has glass markers at the hours and a subsidiary seconds at 6:00. A Swiss, 17-jeweled movement is used in this American case.

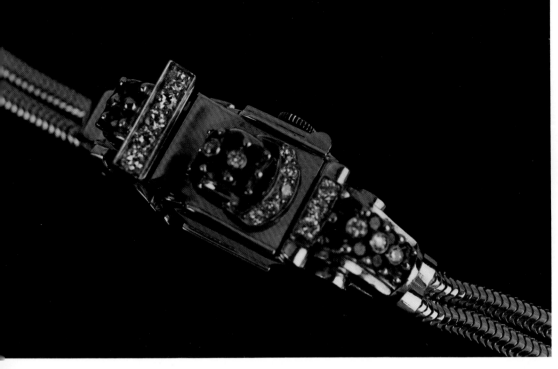

UNKNOWN, 1940s. The jewel-encrusted cover of this hunting case cocktail wristwatch lifts to reveal the time. In high Retro style this lady's wristwatch uses diamonds and rubies set in 14k gold with a double snake bracelet. The white enamel painted dial is white. The case is American and the 17-jeweled movement is Swiss.

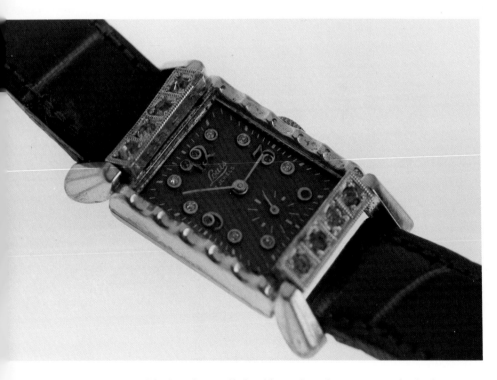

LOUIS, 1940s. This American rolled gold case has glass stones set in the lug edges of the bezel and scalloped edges on the sides. The lugs are mitered and fluted. The black enamel painted dial is set with red glass stones in the Arabic 12, 3, and 9 and clear glass stones at the other hour positions. There is a subsidiary seconds chapter at 6:00. 17-jeweled Swiss movement.

GRUEN, 1950s. This Gruen Precision is unusual for its curved lugs set with glass stones. The case is made by Gruen U.S. and is 14k gold filled. The enamel painted dial is black with glass stones at 12, 3, and 9 o'clock. It has a Swiss Gruen movement with 17 jewels.

LONGINES, ca 1960. Though somewhat late for the Retro-Modern period, this design certainly qualifies it for membership. The 14k gold case has exaggerated sculpted lugs, with the hours chapter on the bezel and marked with diamonds at 12, 3, 6, and 9. Raised gold markers indicate the other hours positions. The enamel painted dial has a minutes chapter and a subsidiary seconds chapter. 17-jeweled Swiss movement.

GENEVA, 1940s. This rectangular wristwatch with sculpted sides has a rolled gold plate case with a stainless back. It has red and clear glass stones set into the bezel at the lugs. Stones are also used on the dial to mark the hours. The movement is 15-jeweled Swiss.

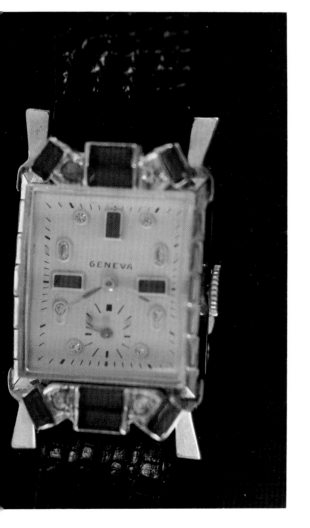

BULOVA, 1945-55. This 14k gold case has diamonds set into its highly sculpted bezel. It has an enamel painted dial with a subsidiary seconds chapter at 6:00. The movement is Swiss with 17 jewels. The style is also available in a gold filled case without diamonds, with a 15-jeweled Swiss movement.

STAR, 1940s. This gold plated square cased wristwatch has glass stones on the bezel to mark the hours of the round dial. The dial itself is enamel painted with Arabic numerals in the hours chapter and a subsidiary seconds chapter. The Swiss movement has 7 jewels and is Monarch-Swiss.

ELMONT, 1940s. This gold filled American case has curved flutes at the sides of the bezel and lugs, and a stainless steel back. The white enamel painted dial is inset with red baguette stones at the 12, 3 and 9 o'clock positions and round inset stones at all the other hour indications. The Swiss, 17-jeweled movement was imported and cased in the United States.

RULON, 1940s. The American rolled gold case is decorated with inset red and white glass on the bezel. 17-jeweled Swiss movement.

HARMAN, 1940s. Fluting decorates the bezel and lugs of this gold filled American case. On the dial the 12, 3, and 9 are set with red glass stones, while clear glass stones are used at the other hours positions. A subsidiary seconds chapter is at 6:00. Swiss movement, 15 jewels.

BENRUS, 1940s. This gold plated tonneau-shaped wristwatch uses red baguette-cut glass stones to mark the hours of 12, 3, and 9, and white brilliant-cut glass for the others. It has a subsidiary seconds chapter and a 17-jeweled Swiss movement.

LE COULTRE, 1940-50. While LeCoultre cased many of their wristwatches in Switzerland for export, they also exported movements to be put into American cases, such as this example. The case is 14k gold and has a painted metal dial, with hours and minutes chapters. The wristwatch has an alarm feature which is set using a movable inner dial. 17-jeweled Swiss movement with a sweep seconds hand.

BULOVA, 1950s. This automatic calendar wristwatch has a cutout for the day and arrow to indicate the date on a chapter within the hours chapter. The gold filled die-stamped case is embossed on the bezel and has curved lugs. In addition to the calendar features the dial has raised Arabic numerals alternating with bar markers in the hours chapter and a subsidiary seconds chapter. The Swiss automatic movement has 23 jewels.

BULOVA, 1950s. This *Wrist Alarm* has a gold plated case with large sculpted lugs. The three crowns are used for setting the wristwatch and the alarm. The center crown is for winding and setting the wristwatch, the upper crown is for winding and setting the alarm, and the lower crown engages the alarm mechanism. The enamel painted dial has diamond and arrow-shaped hours markers. There is a sweep seconds hand and a red-tipped alarm setting hand. The movement is German.

HAMILTON, 1940s. This round gold filled case has slightly exaggerated lugs. The enamel painted sterling silver dial has applied 18k gold numerals. 17 jewels.

HAMILTON, ca 1950. The 14k white gold case has dramatic, geometrically sculpted, pierced lug covers. The dial is two-toned and uses diamonds in the dot markers and Arabic numerals of the hours chapter. The inner minutes chapter and subsidiary seconds chapter overlap in an interesting patterning. 17-jeweled Hamilton movement.

HAMILTON, 1940s. An embossed bezel decorates this 17-jeweled Hamilton. The two-toned enamel painted dial has a subsidiary seconds chapter.

The Forties wristwatches have a color all their own: pink. The pink/red cast of the gold is a constant theme, sometimes echoed in the color of the dial. Dials offered designers another surface to color and the choice was often two tones: one block of color within borders of another color. Some are as dramatic as black and white, others are more subtly tinted in two shades of pink or gold. Pink and gold dials were a favorite of Hamilton. The pin wheel design of Benrus, Bulova and others are subtle renditions of the two tone look with its muted shadings.

Seconds chapters offer another design element to embellish and the variety in the late '40s was nearly as great as the number of wristwatches. Round or square, free-floating or framed, the subsidiary seconds chapter most often echoed the shape and design of the case and dial. Sweep seconds hands are seen largely on round wristwatches.

HAMILTON, ca 1941. The *Midas* is, appropriately, of 14k pink or "coral" gold. That and the covered barrel lugs qualify this as an introduction by Hamilton into the Retro-Modern period. The enamel painted dial carries the color theme and is accented with 18k applied gold markers and Arabic numerals. The warm tones of gold and the rectangular format make this wristwatch pleasing to the eye. 19-jeweled Hamilton movement.

BULOVA, 1940s. This pink gold filled case has flexible lugs and an enamel painted dial. The hours chapter of this rectangular wristwatch has raised markers. The circle within a square design is repeated in the subsidiary seconds chapter. The movement is 15-jeweled Swiss.

BULOVA, 1940s. A gold filled case with an enamel painted dial, it has white Arabic numerals and a subsidiary seconds chapter. 17-jeweled Swiss movement.

BULOVA, ca. 1940s. Rectangular case with a pink dial. The black Roman numerals appear on a white rectangular band. Subsidiary second. (Courtesy of Aaron Faber Gallery)

LONGINES, c.1940s. A 17-jeweled Swiss movement in a 14k yellow gold American-made case. Two-tone enamel painted dial. Subsidiary seconds chapter.

BULOVA, 1940s. Stylized architectural lugs mark this 14k gold case. The white enamel painted dial has painted Arabic numerals at 12, 3, and 9:00 and applied raised markers at the other hours positions. A subsidiary seconds chapter occupies the 6:00 position. Swiss movement, 15 jewels.

BENRUS, 1940s. This rare Benrus has a case of 14k gold with raised, ribbed lugs. This wristwatch was available in yellow and pink 14k gold. The movement is Swiss and has 17 jewels. It has an enamel painted dial, Arabic numerals, an outer minutes track and a subsidiary seconds chapter at 6:00. (Courtesy Time Will Tell)

BULOVA, 1940s. The bezel of this rolled gold plate case has deeply stamped ridges. The dial is painted in a pinwheel pattern, and has Arabic numerals. The movement is Swiss, 15 jewels.

BULOVA, 1940s. With its sculpted bezel and lugs, and its checkerboard dial, this is a striking wristwatch. The case is 14k gold. 21 jewels, Swiss movement.

BENRUS, 1940s. With its offset lugs this rolled gold filled wristwatch is interesting to look at, and its complications make it even more so. On its dial it has a window which reveals the day of the week. The sweep hand points to the day of the month, 1 through 31. There is also an hours chapter with alternating Arabic numerals and marker, and a subsidiary seconds chapter. It is unusual to have this much complexity in an American wristwatch marketed by an American company even if it houses a Swiss movement, as here. 15 jewels.

BENRUS, 1940s. The gold filled case has unusual loops attached to the lugs. The dial is painted in a pinwheel pattern with raised Arabic numerals at 12, 3, and 9:00 and bar markers at the other hours positions. There is a subsidiary seconds chapter. Swiss movement, 17 jewels.

MOVADO, ca 1950. This gold filled, American cased wristwatch tells the day, month and date. The day and month appear in window in the 2 tone enamel painted dial. The date is on the outermost chapter and is indicated by a sweep date hand. The hours chapter has raised Arabic numerals and there is a subsidiary seconds chapter. The two pushers change the month(s) and the date(s). The crown changes the day. 17-jeweled Swiss movement.

DIWEN, 1940s. The regulator dial is a carryover from a design often used in clocks and pocket watches but rarely seen in wristwatches. It has a small hours chapter above a small minutes chapter, and surrounded by a seconds chapter with a red sweep seconds hand. The configuration requires more than a little mental work to interpret the time and for that reason was at odds with the convenience of the wristwatch. The Swiss case is steel. The movement, also Swiss, has 17 jewels.

WITTNAUER, 1940s. 14k gold rectangular American case, with a 15-jeweled Swiss movement.

ORLOFF, 1940s. The American case is rolled gold plate with a steel back. The white enamel painted dial has raised Arabic numerals and a subsidiary seconds chapter. 17-jeweled Swiss movement.

BULOVA, 1940s. The rolled gold plate case is sculpted on the sides of the bezel and on the lugs. The enamel painted dial has a subsidiary seconds chapter. Swiss movement, 15 jewels.

BENRUS, 1950s. This single-crowned calendar wristwatch has a cut-out for the day, and a sweep hand which points to an outer date chapter. This hand is rest by pushing in the crown, and the day is set by turning the crown. The case of this wristwatch is 14k gold. It has an enamel painted dial with Arabic numerals. 17-jeweled Swiss movement.

WARREN, 1940s. The 17-jeweled Swiss movement was cased and timed in the United States. The gold filled case has a white enamel painted dial with stylized Arabic numerals.

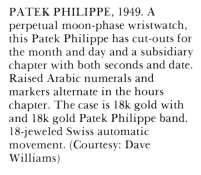

PATEK PHILIPPE, 1949. A perpetual moon-phase wristwatch, this Patek Philippe has cut-outs for the month and day and a subsidiary chapter with both seconds and date. Raised Arabic numerals and markers alternate in the hours chapter. The case is 18k gold with and 18k gold Patek Philippe band. 18-jeweled Swiss automatic movement. (Courtesy: Dave Williams)

UNIVERSAL, 1940s. The *Uni-Compax* is a chronograph with a sweep seconds and minutes recorder operated by the square buttons beside the crown. It also has a continuous subsidiary seconds chapter at 9:00. Swiss movement, 17 jewels.

BULOVA, 1950s. The rolled gold plate case has sculpted batons on its sides. The white enamel painted dial has Arabic numerals at 12, 3, 4, 8, and 10 o'clock with a subsidiary seconds chapter at 6:00. 15-jeweled Swiss movement.

HAMILTON, ca 1954. Using the Illinois name on the dial, Hamilton produced this gold filled automatic wristwatch. It has a power indicator with a digital readout showing the number of hours of wind remaining. The wristwatch can be manually wound. Water resistant case with a 17-jeweled Swiss automatic movement with Incabloc.

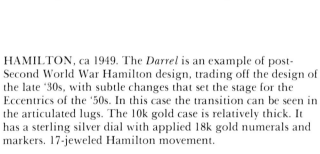

BULOVA, 1940s. This gold filled wristwatch has a highly stylized bezel with an embossed scalloped motif. The dial is enamel painted with a subsidiary seconds chapter at 6:00. The movement is 17-jeweled Swiss.

HAMILTON, ca 1949. The *Darrel* is an example of post-Second World War Hamilton design, trading off the design of the late '30s, with subtle changes that set the stage for the Eccentrics of the '50s. In this case the transition can be seen in the articulated lugs. The 10k gold case is relatively thick. It has a sterling silver dial with applied 18k gold numerals and markers. 17-jeweled Hamilton movement.

The post-war Retro-Modern period continued on into the Fifties when it came up against the new conservatism of the Eisenhower years. War returned to our consciousness very soon, this time in the form of a "police action" in Korea. A homogenization of tastes began, influenced by the expanding reach of television. The Retro-Modern look began to give way to a bland, Danish modern era of design. Once more the pared-down, "nothing but the essentials" look took over, but this was just a brief calm before the storm of the late Fifties. Then a revolution in design—both technical and ornamental—would shake the wristwatch world as it had not been shaken since it first emerged from the cocoon of the pocket watch.

HAMILTON, ca. 1953. Very rare "Gordon" in platinum. 19-jewel movement. The painted matte silver dial has applied diamond indexes. Platinum cases in signed American watches are known to exist only in seven examples. The others are contract cases that do not bear manufacturer's hallmarks. (Courtesy of Harry Stecker)

LONGINES, ca 1954. The *Fleming Sweep* has a 14k gold case with an enamel painted dial. The dial is marked in quadrants with applied markers and Roman numerals in the hours chapter. A distinctive minutes chapter surrounds the hours chapter. 17-jeweled Swiss movement.

LONGINES, 1940s. This 14k gold case is attached to a gold filled expansion bracelet. 17-jeweled Swiss movement.

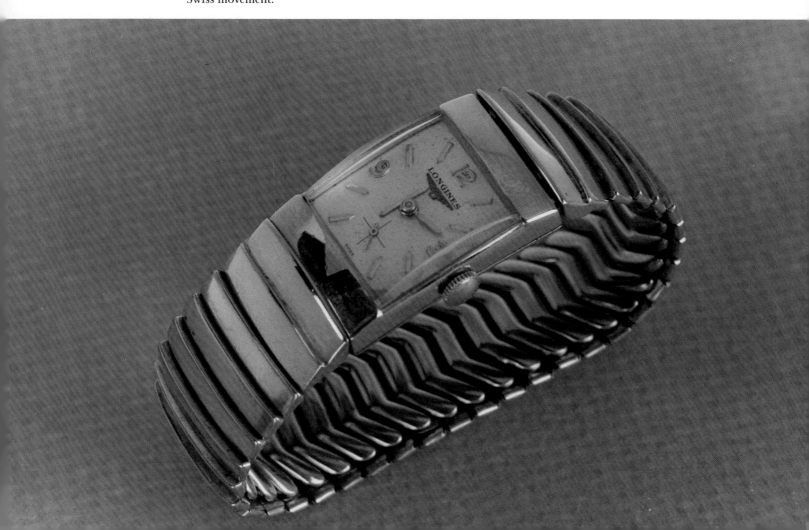

Chapter Seven
The Eccentric Fifties
Hamilton: An Electrifying Idea

The exaggeration of the Retro-Modern period had its moment in the sun before it gave way to the conservative mood that enveloped the country in the Fifties. Re-conversion of factories was completed, and those who survived the difficult post-war years were now engaged in fighting a different kind of battle—to reclaim the domestic wristwatch market.

The technological changes that had taken place during the war were giving way to new ideas and different ways of making timepieces. Within this scientific atmosphere came the newest wristwatch idea from one of America's oldest watch companies, Hamilton.

Never a mass producer, Hamilton had devoted itself to making quality timepieces since 1892. By 1957 it had produced a total of 12,603,207 timepieces including all kinds of watches and clocks. During the Second World War an embargo on imported chronometers sent the government scurrying for a domestic maker. Hamilton was drafted for this work and produced marine chronometers that surpassed the quality standards of the products formerly imported from Switzerland. Its wristwatch production was directed for the man at the front. Soldiers in the U.S. Army, the U.S. Navy, as well as those of the British and Russian military were outfitted with Hamilton wristwatches, most of them employing a slightly altered #987A movement with 17 jewels.

Through the wartime period, Hamilton's attention was directed toward improving and refining the traditional method of watchmaking, based on its modification of the *Elinvar* hairspring which had been introduced in 1919 by Charles E. Guillaume. The improved hairspring, dubbed *Elinvar Extra*, was introduced in 1941. Its benefits would have gone into civilian wristwatches but instead enabled Hamilton to create the much-esteemed marine chronometer and other war era timepieces.

After the war, while Hamilton resumed its regular line of mechanical wristwatches, a new project was started, one that Hamilton would proclaim as "the first basic change in portable timekeeping in 477 years". The change, ironically, was to eliminate the mainspring entirely, the element that Hamilton had worked so tirelessly to improve. This once in five centuries advance was the Hamilton *Electric*. Spokesman for this "milestone in Hamilton's program of research and expansion" was Hamilton's director of research and development, Dr. John Van Horn, but the brains behind the project belonged to Philip Biemiller.

The Hamilton *Electric* that was introduced on January 3, 1957 had been in preparation for ten years. Kenneth Schoenrock, a model-maker who worked for Hamilton from 1950-1970 says, "When I came there in July, 1950, they were starting the electro-magnetic approach to clocks and watches. They started about a year and a half before I got there."

HAMILTON, 1950s. An early eccentric design for Hamilton, this dress wristwatch has a 14k yellow gold case with overlapping lugs. The two-toned dial uses baguette diamonds for the hours markers. The wristwatch foreshadows the *Electric* series to be introduced in 1957. Mechanical movement.

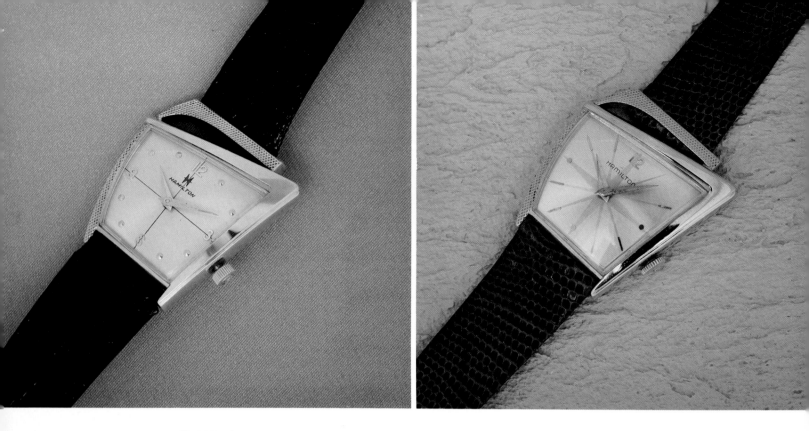

HAMILTON, ca. 1962. The *Flight I* (right) and *II* are among the rarest and most sought after of the eccentric wristwatches, in part because they have mechanical movements. Further, they were produced in limited numbers for only one year. The *Flight I* was made in 14k gold, the *Flight II* in gold filled. They have an offset stem and crown at 4:00. The enamel painted dial has applied gold numerals and markers, and bisectional lines. The *Flight I* always has a sunburst dial. The bezel is asymmetrical and combines polished and embossed finishes. High quality, 22-jeweled movement.

HAMILTON, ca 1960. Textured and smooth surfaces of 14k yellow gold filled mark this Hamilton automatic. The offset round dial is supported by cantilevered lugs. The two-tone, black and gold enamel painted dial has a striking design with a ring of gold running through the hours chapter and a golden arrow pointed to the date window at 3:00. This is the rarest of the Hamilton automatic wristwatches . With its bizarre eccentric design and style, this is a highly sought after wristwatch. 17-jeweled automatic Swiss movement.

HAMILTON, ca 1958. Mechanical production continued for Hamilton after the *Electric* was introduced. The *Chanticleer Alarm* has a 10k yellow gold filled waterproof case with a stainless steel back. The luminous dial has a sweep seconds hand, an arrow to indicate the alarm setting, a power reserve window at 9:00 for the automatic winding, and a window at 3:00 to indicate whether the alarm mechanism is engaged. The crown at 4:00 sets and winds the alarm. 17-jeweled Swiss automatic movement.

HAMILTON, ca 1963. The *Thin-O-Matic* is a fine example of a high style Eccentric. The asymmetrical lugs hold a round case with a dramatic two-toned dial. The lines of the dial carry the angles of the lug into the center of the watch, emphasizing the geometry of the lugs. The wristwatch is available in 10k yellow gold filled with a gold-toned dial and in 10k white gold filled with a gray-toned dial. The dial features hour markers and well-designed hands, with a sweep seconds hand. 17-jeweled automatic Swiss movement.

HAMILTON, ca. 1950s. The *Explorer,* automatic winding with rotating map delineating the four time zones and sweep center second hand. Scroll lugged gold-filled case. (Courtesy of Aaron Faber Gallery)

HAMILTON, ca 1960. For Hamilton and other U.S. manufacturers multi-functioned, complicated wristwatches are unusual, and therefore desirable. The polychrome black rotating discs has registers for five time zones: Greenwich, Eastern, Central, Mountain and Pacific. The hour hand is set independently according to the wearer's location. The case is 10k yellow gold filled with a two-toned enamel painted dial. 17 jewels.

HAMILTON, ca 1963. It is extremely rare to find a mechanical wristwatch in an eccentric case. This 22-jeweled, high grade movement is in a shield-shaped 10k rolled gold plate case.

HAMILTON, 1960s. This highly unusual asymmetric, off-centered Eccentric should, based on its style, be an electric, but it is not. It is one of the few examples of asymmetrical wristwatches Hamilton produced with an automatic movement. The case is 10k gold filled, with the crown placed at the 4 o'clock position. The enamel painted dial has a sweep seconds hand. This is a desirable watch, preferred by some to the troublesome *Electric* series. Swiss movement. 17 jewels.

Because the electric wristwatch had one-third fewer parts than the conventional automatic wristwatch, it was actually a less complex movement. There was no mainspring, and no winding mechanism. This led to a simpler and more efficient operation.

The heart of the *Electric* was a movement powered by a battery the size of a small shirt button. The new movement was described in the introductory press release: "The electric watch operates on chemical energy stored in a tiny energizer. This energy is converted into electrical power as it releases a stream of electrons through a coil of fine wire fixed on a balance wheel. The electrical energy through interaction with permanent magnetic fields causes the balance wheel to oscillate. This oscillation is the mechanical energy which runs the watch." With the power coming from a constant source, rather than a mainspring whose energy could vary as it uncoiled, the accuracy of the new wristwatch was said to be more than 99.995%.

The coil of wire through which the energy passes is five times finer than human hair. The magnets are made of a cobalt-platinum alloy—a material that was not available during the war years when strategic metals were restricted to use by the military. According to Kenneth Schoenrock, Hamilton's magnets were excellent and efficient. They had a good small battery, but "the indexing was a problem. Philip Biemiller and I invented the magnetic indexing system." From the hands of Biemiller and Schoenrock the wristwatch progressed to Ira Fickes, a master watchmaker who joined Hamilton in 1935 and stayed with the company until 1977. Having been through pre-war, wartime, and postwar production, he became a skilled manufacturing engineer. Fickes was involved in setting up designs and procedures to manufacture parts for the Hamilton *Electric*.

Joe Brooks, who was the engineer in charge of producing parts for the *Electrics* and is now retired in Moundville, Pennsylvania, just a short distance from Lancaster, credits Philip Biemiller as the man who invented the concept. (Biemiller died when he was just in his thirties, during the 1950s.) Brooks describes the movement as "a backwards invention. If it was just a little off, a few thousandths, the thing would run backwards. It had an indexing system that Biemiller designed; by all the laws of physics, it wasn't supposed to work."

The first model, the #500, was produced for three years before it yielded to the #505. There was to be a model #502 as well, with a calendar mechanism, developed mostly by Jim Reese, according to Brooks. "He was important to the project. He would play around with the models as they came out of the model shop until we got them to work." Schoenrock says, "There were

HAMILTON, ca 1959. The *Ventura I* is, perhaps, the embodiment of the Eccentric period in design. The shapes, symbols, and color combine to make this the most famous wristwatch of the Hamilton *Electric* series. The exaggeration of the shield shape case is reinforced by the stepped wings that cover the lugs and add drama to this very sought after design. The *Ventura* was manufactured in yellow or white 14k gold, with a black or white dial, and with or without diamond hour markers. There is a double marker at 12:00. The dial is painted sterling silver and has the electronic squiggle symbol bisecting it. Hamilton *Electric* 500 movement.

HAMILTON, ca 1959. The *Pacer*, along with the *Ventura*, was the most popular of the eccentric series of Hamilton *Electrics*. The triangular dial and winged lugs make this a universally prized collectible. Generally it is available in two-toned white and yellow gold filled as shown. It is rare in solid gold. The dial is sterling silver with raised markers. Note the squiggly electronic symbol, a mark of an original dial. The case is by S & W. #500 series Hamilton *Electric* movement.

about 25 or 26 made with the calendar mechanism and they were going to go into production with it. It was very reliable but it would be quite expensive for Hamilton. That was into the 1960s, maybe '61 or '62 and the *Accutron* was taking a big hold, and Hamilton was starting to go downhill. They never went through with it; that was a sad thing." Schoenrock has two of the #502s which are truly collector's items. The *Electrics* were produced until 1965; in all exactly 41,849 pieces were made from 1957 until 1965.

Having worked so diligently to develop the first electric wristwatch, Hamilton now turned its attention to casing these innovative movements. "Since they were introducing the first watch with a battery," Fickes recalls, "they wanted unusually designed cases." And that was exactly what they got. Richard Arbib was a design consultant to Hamilton from 1953-1960 and is the man most responsible for putting the *Electric* into the eccentric cases that so excite today's collector.

"Henri Vermot directed design then," Arbib said during an interview in his New York studio. Designs are spilling out of every crevice, and models of the products of Arbib's many clients fill every available inch, from an airplane suspended from the ceiling to a full size vacuum cleaner next to a

HAMILTON, ca 1957. The shield-shaped *Pacer* was manufactured in 10k yellow gold filled (as here), white gold filled, two-toned (yellow gold filled case and white lugs, the most common configuration), and, rarely, in 14k gold. The choice between a black or white enamel painted sterling dial adds to the possible varieties. The dial uses dot markers in the hours chapter and has a sweep seconds hand. The electronic squiggle is usually not present though it was sometimes used, as here. It is distinguished from the *Ventura* principally by the shape of the lugs and the fact that the *Ventura* was manufactured only in 14k gold, while the *Pacer* rarely was. The *Pacer* has recently been successfully counterfeited in the Far East. The original factory marks inside the movements help determine authenticity. Issued with an optional metal strap for $125. Hamilton *Electric* 500 movement.

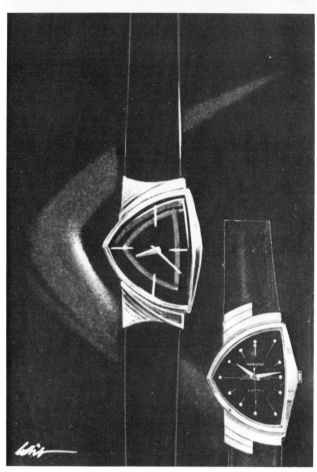

HAMILTON, ca 1958. This *Everest Electric* has an unusual two-toned dial. The 12 is placed on the bezel outside the dial, and the shape of that part of the bezel is carried onto the gold portion of the dial. The *Electric* movement has 5 jewels with a balance wheel.

Arbib rendering. Courtesy: Jeff Hess

HAMILTON, Ca. 1958. The *Van Horn Masterpiece* has an unusual, attractively stepped, heavy 14k gold bezel with applied angled sculpted lugs. It is part of Hamilton's waterproof series. The dial is painted sterling silver with unusual arrow markers at 3,6, and 9 and a pearled seconds track. #500 series Hamilton *Electric* movement.

file cabinet. A metal waste basket holds dozens of scale drawings. "I had been doing some regular designs for them, for the watch line, when they asked me to do some blue sky. I wanted to make different shapes. They had been round, pillow [cushion] and square. I wanted to integrate the design of the crystal with the case; integrate the design of the shape with the watch and the shape of the dial. The first to have this was the *Electric* line. The first one was the long triangle (which became the *Pacer* or *Ventura*). The company was very receptive."

These designs were adamantly asymmetrical—even when a dial started out round it was encased in a bezel that soared off to the side. Up to this time, men's wristwatches were rarely so extroverted. But because of the size of the movement the *Electrics* were restricted to wristwatches for the men's market. Today, however, women are snatching up these and other men's wristwatches in recognition of their exquisite style and workmanship.

Here were wristwatches that were anything but conventional. They had a flair about them that made them soar, almost to take flight, and that visual impression had very real roots in Arbib's other design concepts. He had worked in both the automotive and aeronautical industries before, during and after the war. Visions of wings and tailfins were very much in his mind. "I designed the flying bomb at Republic Aviation during the war." Arbib put the fin on the bomb for guidance. The fin moved into the civilian world as well. "I put those fins on the Cadillacs and designed cars that looked like fighter airplanes." A few years later he was scaling those fins down and replicating them on Hamilton's *Electrics*. Imagine the reception to these designs in the late '50s when the pillbox hat and white gloves were the signature touches of well-dressed women and the man in the gray flannel suit had become the classic cliche.

Each month about three dozen designs were submitted. Of these perhaps two or three were chosen to go to the model maker. And from there, Arbib says, "there were eight or nine watch case companies that worked for them,

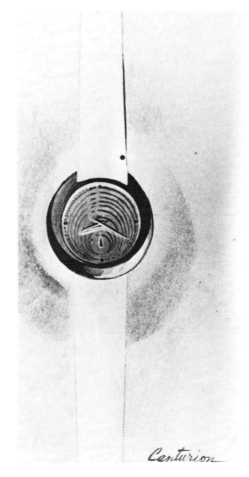

Arbib renderings. Courtesy: Jeff Hess

and we would collaborate with them. Hamilton also got designs from the case companies who wanted the work. There was some competition along that line. Certain case companies did a better job and it came out looking better than the original design. It was a collaborative effort." One of the major firms translating the designs was S & W Watch Case Co.

Jean Wuischpard, now retired to Cocoa, Florida, took charge of S & W Watch Case Company after his uncle, founder Alphonse Wuischpard, died during the Second World War. He remained there until the firm closed in 1965. S & W was an important firm in the world of casemaking, Wuischpard says. "We made 3500 cases a day: gold-filled, or gold plated, stainless steel, 14k and 18k, some platinum." Both Elgin and Hamilton were customers for a long time. Like the watch companies they served, he said, they "managed to survive the war by making some instruments for the Army, Navy, Marines. For Hamilton, we were making 65% of their cases." Included in that number were the first cases for the *Electric* including the *Van Horn*, the *Pacer*, the *Ventura* and many others.

Though the designs were radical, the case making presented no particular problems. "A case is a case," says Wuischpard. "We made everything by tools (stamped cases) so you just make the tools." One quality difference did stand out in his memory. "Ordinarily gold filled was 3.5 thousandths of an inch gold; the electrics were 8 thousandths of an inch because they were diamond turned." Although Wuischpard says "all the designs were made for *Electric* cases; we were very close with Hamilton," it appears that in fact they did work in collaboration as Arbib said. From the original Arbib design sketches of wristwatches that were not made, and are published here for the first time, Arbib's hand and eye can clearly be seen on the *Electrics* that were produced.

Ira Fickes describes the black dials with applied gold numbers that were one of the features of the *Electrics* as well as other Hamiltons. "It gave a three-dimensional look; they were five one-thousandths of an inch in

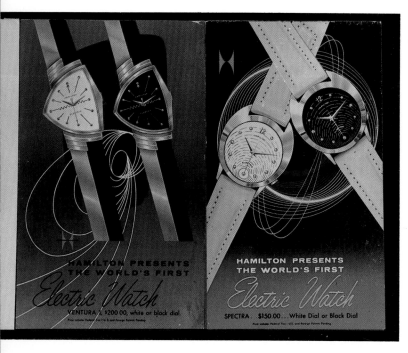

Advertisements for the Hamilton *Electric*. Courtesy: Jeff Hess.

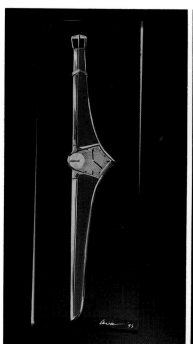
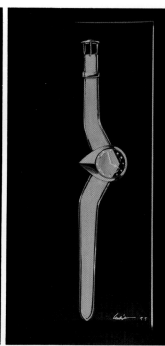

Arbib renderings.
Courtesy: Jeff Hess

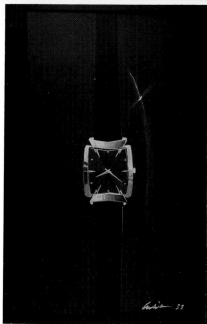

HAMILTON, ca 1958. Known as the *Victor*, the case has lugs offset to the left. The dial comes in black or white and has raised 14k gold numerals and markers. An applied sunburst pattern in gold decorates the dial. The crown is at 2:00. Hamilton *Electric* #500 series.

height so they stood out against the silver background. Although some Swiss companies did this, among the American firms, this was a hallmark of Hamilton.''

Kenneth Derr came to Hamilton in 1944 working in product design and is still there today. He recalls "Some cases for the *Electrics* were made by S & W, some by our own case company—the Wallace Case Company which was a division of Wallace Silversmiths (which Hamilton owned at the time); and some were made by Star. We had to spread it around. Designs were submitted by all of the case companies, as well as our own design department. Henri Vermot was design department head. He may have been there since the '30s. Then there were problems and another fellow came in (that was Steve Fedor who soon left under a cloud of his own)."

Derr, like others involved in this project remembers a woman named Bettye Miller having some role—and like the others can't quite pinpoint what it was. Some think she did do some of the designing, while others say she facilitated turning the designs into models and getting them costed out for production. Derr says it was "teamwork on design, not one individual", although he does recall Richard Arbib having a contract for designs. Arbib

Arbib renderings. Courtesy: Jeff Hess

remembers Bettye Miller as "a designer and director". Ted Lisnow of Belove and Ariente, a firm that embellished watch cases and set them on bracelets, describes her as a buyer and stylist. "They changed buyers frequently. She was a stylist of watch cases. She made sketches and would lay out the price range we had to come in under."

Who is this mysterious Bettye Miller? From her home in Pennsylvania she says, "My whole life was spent in wristwatches. I started with Hamilton around the time of the *Electric* series. I designed a lot of those really wild cases. Henri Vermot was gone by the time I came, around '55 or '56, I don't remember exactly. They had been in development when I got there, and there were a few designs in the works."

Ms. Miller describes working with the case companies. "Schwab & Wuischpard was the best company. They were always our favorite manufacturer. We worked with Jonell Case Co., and Star Case Co. in Ludington, Michigan but they did not get in on the first go-around on the *Electric*. I worked with the case-maker. They would cut the model, we would refine it. I made meticulous drawings. We kept working over it so it could be machined properly to achieve the look.

HAMILTON, ca 1958. The *Spectra* was sold as a waterproof watch. It has a massive 14k gold case with 14k gold applied numerals on a sterling silver dial. The movement is shock resistant and anti-magnetic. There is a hack feature on the sweep seconds hand and the wristwatch is fully adjusted. Note the fine gold markings in concentric circles on the dial. This has the #500 Hamilton *Electric* movement and is difficult to find in good working order. The unusual asymmetrical case makes it a highly prized collectible of the '50s.

HAMILTON, 1960s. The shield-shaped gold filled case is mounted on a bias to give this wristwatch its asymmetric eccentricity. It has cantilevered lugs and is illustrated with an integrated mesh metal bracelet. The round hours chapter has applied hour markers. A desirable eccentric shape. Hamilton *Electric* 505 movement.

HAMILTON, ca 1958. The *Spectra* with the black dial is more unusual than that with the white.

"There was a sense of being revolutionary. We didn't want to be conservative even though the times were. They were remarkably made, and they were really pieces of jewelry. All the dials were sterling silver; the gold markers were all applied."

But there was trouble in paradise. The Hamilton *Electric* was really a watchmaker's version of "Beauty and the Beast", for buzzing inside those exquisite cases was a movement that, though accurate, had a fatal flaw. The electrical contacts proved to be fragile, vulnerable, and difficult to repair. Mention the Hamilton *Electric* to a veteran watchmaker, or anyone knowledgeable about the system, and the same refrain is heard: there was trouble in the contact system—the part where the index wheel and the contact wheel came together.

Jean Wuischpard, the case-maker, says, "Oh yes, they had too much trouble with it; the contacts were burning. We had to change our material many times. There was a ring that was holding the movement in the case which was so complicated that we made it in powder metal. We pressed it and put it in an atmospheric furnace almost to the melting point until it became solid. When they had so much trouble with contacts, they asked us to make it in solid metal."

HAMILTON, ca 1961. The *Vega* is part of the second generation of Hamilton *Electrics*. It has a trapezoidal case with textured angled lugs whose lines continue through the dial. The case is 14k yellow gold filled and was originally available with a matching band. This is one of the six most famous ultra-eccentric designs that are considered a hallmark of the Eccentric period. Hamilton *Electric* 505 movement.

HAMILTON, ca 1960s. The *Railroad Special 52* was approved by the railroad for its accuracy. It has a non-reflecting white enamel dial with black numerals, and a lightning bolt seconds sweep. The crown is at 4:00. There are few examples of wristwatches made for the railroad industry. This is a collectible. Hamilton *Electric* movement.

HAMILTON, ca 1964. The 10k gold filled tear-drop case is supported between faceted lugs on this very desirable asymmetrical *Electric*. The gold dial applied to the black tear-drop silhouette qualifies this design as a great eccentric. Hamilton *Electric* 505 movement: "Only 9 moving parts."

Kenneth Schoenrock remembers, "Indexing was a problem. The spring contact system on the Hamilton #500 was quite critical to adjust. The contact was the index wheel and the contact wheel together; big pivot riding on some gold/silver contact. The contact D pin didn't make contact on the reverse swing. It didn't last as long as the wires because the Contact D pin would wear. After 18-24 months, it would need a new wheel or new balance assembly; the wires would go 4-5 years and as much as 8-10 years and finally just wear out. Jim Reese and I found out that the retail jewelers were having too much trouble trying to adjust those wires."

The model #505 was an attempt to address those problems. In a Hamilton product brochure from 1962, the model #505 is heralded as a "revolutionary new triumph in time, the 505 incorporates new concepts and technologies developed by Hamilton during its 5 years of unmatched experience since creation of the world's first electric watch."

Watchmaker Jesse Medlock, who repairs Hamilton *Electrics*, says the model #500 "is very fragile. Two wires are exposed; 90% of the trouble will be on the contacts. The Hamilton #505 was a different system, not exposed. It was better and corrected the problem." Veteran watch man and writer

HAMILTON, ca 1964. The *Nautilus 500* is typical of the last generation of the Hamilton *Electrics*. Sold as a waterproof, dustproof model, it has a relatively conservative design, considering its Eccentric parentage. The case is stainless steel. The dial features alternating Arabic and bar markers for hour indications and a sweep seconds hand. Hamilton *Electric* 505 movement.

HAMILTON, ca 1964. The 10k gold case of this *Titan III* was manufactured by the Star Watch Case Company. The enamel painted dial has raised 18k gold markers and a sweep seconds hand. This also came in a white gold filled and diamond version called the *Lord Lancaster J.*

Henry Fried agrees: "In the method of making contact sparks occurred, a spark being so hot it would melt the contact spring, and eventually there was no contact. The 505 was an improvement. The first one required a great deal of skill and delicacy to repair. The 505 was much simpler."

Ira Fickes, a veteran of 42 years with Hamilton, describes the contact system in layman's terms: "It's like the ignition in an automobile where you had to get new points every two years. On the #500 model the electric contacts were coming together and breaking apart five times per second. Over time they cause wear. In 1960 they redesigned the movement and brought out the 505. Even that retained a similar system. It was a little better but the problems remained."

Despite the problems, the Hamilton *Electrics* were a landmark in the history of timekeeping and of wristwatch innovation. They have become coveted collectors' items with their original movements.

In Hamilton's consumer catalog for 1964/65, 43 models of *Electrics* were available with straps, with metal link bands, and also set with diamonds, in white or yellow gold filled, in yellow rolled gold plate, and in 14k white or yellow gold. Though movement production had ended in 1965, the 1966/67 catalog still offered 22 *Electric* models. But the *Electric* had already taken its place in history; three years after it sparked onto the wristwatch scene, another innovation stunned the wristwatch world and this one brought with it no inherent movement problems. Virtually all the watchmakers who worked on the *Electric* conclude their reminiscences with the same thought: the *Accutron* was the end of the Hamilton *Electric*.

HAMILTON, ca 1958. The case of this wristwatch is that of the *Spectra*, but the dial is different and may have been substituted from another Hamilton *Electric*.

HAMILTON, ca 1961. The *Lord Lancaster "C"* is from Hamilton's *Medallion* series. The 10k yellow gold case has a sterling silver dial with applied gold markers. The eccentric, asymmetrical right angled bezel is unusual in a mechanical wristwatch from Hamilton. The wristwatch is available with a 4-diamond dial, in white gold, and in white gold filled. The 22-jeweled Medallion movement is fully adjusted, shock resistant, and anti-magnetic.

HAMILTON, 1950s-60s. The *Lord Lancaster* is another mechanical Hamilton in an eccentric case. This yellow gold filled case has a distinctive asymmetrical bezel. It was also available in white gold filled. The black enamel painted dial uses raised markers in the hours chapter and has a subsidiary seconds chapter at 6:00.

HAMILTON, 1960s. wristwatches in original condition and packaging are preferred by collectors. Some boxes are as interesting as the wristwatches . Often in pearlized plastic, the boxes use gold leaf and are lined with velvet. When combined with the appropriate wristwatch they add value to the watch. Hamilton, Elgin, Bulova and others all created interesting packaging, using wood, velvet covered paper, celluloid and other materials in addition to plastic.

HAMILTON, ca 1961. The *Polaris* has an asymmetrical 14k gold bezel, with a cross-over lug at the lower end of the case. The silver dial has applied gold numerals at 12:00 and square gold markers at the other positions. There is a red-tipped hacking sweep seconds hand. Hamilton *Electric* 505 movement.

LONGINES, 1960s. This massive sterling silver case has an elephant hide strap with sterling hardware that is integrated into the overall design. The dial is a blue enameled oval. The crown is at 12:00. 17-jeweled Swiss movement.

LONGINES, 1950s. The 14k gold square case houses a modified mystery dial. The hour hand is on a pinwheel-painted disc, while the minutes hand is traditional. The hours chapter is round and has raised markers for the hours indicators. Swiss movement, 17 jewels.

LONGINES, 1950s. The 14k white gold case is set with diamonds around the circumference of the bezel. The enamel painted dial is two-toned. The hour indicator is on a disc, while the minutes hand is traditional. The hours chapter has raised bar markers. American case, Swiss movement, 17 jewels.

LONGINES, 1950s. An almost traditional, cushion-shaped dial is housed in a sculpted eccentric case. The hour markers are connected to their opposites by diagonal lines. There is a subsidiary seconds chapter above the 6:00 position. The case is American, the movement Swiss, 17 jewels.

LONGINES, 1950s. The smooth raised lugs and oval bezel contrast with the textured background of the round case. The 14k gold case is American with a Swiss movement.

LONGINES, 1950s. The 14k gold case holds an interesting white enamel painted dial. The circular motif on the dial makes this wristwatch unique. The modified "mystery" dial uses a star on the rotating disc to indicate the hours. 17-jeweled Swiss automatic movement.

LONGINES, 1960s. A massive 14k gold tonneau case supports a round dial. The enamel painted dial is textured and has a raised Arabic 12 and teardrop markers at the other hours positions. 17-jeweled Swiss movement.

LONGINES, 1960s. The 14k gold
rectangular case is set horizontally.
The black dial has the movement
set off-center. The applied
triangular hours indicators at 12, 3,
6, and 9 are set with diamonds.
Swiss movement, 17 jewels.

LONGINES, 1950s. An interesting use of juxtaposed geometric
shapes, this case combines a square dial with a round case. The
lugs and the bezel surface abutting the dial have an embossed,
textured brick pattern. Through it runs the smooth outline of the
round case. The case is of 14k white gold with an enamel painted
dial with diamond-set markers at 12, 3, 6, and 9 and enamel-set
slashes at the other hour positions. The case is American, the
movement Swiss. 17 jewels.

LONGINES, 1950s. An unusually constructed pierced 14k
gold case with a black enamel painted dial. Raised gold
markers and a subsidiary seconds chapter at 6:00. Swiss
movement, 17 jewels.

LE COULTRE, 1950s. This mystery-styled wristwatch used diamonds to mark the hours. They are set into the white grooved discs at the center of the enamel painted dial, with the smaller diamond indicating minutes, the larger hours. Applied triangular markers make up the hours chapter. The case is American, the 17-jeweled movement Swiss. This is a variation on the mystery watch which has gemstones for the hour indicators.

LE COULTRE, ca 1950. One of many "mystery" wristwatches issued by various companies, this wristwatch creates the illusion of floating hands by the use of clear rotating discs. The yellow gold plated case holds an enamel painted dial with an hours chapter consisting of a segmented arc from 1 to 11:00 and a small marker at 12:00. 17-jeweled Swiss movement.

LE COULTRE, 1950s. The *Futurematic* has a round 14k gold filled American case with a dramatic black enamel painted dial. The dial has a subsidiary seconds chapter at three o'clock and a power reserve chapter at 9:00. The setting crown of this automatic wristwatch is on the back. 17-jeweled Swiss movement with a hack feature. This wristwatch is also available in 14k gold.

LE COULTRE, ca 1952. The unusual tapered case of this *Aristocrat* is American, 10k yellow gold filled. This is a lady's version, but LeCoultre also produced a larger man's version. The man's version had a subsidiary seconds chapter. 17-jeweled Swiss movement.

LE COULTRE, 1950s. The central white disc of this two-toned enamel painted dial has an arrow which indicates the setting of the alarm on the gold minutes chapter. The case is gold filled with nicely sculpted lugs. Cased and timed in the United States. 17-jeweled Swiss movement.

WITTNAUER, 1970s. The unusual bowed, asymmetrical tank case of this *Sector* houses a rare automatic mechanical sector mechanism. The time is shown on arc-shaped chapters. When they have reached the end of the arc they flip back to the beginning. The case has a gold plated bezel and a stainless steel back. A date window has a cyclops lens crystal. This is one of three models known to exist. Swiss movement, 17 jewels.

WITTNAUER, ca 1960. A gold-plated steel watch, this Wittnauer is the only example of a mechanical perpetual calendar wristwatch. If set and wound properly, it automatically adjusts for the day, month and year, including leap years. The model shown is a ì size, though a full-sized wristwatch was made. Swiss movement, 17 jewels.

WITTNAUER, 1950s. An American gold filled case houses a white enamel painted dial with raised, highly stylized Arabic numerals. Swiss movement, 17 jewels.

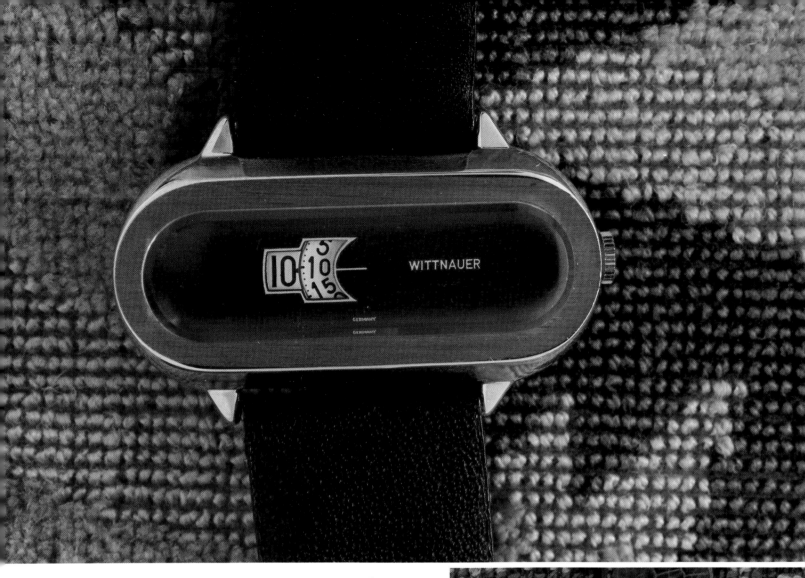

WITTNAUER, 1960s. The wide elliptical steel case has a brown enamel painted dial with a digital readout. Mechanical digitals reached their zenith in the 1960s using a tremendous variety of case designs. The mechanisms were often automatic, as shown, using two rotating disc wheels to indicate hours and minutes. The information appeared in cut-out windows in the polymorphous dial and case designs. Swiss automatic movement.

WITTNAUER, 1950s. The cushion-shaped 10k gold plated case is set with a 45 degree turn between curved sculpted lugs. This is an unusual example of an asymmetric case and lugs being produced in Europe to compete with the eccentric designs of Hamilton. Swiss movement, 17 jewels. Rare.

ELGIN, ca 1961. The *B.W. Raymond* wristwatch is striking in its simplicity. The black numerals and the white dial strongly suggest a railroad watch. The case is 14k white gold filled. The movement has 23 jewels.

ELGIN, 1950s. Manufactured for the Pittsburgh Plate Glass Company as a promotional or premium watch, this Lord Elgin has a sculpted rectangular case of solid gold. The enamel painted dial features the company's logo and raised markers and numerals. 21-jeweled movement.

ELGIN, 1950s. The 14k white gold case of this Lord Elgin is suspended between T-bar lugs extended away from the case. The black enamel painted dial has Arabic numerals at 12, 3, 6, and 9 and diamond-set markers at the other hours position. An Elgin automatic movement, 23 jewels.

ELGIN, 1950s. The round dial sits within a square rolled gold plate fluted case. 17 jewels.

ELGIN, 1951-53. Elgin made some forceful design statements in the '50s. The *Black Knight* is a good example. Exaggerated and faceted U-lugs dramatize a startling dial. The case is by Ross and is 14k yellow gold filled. The black enamel painted dial has a gold honeycomb pattern with stylized numerals at 12, 3, and 9 and a subsidiary seconds chapter at 6:00. 21 jewels.

GRUEN, 1950s. This rather traditional Gruen Precision has one interesting feature: the hours indicators turn from green to blue when the wristwatch goes from A.M. to P.M. This is done with a moving disc under the dial, the color being visible through cut-outs in the hours markers. 10k white gold filled case, 17-jeweled Swiss movement.

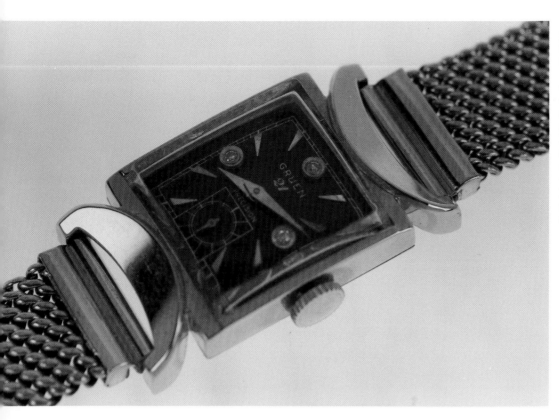

GRUEN, ca 1950. Gruen's plunge into the Eccentric shapes came with gold crescent lugs supporting a rectangular case of 14k white gold. The black enamel painted dial has diamonds at 12,3, and 9 and a subsidiary seconds chapter at 6:00. Other markers and the hands are white. The integrated metal band makes a strong exaggerated style man's dress watch. 21-jeweled Swiss Précision movement. This is an unusual wristwatch for Gruen and desirable.

GRUEN, 1960s. The *Airflight* features a mechanism unique to Gruen: jump hours. The enamel painted dial has cut-outs at the hours positions. Beneath the dial is a wheel that bears the hour numerals. At 1:00 p.m. it "jumps" to change the numbers from 13 to 24. At 1:00 a.m. it jumps back to read from 1 to 12. The round waterproof case is chrome-plated. It was also available in yellow gold-plate. Swiss movement, 17 jewels.

BENRUS, ca 1960. This 14k yellow gold wristwatch is an example of Benrus' attempts at the '50s eccentric style. Cased and timed in the U.S. Swiss movement, 17 jewels.

BENRUS, ca 1957. This *Dial-a-Rama* is fashioned in 10k rolled gold plate. The case has a water proof design. It is interesting for its digital design with windows for the hours and minutes. The star in the center rotates. 17-jeweled Swiss movement.

BULOVA, 1950s. The 10k gold filled triangular case is waterproofed. It houses an enamel painted dial with Arabic numerals and triangular markers. Swiss movement, 23 jewels.

BENRUS, ca 1960. This chromium plated square case has a round enameled bezel with white Arabic numerals in the hours chapter. This very desirable example of enameled bezel wristwatch has a 16-jeweled Swiss movement.

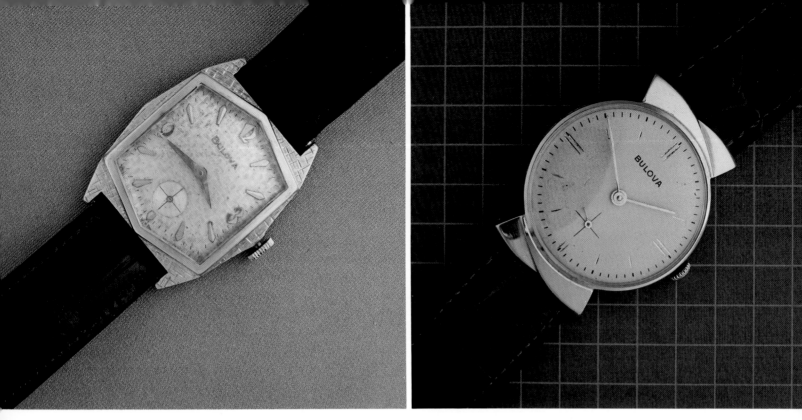

BULOVA, 1950s. The opposing hexagons of the case and the bezel reflector bring a sense of drama to this wristwatch. The case is rolled gold plate with woven-texture embossing. The silvered dial is also patterned and has highly stylized raised Arabic numerals and elongated diamond markers to denote the hours. Swiss movement, 17 jewels.

BULOVA, 1950s. This 14k gold case has unusually designed lugs. The silver enamel painted dial has a subsidiary seconds chapter and gold markers to indicate hours. It has a 17-jeweled Swiss movement engraved "AF11".

WESTBURY, 1950s. The triangular shape of this *Pathfinder* wristwatch has a practical function as well as an aesthetic one. A wheel at the 9:00 point is run along a map and provides a distance readout in the window at 3:00. Two scales are provided for: the blue scale is 1 inch to the mile, and the red is Î inch to the mile. This rare and unusual wristwatch has a 21-jeweled Swiss movement equipped with the Incabloc shock resistance system.

BOREL, 1970s. The lady's and man's Borel *Cocktail* wristwatches have been manufactured from the late 1940s to the present (1988). The dial has two rotating painted plastic discs under the crystal, which work with a pattern on the dial beneath it to create the effect of a flower opening. On one disc is a painted red hours indicator and on the other an indicator for minutes. The hours chapter consists of gold bar markers on the man's wristwatch and a gold ring with black markers on the woman's. The case is gold plated, the movement 17-jeweled Swiss.

LOUVIC, 1950s. A parabolic gold plated case with enamel painted dial. 17-jeweled Swiss movement.

BALL, 1950s. The *Official RR* (Railroad) *Standard* wristwatches of Ball reflect the traditional railroad wristwatch with their porcelain-style dial, bold Arabic numerals and a sweep seconds hand. One innovation in the manual wristwatch shown here is a second, red hours hand to mark the time in a second time zone. The hours hands move in unison. Ball set up the four U.S. time zones at the turn of the century. They were subsequently adopted by the government as the national standards. The wristwatch was available with a 21-jeweled Swiss A. Schild movement and an automatic movement without the second hours hand. Manufactured for the Cleveland transportation industry, these are highly collectible wristwatches.

BALL, 1950s-'60s. The *Trainmaster Official Standard* wristwatch is another example of Ball's railroad wristwatch production. The case is steel and the metal dial imitates the porcelain dials of an earlier era with bold black Arabic numerals on a stark white background. Swiss movement, 21 jewels.

UNKNOWN, 1960s. This woman's fashion wristwatch is highly unusual. The gold plated case is an exaggerated rectangular shape and quite thick. It is worn horizontally and has two individual straps. Swiss movement, 17 jewels.

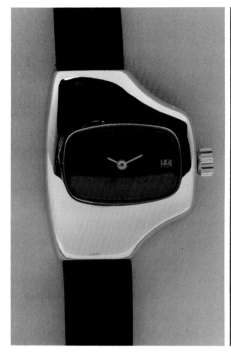

PIERRE CARDIN, 1960s. LONGINES, 1950s. Pierre Cardin, the European designer, and Longines used Swiss manufacturers to produce eccentric cases such as these in sterling silver.

ZODIAC, ca 1960. The *Olympos* has an American gold-plated case with a stainless steel back. The round dial is suspended between angled lugs that extend from the top of the case to the bottom, giving the case an asymmetrical hexagonal appearance. The dial has a modified "mystery" dial with the hours hand affixed to a rotating dial. 17-jeweled, Swiss automatic movement.

LOUIS, 1950s-'60s. The "parking meter" design of this Swiss wristwatch makes for an unusual chronograph. The hands of the dial indicate the time in analog fashion. The digital readout in the window is continuously running but can be set at zero by depressing the button at 2:00, thus engaging the chronograph function. The bezel is rolled gold plate and the back is stainless steel. The hours markers on the enamel painted dial are raised. Swiss movement, 17 jewels.

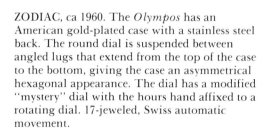

GOTHAM, 1950s. Designed for the blind, the bezel and crystal of this Braille wristwatch are raised by depressing the crown. This allows the blind person to run a finger over the dial to touch the embossed hours dots and the hands to determine the time. An inner hours chapter has full Arabic numerals. The case is American, the movement Swiss. 21 jewels.

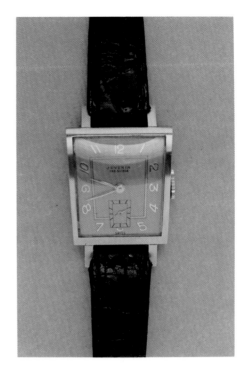

JUVENIA, 1950s. The tapered rectangular case is of steel with an enamel painted dial and Arabic numerals. Swiss, 17-jewels.

SWISS, 1950s. This parabolic wristwatch was made for Spritzer and Fuhrmann, an American retailers. The case is gold plated and has an enamel painted dial with an Arabic 12 and markers for the other hours positions. Several wristwatch manufacturers competed for this custom work, including Louvic and Hilton. 17-jeweled Swiss movement.

SANDOZ, 1950s. The dramatic design of this wristwatch achieves an artistic, abstract quality not often seen in wristwatches. The two-tone target design of the dial has a window through which both digital day and date readings may be made, those being painted on discs beneath the dial. The two red rings on the dial are also rotating discs, one with a square minutes pointer and the other with a pair of squares which mark the hour. Finally, there is a white tipped seconds hand. An identical lady's wristwatch was also manufactured. 17-jeweled Swiss automatic movement.

LOUVIC, 1950s. Though of Swiss manufacture this wristwatch was made for the American market. The shield-shaped wristwatch is plated steel, and the lugs are designed in an overlapping "flying wing" design. The hours chapter follows the shape of the case, the hours markers being set with clear glass stones. The hands are of the "mystery" type, glass markers set on rotating discs to act as hours and minutes hands. Swiss movement, 17 jewels.

UNKNOWN, 1960s. The plated base metal case houses a replica American half dollar. Hour indications are die-stamped on the bezel. 15-jeweled Swiss movement cased and timed in the United States.

BENRUS, ca. 1950s. *Sky Chief* Chronograph with cut-out for the day and month along with a date indicator hand. Manual wind 17-jewel movement with steel case. It is extremely rare. (Courtesy of Steve Jacobson)

LIP, ca 1970. This is an extremely rare sector mechanism in a speedometer display format. A digital date window is above the six o'clock position. LIP is an avant garde French company which produced revolutionary futuristic designs in the late '60s and '70s. This example is probably the rarest of the LIP wristwatches as well as of wristwatches of the sector design and is highly collectible. 17-jeweled Swiss movement.

Chapter Eight
The Sixties
Last Tick of American Dominance

BULOVA, ca 1970. The gold filled wide oval bezel around a small round dial disguises Bulova's use of a man's size movement in this, the first of the lady's *Accutrons*. Lady's *Accutrons* were and are rare. The bezel has a "Florentine" texture. Bulova *Accutron* tuning fork, electro-mechanical movement.

The appearance of the Hamilton *Electric* in 1957 was the distant gun in a battle that would conclude with the end of America's significant role in the design of the wristwatch. Its innovative use of a battery, however, was soon adopted by another, technologically superior wristwatch, which would eclipse the Hamilton *Electric*. According to the press release issued by the company at its arrival, the new wristwatch was seen as the "most significant advancement in timekeeping in more than 300 years." This was Bulova's *Accutron*, billed as the first "Electronic Wristwatch".

The *Accutron* offered timekeeping more accurate than any wristwatch before it—to within one minute per month. This feat was achieved through the use of a tuning fork energized by a small power cell. It eliminated the most familiar parts of the movement: the mainspring, escapement, balance wheel and hairspring, and the winding mechanism. In their place was a tuning fork vibrating at 360 cycles per second, giving the wristwatch its distinctive hum. The public was captivated by the notion of a wristwatch that did not tick. The introduction of the *Accutron* on October 25, 1960 was the culmination of nearly a decade of engineering, planning and commitment. Ironically, it was the last American innovation in wristwatches, and like the Gruen and Hamilton advances before it, was built on European engineering genius combined with American packaging and marketing.

The mainspring, the power source, the heart of the Bulova Watch Company was Arde Bulova. The only son of founder Joseph Bulova, Arde Bulova was a singular man, driven by a can-do attitude, an unwillingness to suffer fools, and an ability to recognize talent and capitalize on it. In a *Harvard Business Review* article published in 1970, Bulova's successor, Harry B. Henschel, wrote, "The late Arde Bulova ran our company as a one-man show for 40 years and built it into one of the world's leading watchmaking corporations. 'Ask Arde' was the theme of the management system; virtually nothing was done without his go-ahead and, usually, his direct participation...Everything started and ended with him." Although Arde Bulova died two years before it was introduced, it was his drive that led to the *Accutron*.

The development of the *Accutron* can be linked to the establishment of a Bulova factory in Switzerland. That was no easy task, and took a man of Arde Bulova's temperament to accomplish. According to one who was on the scene at the time, the Swiss were extremely protective of their watchmaking industry. Through the creation of the Allgemeine Schweizerische Uhrenindustrie AG (ASUAG) in 1931 and consequent (1934) laws which gave the cartel's private agreements the force of law, the Swiss had managed to keep foreigners from buying their technical know-how by prohibiting the export of all watchmaking tools from Switzerland.

So Bulova decided to open a plant in Switzerland to circumvent the ban. The Swiss took a dim view of an American setting up a watch manufacturing operation on their soil, but it was at that plant in Bienne that the *Accutron* was conceived.

The idea for the *Accutron* originated with Max Hetzel, a graduate not of a watchmaking school but of the Eidgenossische Technische Hochschule, considered the MIT of Switzerland. His degree certified him to be an electronics engineer and it was in a treatise developed during his school work that he first entertained the ideas that would lead to the *Accutron*. When he was hired by Arde Bulova to work in the Bienne plant, he was regarded as highly suspect because he did not come out of the horological industry.

But that lack of horological antecedents opened his mind to the idea of combining electronics with timekeeping, enabling Bulova to avoid going down the same path that led Hamilton to its flawed electric movement. By 1953, he had made his first tuning fork timekeeping device, combined with a transistor. Several years of experiment followed, including efforts to reduce the size of the tuning fork and to find a power source that would run reliably for more than three months, the duration of the batteries then available.

Meanwhile, in Bulova's New York plant, William Bennett had come in as a watch engineer in charge of the firm's spring manufacturing operations. During the 1950s, his team worked on improving the accuracy of tools, and rolling spring wire to the finest tolerances. This latter effort would prove crucial to successful mass production of the *Accutron*.

Bennett, who has retired back to his hometown of Lancaster, Pennsylvania after 31 years, recalls that he worked on many things for Bulova. "I was chief engineer for Arde Bulova. I used to travel with him a lot, everywhere. In the early '50s, I met Max Hetzel in Switzerland. I did not know what he was working on at that time but he used to write to me for things he needed—hardware, electronic hardware. I could send him what he needed even though I did not know how he was using it."

In the mid-50s, Hetzel's boss in Switzerland, a Mr. Sudlow, sent Arde Bulova a model of the wristwatch with the tuning fork instead of a balance wheel. Bulova gave it to Bennett to examine. "I looked at this and my people looked and we decided that he had a very good idea. I asked Mr. Bulova to let me work on that, that method and finally he agreed. I worked on it for a long time. Max Hetzel had a very good idea—no question. He had two things that made it interesting. One was the idea of a tuning fork in the wristwatch instead of a balance wheel. The other was his use of magnets and electronic circuitry to make it practical."

But Bennett could see there were problems he would have to resolve before the wristwatch could be put into production. "What he did to make the wheels turn was not practical. It would not work for a long time. I had a lot to do personally with making this thing practical and I had a lot of help from a couple of people who worked for me."

Indeed, Bennett was credited by Bulova as the man who brought Max Hetzel's technical achievement to commercial feasibility. Bennett and the 40-year-old Hetzel, who came over from Switzerland in 1956, headed a team that would ultimately invent more than 100 separate devices needed for electronic watch testing and production.

Instrumental, however, in turning the engineering wizardry of both Hetzel and Bennett into actual production was an unsung hero, August Bozzo, then Bulova's general manager of manufacturing and now retired in Pelham, New York. "The *Accutron* really pushed the state of the art. Max Hetzel was the true inventor. When the transistor became a reality, he invented the tuning fork movement from a theoretical point of view. Bennett rationalized it to a more practical design, and to a prototype. Once the transistor was invented Hetzel was able to translate his idea. But it was an entirely different thing to make it cost effective from the prototype. We

BULOVA, 1960s. An example of Bulova's continued work in mechanical wristwatches , this rectangular wristwatch has a molded bezel framing a black enamel painted dial. White Roman numerals are used in the hours chapter. Swiss movement, 17 jewels.

BULOVA, ca 1973. A nicely exaggerated oval case with graceful lugs has the smaller lady's *Accutron* movement.

BULOVA, ca 1973. A later version of the lady's *Accutron*, this one has a smaller movement allowing for a nicely designed tonneau-shaped case and oval dial. Bulova tuning fork electro-mechanical movement.

always knew we could do it; I knew it was possible. We had the proper people. My responsibility was to make it economically."

Making the tuning fork was the biggest challenge. "It was a very complicated problem. We were working with Nispan-C, a very special temperature compensating nickel alloy, drawing fine wires into a coil for the tuning fork." The material sent by the metal supplier was fairly sophisticated but Bulova's requirements were even more stringent. "We required such a narrow band of the general specification; their tolerances were much broader than ours." Bulova had to test every lot of the alloy that came in to determine the proper temperature at which it needed to be worked. This was an ongoing process. "We had to test every batch to maintain a continuous production line." The lot number appears on the tongue of the tuning fork.

The tuning fork was not the only exacting task carried out in *Accutron* production. The index wheel itself was a remarkable element, extra-ordinarily fine, with "very small teeth. The physical art of cutting those teeth in the wheel required rebuilding existing machines to greater tolerances." Bozzo has preserved a scrapbook depicting each element of the mechanism along with detailed specifications.

Micro-miniaturization of the electro-magnetic and electronic components of the *Accutron* were the technical achievements that occupied much of the inventors' time. The index wheel, which transposes vibratory motions from the tuning fork to the rotary motion that moves the hands, is .0945 inches in diameter, about the size of a pin head, and .0015 inches thick and is notched with 320 ratchet teeth. But it was the coils that keep the tuning fork vibrating that proved to be the biggest obstacle to overcome. Each coil is only ¼ inch long but contains 8000 turns of wire that is .0006 inches in diameter.

The challenge was taken on with pleasure, Bozzo says. "It was very exciting. I really had a good time." And the fun went on: "There was a continuing refinement of the process to increase productivity even after they began production. Even until the end there were always changes to refine the process, reduce the cost, make improvements."

During this period, the first *Accutron* models were given to Bulova executives who were asked to wear them. Bennett recalls, "This is how we found out things that Max Hetzel had tried wouldn't work. We made various attempts to fix that situation and finally make it marketable—that took a couple of years. But people didn't realize, when I went to Bulova they made over one million watches a year. We had a good start on that work." In 1959, the year that led up to the introduction of the *Accutron*, Bulova rang up $55 million in sales.

But just before the wristwatch was put into production, the company, now without Arde Bulova at the helm, had to consider following through on his dream project. By this time Bulova had seen the wristwatch market split dramatically into high-end and low-end merchandise. Timex had exploded onto the market in the mid-50s with an inexpensive, disposable wristwatch; should Bulova go down to the low end to compete with Timex or up to the high? Its middle-market position was the weakest of all. Henschel, a nephew of Arde Bulova and newly appointed president of the company, outlined the problem: after six years in development, a decision had to be made to commit $1 million to tool up for production. Would this innovative, but troublesome product enable Bulova to move into a higher-priced wristwatch market? Was there justification for spending even more money on an untried and radical concept?

In the *Harvard Business Review* article, Henschel described how he had considered the pros and cons:

"The first electric watch developed commercially had just recently been introduced by another company (Hamilton), and had failed in the market.

"We lacked production experience with the tuning-fork concept.

"We did not know whether the public would accept a totally new concept in timekeeping at a high price from Bulova, given our moderate-price image.

"Our retailers were not used to handling such expensive merchandise.

"In a market demanding ever thinner silhouettes, the product was comparatively thick.

"At that time, men's watches, unlike women's watches, did not move well in the higher ranges.

"The company had a weak track record in experimental projects."

Quite a list of negatives. Added to it was the image conveyed by the Bulova name. It was so low-brow, The *New Yorker* would not even accept Bulova advertising. To get around this, Bulova placed the *New Yorker* advertisement through Tiffany and emphasized the *Accutron* name throughout. The front of the wristwatch carried only the *Accutron* name; Bulova appeared on the back of the case. (Later models would carry both names. The product overwhelmed the stigma.)

BULOVA, 1960s. This sterling silver case is of a wide cushioned design with large oval lugs. The black enamel painted dial has full Roman numerals. Swiss movement, 15 jewels.

On the positive side, Henschel points out the amazing accuracy of the wristwatch—to within one minute a month. Granting that few people actually had need for such accuracy, still, he maintained, "There seemed to me to be a strong appeal in the fact that here was the first watch with demonstrable and continuous accuracy, to a guaranteed in-use exactness."

But then he put his finger on the ultimate selling point: "American men are intrigued by complex, scientifically oriented equipment...the watch developed close associations with the then-new and extremely glamorous space effort." And this latter connection was heightened by the product's name, *Accutron*. The name was part of the mystique. It was taken from the phrase, "Accuracy through electronics."

All the miniaturization and technical innovation, however, were not enough to bring the movement down to a size acceptable for a woman's model—at least not in 1960. The *Accutron* was produced only as a man's wristwatch for ten years. The size was no drawback for men who found this technical wizardry most appealing, according to Robert Weber, Bulova's current operations manager, who says, "Men are technophiles," echoing Henschel's comments.

Two men's models were made. The original #214 movement, identified by its thickness and the absence of a crown, was produced until late 1965; more than one million pieces were made. It was followed by the #218, a calendar model with the setting crown placed at 4:00—just to be different. Technically, there was no reason for that placement. This movement, with its reduced bulk, proved enormously popular and outsold the original model by a considerable margin. With the various options offered, 2.75 million were made. *Accutron*, says Weber, was the dominant brand in the over $100 market in the U.S. market.

Ten years later, Bulova introduced its first woman's *Accutron*. The styling concealed the actual size—it was the man's model simply disguised with an oversized bezel. But two women's models were produced, according to Robert Weber. "The first lady's *Accutron* used the #218 movement, but there were two lady's movements made after that. The Swiss-made #230, which had a tuning fork of Swiss design and manufacture, and the U.S. designed and manufactured the #221 movement which was a tonneau shape, about 6 x 8. A smaller magnet made possible by more exotic and more recent developments in magnetic materials made the smaller movement possible." The #221 sold more than half a million pieces.

Weber reveals a quirk of the *Accutron* that only an insider would know: "It had position deficiencies. It kept time differently in vertical and horizontal modes. Because of the pull of gravity, you could change it by the way you laid it down on the night table, making it run a little faster or slower."

BULOVA, ca 1972. Shown with its movement, this *Accutron* had a twenty-four hour registration and an adjustable, moving wheel that allowed one to keep track of the times around the world. There are also day and date chapters. Bulova *Accutron* tuning fork, electro-mechanical movement.

BULOVA, 1960-'70s. An unusual multi-time zone *Accutron* has a digital window at the bottom which can be set to a second time zone using the crown at 4:00. Another window, in the 12:00 position, gives the date. The gold filled case is in a beveled cushion shape with a round enamel painted dial. Bulova *Accutron* tuning fork, electro-mechanical movement.

CASING THE JOB

While the technicians were putting the finishing touches on the insides of the *Accutron*, equally intense preparation was going into casing the wristwatch. It was clear to everyone involved that the package had to be an advance in style in the same way that the movement was an advance in technology. The first steps were false ones. Trying to get the *Accutron* off with a pretty fair bang, as one Bulova executive describes it, the sales and marketing people approached the renowned industrial designer, Raymond Loewy. Loewy was the father of industrial design, the man whose original, streamlined designs in the 1930s had led imitators to streamline everything. But he was an outsider, and not a watch designer. He was brought in for his name. Not surprisingly, the case design people on staff were unimpressed with the designs he submitted. This was clearly not going to be a repeat of the success Hamilton had had with industrial designer Richard Arbib. Nearly all the Loewy designs were discarded and the job was given to Bulova's own, on-staff designers.

BULOVA, 1960s. A railroad-styled *Accutron* emphasizing large black Arabic numerals against a white background. The minutes chapter has red numerals at 5 minute intervals. The case is stainless steel. Bulova *Accutron* tuning fork, electro-mechanical movement. Collectors are showing more interest in this style of watch.

BULOVA, 1960s. Curved lugs grace this railroad-styled *Accutron*. Marked "Railroad Approved" on the white enamel painted dial, with its black bold figures it recalls earlier wristwatches. Bulova *Accutron* tuning fork, electro-mechanical movement.

Werner Koeningsberger was another Arde Bulova import. A noted designer in his native Pforzheim, Germany, Koeningsberger was originally hired to work for Bulova in Germany. The dynamism of Arde Bulova was remembered fondly by Koeningsberger who is now retired but still comes in to help out at his son's Long Island-based watch import business every day. "I worked for Bulova for six months in Germany. Arde Bulova was a race horse; he worked by instinct. He was already about 67 or 68 when I met him. Arde Bulova asked me to build a factory for him in Pforzheim. (This factory would later make the Caravelle cases.) He saw some people he liked in Vienna and asked me to hire them and bring them to Pforzheim. I would just get a telex: 'Arde Bulova wants to manufacture transistors in Pforzheim. Go find a room and people.' And I would do what he wanted.

"When he and Emil Fachon hired me, I could not speak English." (Fachon, who was running the Bulova case factory in Providence at this time, was also from Pforzheim and interpreted for him.) Arde Bulova

BULOVA, 1960s. A round dial is set within this cushion-shaped steel case, the cushion design being picked up again in the black center of the two-toned dial. A digital date chapter is above the 6:00 position. Bulova *Accutron* tuning fork, electro-mechanical movement.

BULOVA, 1960s. An offset pinwheel design decorates the dial of this *Accutron*. It has a date window and raised bar markers in the hours chapter. Bulova *Accutron* tuning fork, electro-mechanical movement.

BULOVA, 1960s. An offset eccentrically shaped steel case distinguishes this *Accutron*. The black enamel painted dial uses bar markers for the hours and minutes chapters. It has day and date windows and a sweep seconds hand. Bulova *Accutron* tuning fork, electro-mechanical movement.

courted Koeningsberger and asked him to come to New York to be the chief stylist for Bulova. "The situation was so fascinating; Arde Bulova was three times in my home." said Koeningsberger. Already a married man with a child and well-established in Germany, he decided to come to the United States. "Why did I come? I believed in Bulova, I believed in the United States, and I believed in my success.

"When I came from Europe I landed in New York at Idlewild—now it's JFK; with the next plane I landed in Providence. In Providence were the sample makers and I was seated next to them—we understood ourselves very well, Fachon and myself." Soon enough, Koeningsberger was working on the regular Bulova line in Bulova's big Jackson Heights, New York plant and commuting regularly to Providence.

"The marketing policy of Bulova was that each season, Spring and Fall, there would be a new feature and that's where I came in. I created the feature and I decided to do it, working with Harvey Whidden who was the vice president for sales. I brought my designs to Providence every week, every second week, sometimes twice a week. Sometimes I proposed designs to Whidden in a letter and he would say it was too early for them." Koeningsberger remembers when the Loewy designs for the *Accutron* came in. He stretches his arms as wide as they can go to describe the actual artwork: "The designs were so big. It was typical Raymond Loewy design; they wanted to go for a name. He designed the first *Accutron* but they were never made. The samples were made by Emil Fachon and Steve Hedor and myself."

BULOVA, 1960s. The *Astronaut Mark II* has a round dial within a cushion-shaped case. There are two crowns, one for setting the time and the other for the date, which appears in a window at 3:00. Bulova *Accutron* tuning fork, electro-mechanical movement.

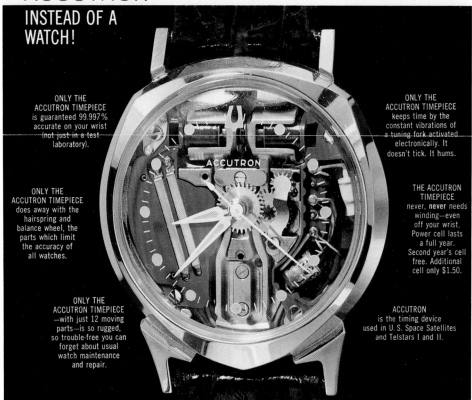

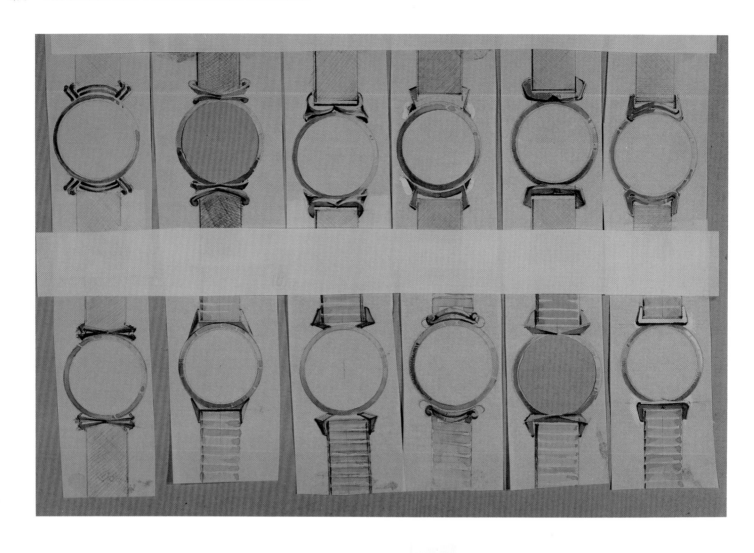

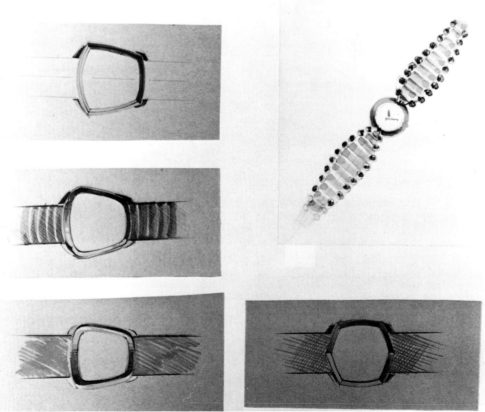

Renderings by Werner Koeningsberger, courtesy of the artist.

BULOVA,1960s. This *Accutron Space View* has numbers painted on the crystal. The clear crystal permits the movement to be viewed. A setting crown is located on the back of the stainless steel case. Bulova *Accutron* tuning fork, electro-mechanical movement.

Koeningsberger describes the most revolutionary *Accutron* case design, the *Space View*, simply as an accident. In talking with other Bulova veterans, the idea seems to have been one of committee design. Koeningsberger describes having a tablefull of movements in front of him. It was common practice to put a crystal over the back of the movement for convenience in handling. One day, he put one over the front as well and then thought he would just add dots to it. The result was a startling look into the heart of the *Accutron*. But it was not the first "skeleton" design for a wristwatch. That, Koeningsberger remembers, was done by a European watch manufacturer early in the 1950's. The name, *Space View*, came from the marketing people who were eager to capitalize on Bulova's association with the then infant space program.

The sales of the *Accutron*, he says, were fantastic. The company could not keep up with demand and sold all it could make. The biggest hindrance was making the wire thin enough for the tuning fork. But Bulova was used to big numbers: the company overall was turning out 16,000 watches a day. And that was the problem, according to Koeningsberger, and for him the beginning of the end. "Money was most important to Bulova; the same thing happened to me; I became a money man." But not at Bulova.

After three years on the *Accutron* (and the death of Arde Bulova in 1958), Koeningsberger left the firm. There was, he says, a complete vacuum when Arde Bulova died. A few years later, Emil Fachon left too. "After all these people left it was no inducement to work for Bulova; not for money, not for glamour.

BULOVA, ca 1966. This extremely rare *Space View Accutron* model has a partially skeletonized movement and a digital date at 3 o'clock. It is available in 14k gold only. Bulova *Accutron* tuning fork mechanical movement.

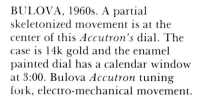

BULOVA, 1960s. A gold plated case holds this *Space View Accutron*. There is an enamel painted hours/minutes chapter surrounding the open center of the dial revealing the movement. Setting is from the back. *Accutron* tuning fork electro-mechanical movement.

BULOVA, 1960s. This 14k gold *Accutron* has a dial with a skeletonized center surrounded by an enameled hours and minutes chapter. The crown is at 4:00. At 3:00 there is a window that reveals the date. *Accutron* tuning fork movement, electro-mechanical.

BULOVA, 1960s. A partial skeletonized movement is at the center of this *Accutron's* dial. The case is 14k gold and the enamel painted dial has a calendar window at 3:00. Bulova *Accutron* tuning fork, electro-mechanical movement.

But the *Accutron* went on. "The tuning fork movements were manufactured until 1976," Weber says, when "the company decided to consolidate its manufacturing in Switzerland and to concentrate efforts on the transition to quartz in the technical environment of Switzerland."

With its patents running out and quartz coming in, there was no reason to keep the *Accutron* production going. Weber lists the drawbacks with the unemotional precision of a surgeon cutting into a warm body: "It did not have shock resistance, it did not have the accuracy of quartz. The resistance to temperature, vibration, shock, and stability are far superior with quartz. Price used to equal accuracy. Quartz has taken the definition of accuracy out of the realm of quality on a watch." The accurate, inexpensive, supremely reliable quartz wristwatch was storming the barricades. The inventive, beautiful, free-spirited American wristwatch manufacturing era was over.

BULOVA, 1960s-70s. This is an LED quartz wristwatch giving a digital display of hours and minutes. To activate the display a button on the side must be depressed. The modernistic case is gold plated. Battery operated.

Epilogue

Vibrating to a New Beat

The Bulova *Accutron's* technical wizardry was an exciting chapter in the American wristwatch business, but it was to be eclipsed by another advance that carried within it the seeds of the industry's demise. The introduction of the first quartz wristwatch, the Hamilton *Pulsar*, on May 6, 1970, truly marked the end of American wristwatch manufacturing. It also would have a strong, detrimental impact on the Swiss watch industry. As Hamilton was excitedly trumpeting that date as the start of "a new era in the science of measuring time," the Japanese watch industry was becoming the dominate force in the wristwatch business.

The quartz was the wristwatch with no moving parts. Instead of a mainspring, it featured a quartz crystal, vibrating at exactly 32,768 cycles per second. Instead of the careful work of watchmakers, it was created by a factory worker who was most likely to be young and Japanese, and whose principal attributes were patience and manual dexterity. The quartz wristwatch did not need anyone to repair it. The movements, or modules as they were more correctly called, quickly became so inexpensive it was cheaper to replace them than to even attempt repairs of the circuits.

Above all, the quartz wristwatch was accurate beyond the wildest dreams and best efforts of the world's finest watchmakers. The watch industry became an adjunct of the electronics industry. The difference in price between the cheapest of the quartz movements and the very best was measured in pennies, not in thousands of dollars as with mechanical wristwatches. All the traditional standards by which fine wristwatches were measured simply didn't matter anymore.

MOVADO, 1960s. Created for Tiffany & Company, this 14k gold rectangular wristwatch has a white enamel painted dial with Roman numerals. The Swiss movement has 17 jewels. Note the gem in the crown.

CARAVELLE (A Division of Bulova), 1970s. This 17-jeweled mechanical wristwatch has an exhibition window at the 6:00 position giving a view of the balance wheel. The black enamel painted dial has gold markers for the hours and a sweep seconds hand. The crown is at the 2:00 position. Swiss movement, 15 jewels.

GRUEN, 1960s. A lady's version of picture on right.

LONGINES, 1960s. This Longines *Comet* has a two-toned, blue and white enameled dial. The blue center has a disc with white revolving arrow indicating the hours on the surrounding white hours chapter. Outside of that is another blue enameled ring with a white dot which indicates the minutes on the outward-most white minutes chapter. The case is steel in a modified rectangular shape. Swiss movement, 17 jewels.

The first quartz wristwatches were designed around digital displays, either LED (light emitting diode) or LCD (liquid crystal display), following the electronics industry's lead. Clocks in railroad stations went to digital displays which were considered more modern, more accurate, more in keeping with schedules which were, after all, expressed in digital time.

All the care that had gone into the design of a wristwatch dials and cases was left without a surface to enhance. The digital displays sat uneasily on round wristwatches, with most of the canvas remaining blank. Technology was everything and it had to run its course. The first digital was extremely bulky and heavy. Efforts were directed to slimming down the movement, and getting rid of that weight, and the goal was quickly achieved. Indeed, the rush to thinner wristwatches became an obsession within the industry, with each millimeter shaved off the profile of the wristwatch celebrated with parties and advertising campaigns.

As the quartz wristwatch industry matured, however, the analog began a comeback. Even the railroad stations changed back to the old familiar face of the traditional wristwatch dial. As earlier wristwatch designers had found years before, the visual presentation of an analog dial gives important information at a glance. Normally, it was not important to know that it was exactly 12:43, but that you had about a quarter of an hour left to be on time for a 1:00 appointment. The brain resisted the transition to digital time and the further computations it required.

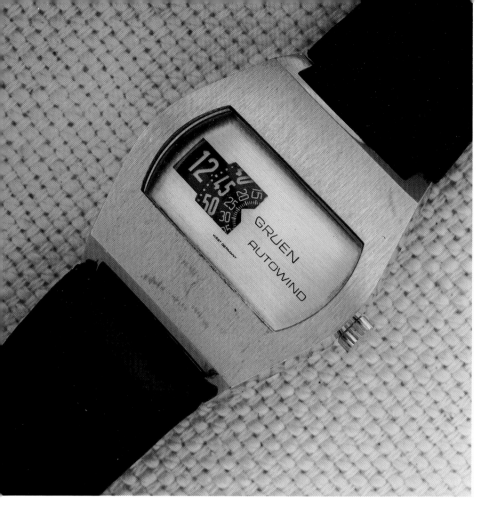

GRUEN, 1960s. This mechanical digital *Autowind* reads West Germany on the dial. It is gold plated with an enamel painted dial. Windows reveal the hours, minutes, and seconds in such a way as to allow them to be easily read in order. 17 jewels.

CARAVELLE (A Division of Bulova), 1970s. The dial of the gold plated wristwatch has a white enamel painted hours chapter around a skeletonized movement. Mechanical Swiss movement. Sweep seconds hand.

The quartz revolution was complete. With it the emphasis in watch-making shifted away from design and toward volume. With the inexpensive movements came a great leap in the production of wristwatches. And with the growth in production came a disregard for design. To be sure it is possible to find some well-designed quartz wristwatches, but often the design is from the past. The *Curvex*, the *Piping Rock*, and the doctor's wristwatch are now all available in quartz versions, in cases that emulate the look of the originals. These hybrid creations only serve to enhance the appreciation for the original mechanical models...the ones that can now be advertised as the wristwatches that never need a battery.

The American watch companies that survived into the Seventies and beyond were either marketing companies, such as Gruen, or firms whose movements, and often complete wristwatches, were made offshore. They continued under the fine old names but their nationalities were very mixed. As movement production ended in the United States, virtually all the watch case companies closed. The last remaining major firm, Star Watch Case Company, closed in 1985. Only specialty watch case firms remain.

While the American wristwatch industry has essentially passed, the beauty and quality of the products it produced during its brief history are enduring. Year by year, as more and more people discover the pleasure of wearing and collecting these examples of the American ingenuity and creativity, they become more valued and valuable.

ZODIAC, 1960s. The unusual target dial has a rotating dot to indicate the seconds and a rotating white arrow for the hours. The outer white marker indicates the minutes. The case is waterproof, the movement automatic.

ACCUTRON...the only timepiece guaranteed† 99.9977% accurate on your wrist. It makes the finest watches—even electric watches—obsolete.

Accutron "202"
Railroad model with full figured easy-to-read dial. Calf strap. Waterproof*, shock-resistant. Also in stainless steel.

$125.00

Accutron "213"
Handsome stainless steel case, with raised, faceted hour markers. Alligator strap. Waterproof*, shock-resistant. Also with full figured dial or in white case.

$125.00

Accutron "401"
Handsomely designed case, dial with raised, faceted characters, dial lets you see the electronic movement in action. Stainless steel case and adjustable band. Waterproof*, shock-resistant.

$150.00

Accutron "Spaceview B"
A conversation piece. Transparent and adjustable band. Applied hour markers. Waterproof*, shock-resistant.

$150.00

Accutron "403"
Smart styling in a gold filled case and adjustable band in gleaming stainless steel. Luminous dial with hand-applied markers. Waterproof*, shock-resistant.

$175.00

Accutron "216"
Uniquely styled case and adjustable band in gleaming stainless steel. Luminous dial with hand-applied markers. Waterproof*, shock-resistant.

$175.00

Accutron "500"
The look of leadership crafted in 14 karat gold...with adjustable 24-hour outer ring and separate hand that revolves once every 24 hours. Thus, can be set instantly for any two time zones in the world. Can also measure elapsed time. And can tell both local and Greenwich Mean time simultaneously. Stainless steel case and link bracelet. Waterproof*, shock resistant.

$300.00

Accutron Astronaut
Regular dial and hands plus adjustable 24-hour outer ring and separate hand that revolves once every 24 hours.

$175.00

ACCUTRON®
A Research breakthrough by
BULOVA

†We will adjust your Accutron Timepiece to the required tolerance if necessary, free of charge within one year from date of purchase
*Prices plus tax
*When case, crystal, and crown are intact.

Watch Company Histories

Bulova Watch Company

Bulova, the biggest maker of watches in the United States, during its decades long success story, was really the product of two men: Arde Bulova, son of founder Joseph Bulova, and John Ballard, a long time employee who rose from office boy to company president. Bulova's success was always tied to its innovative and aggressive marketing and advertising programs. The trademark advertising—"It's 9:00 B-U-L-O-V-A watch time"—originated in the 1926 and continued for decades. The company manufactured watches by the millions, casing movements made in its own Swiss plant. It was a mass maker into the 1960s, culminating with its technological wonder, the *Accutron*. That innovation found its way into nearly five million watches before quartz ended this firm's dominance. Today, Bulova is a totally imported product though the heart of the watch comes from Japan technology rather than Switzerland.

Bulova Watch Company, New York

1875	Joseph Bulova starts a wholesale jewelry business.
1920s	John Ballard markets the first wristwatches for Bulova.
1926	B-U-L-O-V-A radio time announcements.
1927	*"Lone Eagle"*, Charles Lindbergh watch.
1941	Bulova creates television's first commercial which was for wristwatches.
1950s	The company begins work on tuning fork principle.
1958	Arde Bulova, son of Joseph Bulova, dies.
1960	*Accutron* introduced.
1976	*Accutron* production ends.

Elgin National Watch Company

From nearly the beginning, Elgin was both the symbol, and the essence of its home town, Elgin, Illinois. The company was owned by shareholders and took price in its "family" of investors.

The company positioned itself as a style leader during the '20s and '30s, and offered a series of exquisite Art Deco enamel watches for women that demonstrated the best of this decorative style. At the same time, its output was enormous: an average of one million movements a year from 1920 through 1928, double the production of Waltham, its nearest competitor. Factory production took fullest advantage of the assembly line techniques popularized by Henry Ford, keeping costs low. Loyalty to the firm was noteworthy, with many employees counting forty or more years with the company.

Like Waltham, Elgin profited from the Second World War. It anticipated the entry of the United States into the war by several years and was already producing timing fuses when President Roosevelt declared the United States to be in the war following the bombing of Pearl Harbor.

Innovations that were on the drawing boards in the 1950s, including a battery powered watch, were announced but never produced. The firm's 50 millionth movement, produced in 1951, was celebrated with great fanfare but it was really the end of the glory days. Swiss watches had taken over the market during the Second World War and Elgin, like other American firms, never really recovered their share. Bit by bit, the firm was dismantled. The towering symbol of its presence in Elgin, the clock tower, came down under the wrecker's ball in 1966. Little remained of Elgin but the name.

Elgin Watch Company

1867	Founded in Elgin, Illinois.
1912	Introduces the lady's convertible wristwatch.
1916	Produces military wristwatches.
1942	All production turned over to military needs.
1947	*Durapower* mainspring introduced.
1950	Lays off 300 workers and slows to a four-day week.
1951	Makes its 50 millionth timepiece.

Gruen Watch Company

1874	Dietrich Gruen starts watchmaking business in Columbus, Ohio, later moving it to Cincinnati.
1904	Introduces Gruen *Veri-Thin*.
1908	Makes wristwatches for both men and women.
1911	Runs national advertising in the *Saturday Evening Post*.
1921	Develops the Gruen *Cartouche*, an oblong movement for small watches.
1924	50th Anniversary watch produced.
1925	Gruen *Quadron*, rectangular man's wristwatch movement.
1928/30	*Techni-Quadron* (Doctor's watch) movement #877.
1931	Jump hour model introduced.
1935	Benjamin S. Katz named president, staying until 1950.
1935	*Curvex* model #311 offered to the public.
1936	Woman's *Curvex* #520 makes its debut.
1937	*Curvex* #330, side-of-the-wrist model introduced.
1940	Compact *Curvex* #440 marketed.
1947	A man's bumper-type *Autowind* Model #460 developed.
1948	*Curvametric* Model #370 shows Retro-Modern influences.
1954	The company is sold.
1958	The company moves to New York.

Hamilton Watch Company

In 1893, railroad accuracy was the highest compliment a pocket watch could receive. Hamilton achieved that renown and maintained it through its years of both pocket and wristwatch manufacture. The firm, located in Lancaster, Pennsylvania from its beginning through the present time, was always devoted to quality, not quantity. Its total production was relatively low, its quality exceptional. It has been called by many the Patek Philippe of America, but that company should be flattered to be known as the Hamilton of Europe.

Hamilton's first period of design excellence came in the late 1920s with the enamel-bezel watches known as the *Coronado*, the *Spur*, and the *Piping Rock*. Three decades later, in 1957, Hamilton re-invented the wristwatch, startling both the public as well as the trade with its *Electric* series. Using a battery as the power source, the watch electrified both the movement as well as the idea of watchmaking. Hamilton packaged its revolutionary technology in a case designed to capture attention: the asymmetric *Ventura* and

Here, in the Bulova Observatory atop Fifth Avenue, New York, are but a few of the craftsmen who put together, time and case Bulova Watches. These men work in a dust-proof room, scientifically ventilated by purified air so that no dust can enter your Bulova Watch.

In the Bulova plant at Providence, Rhode Island, hundreds of artisans such as these make standardized parts so necessary to the time-keeping accuracy of your Bulova Watch.

A glimpse of the Order Department in the Bulova Observatory high up above Fifth Avenue, New York.

These workers, in the Bulova plant at Providence, with infinite skill, are performing one of hundreds of operations — each necessary to the timekeeping accuracy of a Bulova Watch.

Here you see a part of the Correspondence Department in the Bulova Observatory, atop Fifth Avenue, New York, where thousands of letters are handled daily from every section of the country.

Another corner of the great Bulova plant in Providence, Rhode Island. Here again are skilled craftsmen where the making of a fine timepiece a Bulova timepiece, is their life's work.

Where BULOVA watches are made!

FACTORY   Woodside, Long Island   ASSEMBLY PLANT   Waltham, Mass.

FACTORY   Bienne, Switzerland   ASSEMBLY PLANT   Jersey City, N.J.

FACTORY   Providence, Rhode Island

EXECUTIVE OFFICES

Fifth Avenue, N. Y.   Toronto, Canada

Pacer. This was followed by a series of eccentric shapes that had never before been used on watches. The Hamilton *Pulsar* created its own revolution in the next decade, but with the quartz watch the American watch industry sealed its fate. Production moved offshore.

With minor exceptions, Hamilton ceased making watch movements in this country in 1969.

Hamilton Watch Company

1892	The company is established in Lancaster, Pennsylvania, producing railroad-accuracy pocket watches.
1915	Produces the #986 movement for both men's and women's wristwatches.
1917	Produces a military-style wristwatch.
1927	Buys Illinois Watch Co.
--28/29	Produces the *Coronado, Spur* and *Piping Rock* enamel designs.
Mid-1930s	Designs the 6/0, rectangular #980 movement.
1930s	Introduces silver dials with applied gold numbers.
1931	Begins use of the *Elinvar* hairspring.
pre-1935	Operates its own watchmaking school.
1936	Makes *Seckron*, a "Doctor's" watch.
1938	Markets the reversible *Otis* model.
1940s	Produces marine chronometers waterproof watches for U.S. Navy and Marine Corps; military watches for Army and Army Air Corps.
late-1950s	Designs its 12/0 movement.
1956	Wins *Diamonds USA* award for diamond watch.
Pre-1965	Hamilton owns Wallace Case Co., of Stamford and later Wallingford, Connecticut.
1957	Hamilton *Electric* Model 500 introduced.
1960	Hamilton Model 505, a redesigned electric movement introduced.
1957-65	Production of 5/0 size men's electric watch: 41,849 pieces.
1952	Swiss movements are imported.
1970	Hamilton reduces its workforce by 1700 people.
1970s	Hamilton is sold and dispersed among three companies.
1892-1957	Total production of all timepieces: 12,803,207.

Illinois Watch Company

The short, decorative life of the Illinois Watch Company added its own special chapter to the history of the American wristwatch. Perhaps more appreciated and valued in our own time than in its heyday, Illinois created a series of highly ornamented watches in the Art Deco mode that set them well apart from other manufacturers. The eccentric placement of the subsidiary seconds chapter at 9:00, purely an expedient gesture for a watch built on pocket watch movement, added its own special charm.

As was typical of the American watch firms, one family —the Bunns— created and lovingly nurtured the firm. With the death of a key family member, Jacob Bunn, Jr., the firm was sold to the Hamilton Watch Company. That marked the end of the Illinois "look". Watches made after the 1930s may carry the Illinois name, but are really Hamilton products.

Illinois Watch Company

1869	Company founded in Springfield, Illinois.
1905	Begins making women's wristwatches using 0/size pendant moves.
1921	Adds men's wristwatches to its product line.
1927	Sold to Hamilton Watch Company.
1933	Illinois factory in Springfield closed, though Hamilton continues making Illinois brand watches until 1939.
1905-1933	Total wristwatch production: 820,000 pieces. Illinois made six watch movements.

Ingersoll

1881	Founded by Robert H. and Charles H. Ingersoll.
1905	Producing 3 million pocket watches per year at $1 each.
1906	*Midget* watch offered with strap or holder so women could wear it on the wrist.
1914	Waterbury Watch Co., formerly the New England Watch Co., buys Ingersoll Co. and continues Ingersoll trademark.
1933	Mickey Mouse watch introduced at Chicago World's Fair. Ingersoll cases many character watches.
1944	Company bought by U.S. Time which continues Ingersoll trademark.
1956	U.S. Time becomes Timex.

Waltham Watch Company

If it weren't for the various wars in which this country has been engaged, the Waltham Watch Company would probably not have survived past the 19th century. Even before the company was organized under this name, it was engaged in military production. Both the First and Second World Wars found it working at full capacity. In between, a series of financial crises, real and impending, separated the chapters of its history with the threat of bankruptcy. Under the stewardship of Frederic C. Dumaine, beginning in 1922, the company's finances were put in order but at the expense of its future. Dumaine's neglect of the plant and capital improvements made it impossible for Waltham to keep up to date. Its resources sold, the company ended not with a bang, but with yet another whimper in 1955. The name continues to be used on watches made abroad.

Waltham Watch Company

1851	Organized by Messrs. Davis, Howard, Dennison, and Sam Curtis as The American Horologe Company.
1885	Becomes the The American Waltham Watch Co., Waltham, Massachusetts.
1886-1921	The company thrives under its president, Ezra C. Fitch.
1912	Starts offering women's bracelet watches using 8/0 size movement.
1914	Introduces men's wristwatches.
1915	Produces time fuses for military use; devotes itself to wartime production of timing equipment.
1922	Frederic C. Dumaine appointed president.
1923	Name changed to Waltham Watch Co.
1927	Wristwatch production surpasses that of pocket watches.
1931	Baguette model #400 introduced.
1933	Baguette model #450 marketed.
1942-44	The company employs 1/5 of all workers in Waltham, Massachusetts, producing military watches, speedometers, fuses; almost exclusively engaged in war work.
1948	2300 workers laid off as the company files for reorganization.
1949	Another reorganization action takes place.
1955	Bought by Bellanca which disposes of watch inventory.

Additional Company Histories

Agassiz Founded 1878, made fine quality Swiss wristwatch movements; active in wristwatches from as early as 1915 through the 1950s. Contractor for Tiffany, J.E. Caldwell and other prestigious United States retail stores.

Ball Watch Co. Organized by Webb C. Ball of Cleveland, Ohio in 1879, manufactured accurate timepieces for railroad industry; active in wristwatch manufacture from the 1950s until 1969. The firm never made movements.

Dueber Hampden, Canton, Ohio. Began as Dueber Co., a pocket watch maker. The name Dueber Hampden was used for the company's wristwatches which were made from 1921 to 1931. The firm and its factory were sold to Antorg, in the USSR where it has remained active to the present.

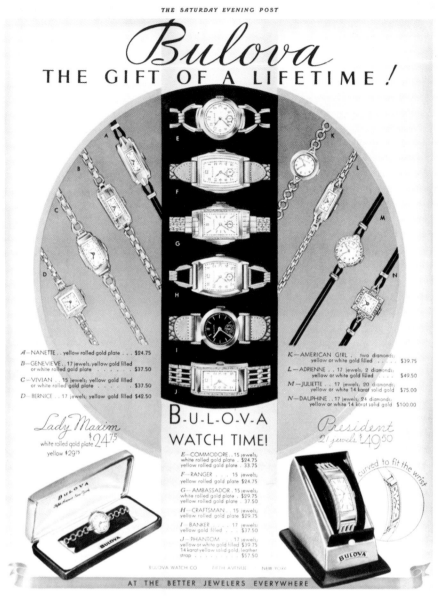

Production Dates

By referring to the serial numbers of wristwatches by the following watch companies, the date of manufacture may be determined.

Serial No.	Date
Elgin	
17,000,000	1912
20,000,000	1917
25,000,000	1922
30,000,000	1927
33,000,000	1929
35.000.000	1934
40.000.000	1941
45,000,000	1948
50,000,000	1953

Hamilton	
1,330,000	1912
1,516,000	1916
1,780,000	1920
2,050,000	1923
2,300,000	1926
2,450,000	1929
2,500,000	1930
2,600,000	1935
2,900,000	1940

Grade #		
980G101-G6694001937	1946
982J1001-J6706001935	1951
987001-04863001937	1948

Illinois	
2,480,000	1905
3,220,000	1908
4,000,000	1912
4,250,000	1918
4,300,000	1919
4,500,000	1921
5,049,000	1924
5,600,000	1927

Waltham	
14,000,000	1905
15,000,000	1907
18,000,000	1910
20,000,000	1914
25,000,000	1926
27,200,000	1930
28,500,000	1935
30,000,000	1939
32,000,000	1945
33,558,000	1950
33,830,000	1953

Helbros A marketing company active from mid-1920s to the present, importing Swiss movements housed in gold, gold filled and stainless steel.

E. Ingraham Co. Active 1912-1968; comic character wristwatches made 1930-1968.

LeCoultre Founded in Switzerland in 1833. Became Jaeger-LeCoultre in 1930; introduced the *Reverso* in 1931. This model is still made today.

Longines Founded in 1867. Began making wristwatches at the turn of the century. Cased Swiss movements in American cases and marketed them in United States; also sold totally Swiss made watches, from the early 1900s to the present.

Mohawk An American marketing company importing Swiss movements; active in wristwatches during 1930s and 1940s.

Movado Founded by Achille Ditesheim in 1881. A Swiss company active in marketing wristwatches to the American market. Began making women's wristwatches in 1890 and has continued to manufacture wristwatches to the present. The name 'Movado' comes from Esperanto, the universal language, and means 'always in motion'. Nate Horwit's stark design, the dial with a single dot at 12:00, set a new standard for design and was made part of the permanent collection of the Museum of Modern Art in 1959.

New Haven Clock & Watch Co. New Haven, Connecticut, 1853-1956. Active in wristwatch production from the 1930s to 1956. Comic character watches with automata, 7 jeweled movements, and base metal cases.

Rockford Watch Co., Ltd. Rockford, Illinois. Active in wristwatches 1900-1915.

South Bend Watch Co. South Bend, Indiana. Active from March, 1903 through December, 1929.

Tiffany This high-end New York retail jeweler marketed major European and American wristwatches as early as 1915. The Tiffany name appeared on the dial and the case, sometimes along with the manufacturer's name.

Vacheron-Constantin The company was organized in 1819, and is the oldest watch factory in Geneva. It began making wristwatches early in the 20th century.

Watch Case Companies

Bulova Watch Case Co., Providence and Pforzheim, Germany. Made cases for Bulova watches; the only firm to have its own case factories on an on-going basis.

Cress-Arrow. made cases for many imported European makers including International Watch Co., LeCoultre and others.

Denison. Cased Waltham movements.

DiVencenzo and Ariente. Made cases for Hamilton.

Dubois Watch Case Co., New York City. Cased Waltham movements, ca 1918.

Gruen Watch Case Co., Cincinnati, Ohio. By 1931 90% of the cases produced were for wristwatches. Gruen Watch Case Company produced *Curvex* cases and regular cases for Gruen in karat gold and, after 1924, gold filled.

I.D. Case Co., New York. Cased generic Swiss movements. Active in the middle third of the 20th century.

Illinois Watch Case Co., Elgin, Illinois. Made cases for Elgin.

Jacques Depollier & Son, New York City. Cased Waltham movements, ca 1919.

Katz & Ogush, New York City. Made many lady's wristwatch cases in 14k gold, 18k gold and platinum for Gruen.

Keystone Watch Case Co., Philadelphia. Manufactured cases for Waltham and Illinois.

Major Watch Case Co. New York.

Schwab & Wuispard Case Co. (S & W). Made many cases for Hamilton including *Electric* series, and also made cases for Elgin.

Star Case Co., Ludington, Michigan. Star was the last major case company operating in the country, going out of business in 1985. It made cases for Hamilton, lower priced Gruen cases, and cases for Elgin.

Wadsworth Case Co., Cincinnati, Ohio. Made most of the gold filled and some *Curvex* cases for Gruen, as well as cases for Hamilton, Longines, and Wittnauer. Principal maker for Elgin; owned by Elgin in 1951.

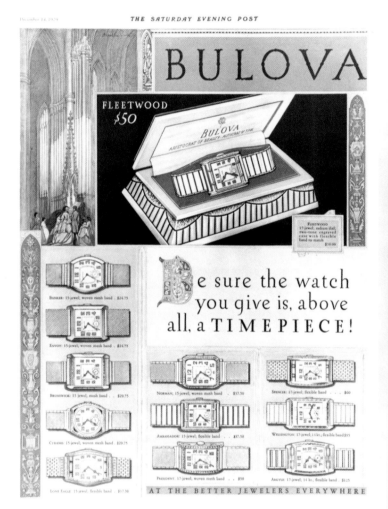

This forceful holiday presentation of Bulova Watches appears in the December 15th issue of Saturday Evening Post—a color page as timely as it is arresting— *a color page that will sell watches!*

Glossary

Accutron: trademark of Bulova Watch Co. for its tuning fork movement.

Arabic numerals: numbering system in everyday use employing digits 0 through 9, most commonly used to indicate hours, minutes and seconds on wristwatch dials.

automata: moving parts displayed on the dial other than time and calendar functions, usually cut out and in relief.

baguette: a french term for "rod, wand or stick" which describes these narrow, rectangular, small stones, usually made from cleavage fragments of a larger stone.

bezel: the frame, usually metal, surrounding the dial and crystal.

chapter: the frame or track on which numbers, dots or markers are placed to indicate seconds, minutes or hours.

chronograph: a mechanical watch with hour and minute hands and a center sweep-second hand which can be controlled by one or more special buttons, on the side of the case or through the crown. The sweep second hand may be started stopped, and made to return to zero without interfering with the timekeeping of the watch.

chronometer: a specially adjusted watch whose precision meets officially accepted standards as defined by the Swiss Institute and the English Kew certificate. Together these represent the highest standard of accuracy for mechanical watches.

crown: a small serrated wheel extending from the bezel which permits winding of the watch; it is attached to the winding stem. Note: some crowns perform other functions such as setting the day or date.

crystal: the transparent covering, usually glass or plastic, that protects the dial.

Curvex: trademark of Gruen Watch Co. for its curved watches.

cushion shape: a square or rectangle whose sides curve outward.

decorative: the design period of the 1920s: 1930s characterized by richly engraved surfaces, the use of color and curved lines.

demi-hunter case: a metal case that partially covers the dial of the watch like a picture frame; in some designs, this frame lifts up to reveal the dial.

dial: also called the face; indicates the time in hours and minutes with hands and chapters placed on a metal, porcelain or pasteboard surface and records all the various activities of the wristwatch.

digital: a name given to watches circa 1930s that use rotating discs under the main dial; windows, cut out on the dial, display hours, minutes and seconds.

doctor's watch: a popular term for a split-dial watch in which hours and minutes are indicated on one dial, seconds on another of equal size (duo-dial). The name is also applied to a wristwatch having a concentric chapter of enlarged seconds inside the hours and minutes chapters allowing a sweep seconds hand to indicate accurately the passing seconds.

ebauche: a term used by Swiss watch manufacturers to denote the raw movement comprising jewels, escapement, plating, engraving.

eccentric: a design period of the 1950s and 1960s based on asymmetrical lines.

embossed: usually achieved through die striking.

enamel painted dial: metal plate with painted symbols using stenciled chapters indicating the time and functions of the watch.

gold: Malleable, ductible yellow metallic clement Green gold: karat gold alloyed with silver Pink gold (rose): karat gold alloyed with copper White gold: karat gold alloyed with nickel.

gold filled: the fusing (laminating) of two layers of gold with a middle layer of base metal by heat, time, and pressure. The gold is lOk or better and is at least three thousandths of an inch thick.

gold plated: this is an electroplating process, coating a base metal with gold. The electroplating must be at least .00075 of lOk gold or better.

hack: a control from the crown that permits the sweep seconds hand to be stopped and re-started at the precisely desired moment by applying a brake to the escapement or the primary wheel.

hunting case: a hinged metal cover that protects the dial and crystal of a watch; it springs up at a touch so the time can be read.

jeweled movement: gemstones such as rubies are placed at key points of friction to lengthen the life of the movement; the more jewels, the longer the life of the movement, up to a maximum of 37; the jeweling is not a guarantee of the quality of the movement.

karat gold: alloys of gold and other metals, measured in 24 parts, for example, 14k gold combines fourteen parts of gold with ten parts of other metals; the alloying metals add strength and affect the color.

lugs: the metal extensions that connect the watch case with the band or strap.

markers: slashes, dots or sticks used instead of numbers to indicate the hours.

movement: the working mechanism of a wristwatch. pin lever movement: an inexpensive movement with one or no jewels; most character watches were made with these movements; although they are inexpensive, many function quite well for many years.

retro-modern: the period following WW II in which exaggerated motifs and bold metal surfaces dominated.

rolled gold plate: the fusing (laminating) of two layers of gold with a middle layer of base metal by heat, time, and pressure. The gold is lOk or better and is at least one and half thousandths of an inch thick. Note: in England and, occasionally in the United States, the rolled gold plate process consists of a single layer of gold fused (laminated) by heat, time, and pressure on a base metal. The reverse side of the base metal will be electroplated.

Roman numerals: system used to indicate hours employing letters of the alphabet: I, II, III, IV, V, VI, VII, VIII, IX, X, XI, XII.

streamlined: a design idea growing out of the functional process of stripping surfaces of unnecessary decoration in order to provide less wind resistance.

subsidary seconds: a small 60-second dial demarcated in 5, 10, or 15 second segments and usually placed at the 6:00 position.

sweep seconds: a centrally rotating hand sweeping around the dial to indicate the passage of seconds; sometimes called center seconds.

tank watch: a rectangular case design of the 'teens; the shape is meant to evoke the military tank.

tonneau shape: a rectangle whose sides are curved outward.

transitional: the period of design experimentation that led from the pocket watch to the wristwatch.

window: a cut out section on the dial permitting changing displays for day, date, and other information; on mechanical digital watches, all the time displays are on discs that revolve and indicate the hours, minutes and seconds through windows.

Bibliography

Barracca, Jader; Giampiero Negretti and Franco Nencini. *Ore D'Oro 2.* Milan, Italy: Wrist Editoriale, 1987.

Bolino, August C. T*he Watchmakers of Massachusetts.* Washington, D.C.: Kensington Historical Press, 1987.

Brown, Hy. *Comic Character Timepieces: Seven Decades of Memories.* Atglen, PA: Schiffer Publishing Ltd., 1992

Brunner, Gisbert and Christian Pfeiffer-Belli. *Swiss Wristwatches: Chronology of Worldwide Success.* Atglen, PA: Schiffer Publishing, Ltd., 1987

Brunner, Gisbert L. and Christian Pfeiffer-Belli. *Wristwatches.* Atglen, PA: Schiffer Publishing Ltd., 1993

Doensen, Pieter. *Watch: History of the Modern Wrist Watch.* Utrecht: Snoeck-Ducaju & Zoon, 1994

Ehrhardt, Sherry; Roy Ehrhardt and Joe Demesy. *Vintage American & European Wrist Watch Price Guide,* Book 2. Kansas City, MO: Heart of America Press, 1988.

Ehrhardt, Sherry and Peter Planes. *Vintage American & European Wrist Watch Price Guide,* First Edition. Kansas City, MO: Heart of America Press, 1984.

Good, Richard. *Watches.* Dorset: Blanford Press Ltd., 1978.

Hampel, Heinz. *Automatic Wristwatches from Switzerland: Watches that Wind Themselves.* Atglen, PA: Schiffer Publishing Ltd., 1994

Huber, Martin, and Alan Banbery. *Patek Philippe.* Geneva: Antiquorum, 1988.

Jaquet, Eugene, and Alfred Chapuis. *Technique and History of the Swiss Watch.* London: Spring Books, 1983, 1986.

Kahlert, Helmut, Richard Muhe and Gisbert L. Brunner. *Wristwatches: History of a Century's Development.* Atglen, PA: Schiffer Publishing Ltd., 1983, 1986

Landes, David S. *Revolution in Time.* Cambridge, MA: Belknap Press, 1983.

Lang, Gerd-R., and Reinhard Meis. *Chronograph Wristwatches: To Stop Time.* Atglen, PA: Schiffer Publishing Ltd., 1993

Levenberg, Juri. *Russian Wristwatches: Pocket Watches, Stop Watches, Onboard Clocks & Chronometers.* Atglen, PA: Schiffer Publishing Ltd., 1995

McCarthy, James R. *A Matter of Time, The Story of the Watch.* New York: Harper & Brothers, 1947.

Meis, Reinhard. *Pocket Watches.* Atglen, PA: Schiffer Publishing Ltd., 1996 (rev.)

Moore, Charles W. *Timing a Century: History of the Waltham Watch Co.* Cambridge, MA: Harvard University Press, 1945.

Negretti, Giampiero, and Franco Nencini. *Ore D'Oro.* Milan: Editoriale Wrist, 1984.

Ordnance Maintenance, War Department. *Technical Manual: Wristwatches, Pocket Watches, Stop Watches, and Clocks.* April, 1945

Patrizzi, Osvaldo. *Rolex: Wristwatches,* 2nd Edition. Geneva: Antiquorum, 1992, 1993.

Richter, Benno. *Breitling Timepieces: 1884 to the Present.* Atlgen, PA: Schiffer Publishing Ltd., 1995.

Rondeau, René. *The Watch of the Future: The Story of the Hamilton Electric Watch,* 2nd Edition. Corte Madera, CA: Published by the author, 1989, 1992.

Shugert, Cooksey and Tom Engle. *The Complete Guide to American Pocket Watches.* Cleveland, TN: Overstreet Publications, Inc., 1987.

Viola, Gerald and Gisbert L. Brunner. *Time in Gold: Wristwatches.* Atglen, PA: Schiffer Publishing Ltd., 1988

Index

AARON FABER GALLERY

666 FIFTH AVENUE (ENT. ON 53RD ST.) NEW YORK, NY 10019 212-586-8411 FAX: 212-582-0205

TIME WILL TELL

ANTIQUE WRISTWATCHES

962 Madison Avenue
(75th Street)
New York, New York 10021
Phone: (212) 861-2663
Fax: (212) 288-4069

New York's finest collection. Rare
and unusual vintage and classic
wristwatches. Prized collectables,
sound investments, fashionable and
superb timepieces. Fully warranteed.
Expert repairs and restorations.
Free catalog available.

bought/sold
consignments accepted

Price Guide to American Wristwatches
Five Decades of Style and Design
Copyright © 1996

The market for American wristwatches continues to grow and change. Because of this, any price guide must be used only as a guide and should not be the sole determinant of the value of a wristwatch. The price range covered in this Price Guide begins at the price the consumer may pay at a flea market or other such place for a wristwatch in "as is" condition. At the higher end of the scale is the price a consumer may expect to pay at a reputable dealer of fine wristwatches. The watch from the dealer may be expected to be in excellent and correct condition, and backed by the dealer with a warranty and service agreement. This Price Guide is organized by page and position. The position codes used in the second column are as follows; they may be used singly or in combination.:   T = top; C = center; B = Bottom; L = Left; R:Right

Pos	Brand	Price		Pos	Brand	Price
2R	Illinois	$300-700		CR	Westfield	$75-550
3L	Illinois	$480-1200		BL	Omega	$100-900
3C	Illinois	$300-700		92 TR	Patek Philippe	$1900-5200
3R	Illinois	$160-400		CL	Longines	$100-800
4L	Illinois	$160-400		BR	Wittnauer	$250-1100
4C	Illinois	$250-600		93 TL	Patek Philippe	$4000-8500
60 TL	Waltham	$800-2000		CR	Westfield	$85-575
TR	Waltham	$90-625		BL	Waltham	$100-900
BL	Illinois	$90-650		94 TR	Gruen	$100-800
61 TL	Illinois	$250-1800		CL	Waltham	$85-575
BR	Illinois	$125-625		BR	Waltham	$85-675
62 TL	Illinois	$100-550		95 TL	Gruen	$80-475
BL	Illinois	$200-500		BL	Illinois	$150-1250
BR	Illinois	$125-1200		BR	Waltham	$175-1000
63 TR	Illinois	$100-550		96 T	Bulova	$85-750
BL	Illinois	$100-570		BL	Longines	$100-650
BR	Illinois	$100-650		BR	Bulova	$100-675
64 BR	Illinois	$100-800		97 TL	Hamilton	$450-1700
C	Illinois	$120-725		BR	Hamilton	$90-550
BL	Illinois	$100-1250		98 TL	Hamilton	$80-850
65 TL	Illinois	$100-600		TR	Waltham	$75-450
C	Illinois	$100-600		BR	Benrus(RGP)	$100-490
BR	Illinois	$100-750		99 TR	Gruen	$100-575
66 TR	Hamilton	$200-1500		C	Illinois	$90-550
BL	Hamilton	$85-750		BL	Illinois	$125-1250
67 TL	Hamilton	$85-550		100 TL	Gruen	$90-690
BR	Hamilton	$85-800		TR	Gruen	$250-950
68 CL	Gruen	$150-780		BL	Gruen	$100-625
69 TR	Illinois	$300-700		101 TL	Bulova	$85-490
CR	Gruen	$100-525		TR	Bulova	$85-650
70 TL	Gruen	$600-2400		BL	Bulova	$85-650
TR	Gruen	$225-1200		BR	Patek Philippe	$4500-7500
BL	Gruen	$250-1700		102 TL	Elgin	$75-425
71 TR	Gruen	$250-1500		C	Elgin	$125-675
B	Gruen	$250-1700		BR	Gruen	$225-925
73 BL	Gruen	$1200-2500		103 TR	Hamilton	$180-825
CR	Hamilton	$600-1500		C	Hamilton	$90-550
BR	Gruen	$500-1500		BL	Hamilton	$90-580
74 T	Gruen	$250-1800		104 TL	Bulova	$110-600
B	Gruen	$250-1900		TR	Bulova	$110-650
75 TL	Gruen	$250-1200		BL	Hamilton	$400-1200
TR	Gruen	$300-950		105 TL	Hamilton	$150-850
BR	Gruen	$80-625		BR	Ball	$150-625
76 TR	Bulova	$175-900		106 TR	Swiss	$100-900
BL	Gruen	$350-1600		CL	Swiss	$100-525
77 TL	Patek Philippe	$7000-15000		BR	Gruen	$200-1000
TR	Bulova	$175-700		107 TL	Elgin	$250-1075
BR	Omega	$150-950		CR	Elgin	$200-1200
78 TL	Bulova	$150-750		BL	Elgin	$100-725
CR	Benrus	$85-550		108 TL	Hamilton	$80-525
BL	Waltham	$100-700		CR	Geneve	$85-525
79 TR	Bulova	$125-700		BL	Rolex	$1300-3900
CL	Bulova	$125-600		109 T	Waltham	$85-575
CR	Hamilton	$950-1900		BR	Waltham	$250-1200
80 TL	Gruen	$900-2500		110 TL	Illinois	$85-550
CR	Gruen	$120-850		TR	Illinois	$110-625
BL	Gruen	$190-1600		BR	Hamilton	$85-550
81 TL	Gruen	$90-500		111 TL	Elgin	$85-625
CR	Gruen	$200-800		TR	Elgin	$125-600
BL	Gruen	$300-1400		BL	Elgin	$80-525
82 TL	Bulova	$150-900		112 TL	Waltham	$150-750
TR	Bulova	$85-525		TR	Waltham	$150-650
BL	Bulova	$75-600		BL	Hamilton	$90-600
BR	Bulova	$150-600		113 TL	LaSalle	$150-575
83 BL	Bulova	$125-800		TR	Illinois	$110-625
R	Bulova	$150-900		BR	Hamilton	$1200-2500
84 TR	Waltham	$85-525		114 TL	Hamilton	$2300-3900
BL	Hamilton	$400-1700		CR	Hamilton	$1100-2500
BR	Hamilton	$600-1800		BL	Hamilton	$250-900
85 T	Elgin	$150-725		115 TL	Hamilton	$1225-2400
BL	Elgin	$200-900		TR	Elgin	$150-500
BR	Elgin	$250-1050		BR	Elgin	$1400-3300
88 TL	Elgin	$100-650		116 TR	Gruen	$1200-3800
TC	Elgin	$80-425		117 T	Gruen	$3500-6000
TR	Elgin	$75-525		BL	Gruen	$1200-3800
BR	Elgin	$125-925		BR	Gruen	$1200-3800
89 TL	Elgin	$90-900		118 L	Gruen	$900-2200
CR	Elgin	$600-1700		TR	Gruen	$2500-6000
BL	Elgin	$125-900		119 T	Hamilton	$900-2300
90 TL	Elgin	$125-950		120 T	Swiss	$1200-1850
CL	Paul Breguette	$150-725		121 TL	Bulova	$900-1800
91 TL	Omega	$90-790				

Pos	Brand	Price		Pos	Brand	Price
9 R	Waltham convertible	$150-750		CL	Omega	$1200-3000
10 TR	Hampden convertible	$100-450		BR	Omega	$1200-3000
BL	Elgin convertible	$100-525		BL	Sopra	$200-600
11 TL	Waltham	$100-500		30 TL	Patek Philippe	$1200-3600
BL	Waltham	$105-600		BL	Blancpain	$300-1250
BR	Waltham	$90-600		BR	Audemars Piguet	$1500-4500
12 TL	Waltham	$90-600		31 BR	Elgin	$200-1250
TR	Elgin	$300-1500		32 TL	Swiss	$200-850
BL	Waltham	$250-1500		BR	Swiss	$150-750
13 TL	Ingersoll	$85-250		33 TR	Swiss	$300-2500
TR	Ingersoll	$85-250		BL	Swiss	$150-1500
BR	South Bend	$375-450		BR	Swiss	$500-2500
14 TR	Waltham	$100-700		34 TL	Gruen	$200-700
BL	Elgin	$100-585		TR	Gruen	$150-600
15 T	Waltham	$100-650		BL	Gruen	$250-1250
BL	Swiss	$150-850		BR	Elgin	$80-600
BR	Waltham	$85-475		35 TL	Elgin	$100-650
16 TL	S. Kirk & Son	$100-525		BL	Gruen	$100-500
CR	Elgin	$75-475		BR	Elgin	$125-700
BL	Waltham	$250-900		36 TL	Gruen	$190-1600
17 TL	Elgin	$70-425		CR	Gruen	$250-1200
CR	Elgin	$250-1400		BL	Elgin	$200-1100
BL	Elgin	$85-625		37 TL	Waltham	$125-490
18 TL	New Haven	$50-250		TR	Elgin	$125-425
CR	Waltham	$70-700		BL	Elgin	$150-400
BL	Waltham	$60-675		BR	Elgin	$450-2000
19 TR	Hampden	$90-550		38 TR	Waltham	$250-500
BL	Elgin	$100-750		BL	Elgin	$150-400
20 TR	Patria	$200-1000		BR	Elgin	$125-700
CL	Swiss	$150-1250		39 TL	Harwood	$200-450
BR	Liverpool	$150-1600		TR	Benrus	$120-700
21 TR	Dublin	$350-1500		BL	Swiss	$125-700
CL	English	$750-2800		BR	Elgin	$150-950
BR	Rolex	$350-1800		40 TL	Longines	$125-550
24 TR	Movado	$900-2500		BL	Gruen	$150-650
BL	Longines	$400-1900		BR	Benrus	$90-700
25 TR	Harwood	$100-600		41 TL	Gruen	$500-1500
CL	Harwood	$100-600		TR	Bulova	$125-750
BR	Harwood	$100-600		BL	Elgin	$155-700
26 TL	Oyster	$500-2900		BR	Gruen	$100-625
BR	Waltham	$100-590		42 TL	Elgin	$200-1500
27 B	Illinois	$200-800		BL	Elgin	$100-450
28 TL	Unknown	$300-1000		BR	Elgin	$200-1300
BL	Swiss	$400-2000		43 TL	Elgin	$100-650
BR	Omega	$250-1200		TR	Gruen	$175-1400
29 TR	Rolex	$1000-3600		BR	Hamilton	$600-2300
				44 TL	Elgin	$200-900

Pos	Brand	Price
TR	Gruen	$100-550
BL	Benrus	$150-700
BR	Elgin	$125-925
45 TL	Elgin	$125-700
TR	Elgin	$100-550
BL	Ingraham	$225-675
BR	Dueber Hampden	$100-900
46 TL	Benrus	$100-600
CR	Patek Philippe	$5500-9500
BL	Gruen	$1200-2500
47 BL	Elgin	$75-450
BR	Bulova	$250-1050
50 TL	Illinois	$100-600
TR	Illinois	$100-690
BL	Illinois	$100-750
51 TL	Bulova	$200-1250
TR	Bulova	$90-400
BR	Bulova	$100-600
54 TR	Bulova	$65-525
BL	Bulova	$65-600
BR	Bulova	$125-850
55 TL	Bulova	$90-550
CR	BulovaBB	$85-525
BL	Bulova	$85-550
56 TL	Waltham	$225-750
TR	Waltham	$85-600
BL	Waltham	$200-1800
57 TL	Waltham	$125-600
TR	Waltham	$85-600
BR	Waltham	$100-800
58 1L	Waltham	$500-1200
1C	Illinois	$300-700
1R	Illinois	$300-700
2L	Illinois	$400-1000
2C	Illinois	$300-700
2R	Illinois	$200-500
3L	Illinois	N/A
3C	Illinois	$200-500
3R	Illinois	$160-400
4L	Illinois	$300-700
4C	Illinois	$300-700
4R	Illinois	$160-400
59 1L	Illinois	$500-1200
1C	Illinois	$160-400
1R	Illinois	$200-500
2L	Illinois	$150-350
2C	Illinois	$160-400

	BR	Hamilton	$900-2400
122	TL	Elgin	$750-1800
	BL	Bulova	$225-750
	BR	Lord Elgin	$800-1700
123	CR	Exacta Time w/ball package	$450-1200
124	CR	Ingersoll	$375-1250
	BL	Ingersoll	$350-1150
	TL	Mickey Mouse Ingersoll w/box	$800-2400
125	TR	Ingersoll w/box	$150-750
	CL	Ingersoll	$150-550
126	TL	Ingersoll w/box	$135-450
	CR	Ingersoll w/box	$120-400
127	TR	U.S. Time	$125-575
	CL	Ingersoll	$115-525
	BR	Ingersoll	$75-300
128	TL	Timex	$100-600
	BR	Timex	$65-325
129	TL	Swiss	$125-525
	CR	Honest Time	$65-225
130	TR	Agon Chromatic Watch Co.	$65-275
	BL	Unknown	$50-300
131	TR	Unknown	$150-450
	BL	New Haven	$150-550
	BR	New Haven	$300-1250
132	TL	U.S. Time	$85-425
	CR	Ingersoll	$50-425
	BL	Minnie Mouse Ingersoll (U.S. Time) w/box	$50-450
133	CL	Helbros	$750-1500
	BR	Bradley	$60-275
134	TL	U.S. Time	$150-525
	CR	U.S. Time	$130-575
	BL	U.S. Time	$110-450
135	TL	New Haven	$200-700
	TR	New Haven	$200-700
	BC	New Haven	$200-700
136	TR	Chancellor	$60-350
	BL	New Haven	$200-700
137	BL	Ingraham	$85-350
	BC	Ingraham	$85-375
	BR	Ingraham	$85-375
138	TR	Ingraham	$85-375
	BL	Ingraham	$190-700
139	T	Bradley w/original display & box	$50-400
	BR	U.S. Time w/original display & box	$85-400
140	T	U.S. Time	$85-290
	B	U.S. Time w/original display & box	$85-450
141	TL	U.S. Time w/original saddle	$150-450
	TR	New Haven	$150-650
	BL	New Haven	$135-635
	BR	Unknown	$100-425
142	T	Ingraham w/original box	$150-900
	BL	Ingraham	$135-600
143	TL	Ingersoll	$75-225
	TR	Ingraham	$200-700
	BR	Sheffield	$80-300
144	TL	New Haven	$125-700
	CR	New Haven	$100-650
	BL	New Haven w/box	$100-550
145	TR	New Haven	$150-675
	CL	Marvel Importing	$85-350
	BR	New Haven w/orig. box	$150-800
146	TL		$125-325
	TC	Dabs	$125-325
	TR	Dabs	$125-325
147	TL		$110-330
	BR		$100-330
148	TR	Swiss	$85-400
	CL	Timex	$85-425
	BR	U.S. Time	$50-190
149	TL	U.S. Time	$60-325
	BL	Timex w/"Glass Slipper" box	$50-400
150	TL	Ingraham w/box	$150-600
	TR	Patent Watch Co.	$150-550
	BR	U.S. Time w/box	$110-350
151	TL	U.S. Time	$150-525
	CR	U.S. Time	$135-525
	BL	Unknown	$135-400
152	TL	Swiss	$125-425
	TR	Unknown	$85-225
	BL	Ingersoll	$150-550
	BR	Ingersoll	$600-1800
153	TR	Ingraham	$85-295
	BL	Ingraham	$120-325
	BR	Ingraham	$90-250
154	TL	Abra	$150-600
	TR	Illinois	$150-800
155	TL	New Haven	$85-300
	TR	New Haven	$110-525
	BR	Elgin	$100-500
156	TL	Swiss	$90-375
	TR	Swiss	$100-375
	BL	U.S. Time	$75-225
157	TL	Royal Roulette	$100-600
	TR	Unknown	$350-1200
	BR	Hong Kong	$100-400
158	TL	Customtime	$85-375
	TR	Swiss	$200-800
	BR	Old England Watches Ltd.	$100-375
159	CR	Ingersoll	$150-450
160	TL	Benrus	$130-400
	TR	Depollier	$800-1700
	CR	Benrus	$100-350
	BR	H. Moser	$250-850
161	TL	Swiss	$350-1500
	TR	Benrus	$80-350
	BL	Benrus	$100-300
	BR	Elgin	$450-950
162	TL	Longines	$300-860
	TR	Longines	$1500-2800
163	TL	Elgin in Depollier Case	$800-1700
	TR	Elgin	$100-550
163	BR	Elgin	$175-700
164	TL	Elgin	$220-1100
	TR	Elgin	$80-550
	BL	Elgin	$85-325
165	TR	Hamilton	$85-350
	BL	Hamilton	$85-350
166	TL	Bulova	$85-325
	BR	Bulova	$85-350
167	TL	Bulova	$85-350
	TR	Waltham	$85-350
	BR	Waltham	$450-1600
168	T	Gruen	$90-525
169	CR	Wittnauer	$90-575
	BR	Hamilton	$350-1250
170	TR	Hamilton	$90-550
	CL	Bulova	$100-525
	BC	Wittnauer	$90-525
171	TL	Waltham	$700-1500
	TR	Bulova	$200-800
	BR	Elgin	$100-490
172	TL	Elgin	$250-925
	C	Elgin	$250-950
	BR	Elgin	$100-550
173	TR	Elgin	$110-560
	C	Elgin	$150-600
	BL	Elgin	$110-450
174	TL	Elgin	$110-550
	TR	Bulova	$225-475
	BL	Elgin	$110-470
	BR	Elgin	$110-500
175	TL	Elgin	$110-475
	TR	Elgin	$120-675
	BL	Elgin	$120-650
176	TL	Elgin	$140-600
	TR	Elgin	$100-490
	BR	Elgin	$90-400
177	T	Elgin	$1200-2800
	BL	Elgin	$120-525
178	TR	Elgin	$210-950
	CL	Elgin	$100-440
	BR	Elgin	$110-360
179	TR	Gruen	$200-1100
	CL	Gruen	$100-475
	BR	Gruen	$200-1400
180	TL	Gruen	$180-500
	BL	Gruen	$150-600
	BR	Gruen	$200-550
181	TL	Gruen	$300-750
	TR	Gruen	$120-450
	BL	Gruen	$100-400
	BR	Gruen	$100-575
182	TL	Gruen	$90-450
	TR	Gruen	$90-450
	BL	Gruen	$300-1500
183	TR	Hamilton	$110-550
	CL	Simmons	$80-400
	BR	LeCoultre	$150-1200
184	TL	Bulova	$100-450
	TR	LeCoultre	$250-900
	BL	Helbros	$100-375
185	TL	Longines	$100-525
	CL	Hamilton	$120-600
	BR	Hamilton	$100-425
186	BL	Hamilton	$400-1075
	BR	Vacheron & Constantin	$1800-3600
187	TL	Hamilton	$200-800
	TR	Wittnauer	$120-600
	BR	Bulova	$85-450
188	TL	Bulova	$90-500
	TR	Hamilton	$90-625
	BR	Elgin	$90-525
189	TR	Eberhard	$190-600
	BL	Wittnauer	$110-550
190	TR	Helbros	$90-375
	CL	Hamilton	$95-900
	BR	Hamilton	$150-800
191	TL	Wittnauer	$120-650
	TR	Bulova	$90-425
	BL	Hamilton	$90-675
	BR	Elgin	$100-550
192	TL	Wittnauer	$250-800
	TR	Gubelin	$350-1500
	BL	Norman	$120-450
193	TR	Hamilton	$100-475
	BR	Bulova	$100-490
194	TR	Benrus	$225-800
	CL	Wittnauer	$225-775
	BR	Lee	$120-450
195	TL	Gruen	$450-1800
	TR	Gruen	$130-675
	BL	Bulova	$95-425
196	TR	Buren	$150-850
	CL	Bulova	$200-925
	BR	Benrus	$90-580
197	TL	Benrus	$90-650
	CR	Geneva	$90-570
	BC	Benrus	$150-600
198	TL	Bulova	$95-525
	TC	LeCoultre	$300-900
	TR	Gubelin	$350-1400
	R	Longines	$100-450
199	TL	Bulova	$90-475
	CL	Hamilton	$650-2200
	BR	Bulova	$100-525
200	TR	Longines	$300-1500
	CL	Longines	$90-425
201	TL	Bulova	$95-450
	CR	Bulova	$90-700
	BL	Bulova	$190-890
202	TL	Benrus	$150-600
	TR	Wittnauer	$200-750
	BR	Cort	$100-590
203	TL	LeCoultre	$350-1400
	CR	Bulova	$120-750
	BL	Geneva	$125-650
204	TL	Unknown	$800-1800
	BL	Louis	$125-500
	BR	Gruen	$125-550
205	TR	Longines	$450-1350
	BL	Geneva	$150-650
	BR	Bulova	$300-950
206	T	Star	$130-550
	BR	Elmont	$100-450
207	TL	Harman	$110-475
	TR	Rulon	$110-600
	BR	Benrus	$100-425
208	TL	Bulova	$135-725
	TR	LeCoultre	$600-2400
	BR	Bulova	$130-600
209	TL	Hamilton	$90-525
	TR	Hamilton	$300-1800
	CL	Hamilton	$100-450
210	TL	Bulova	$100-425
	TR	Hamilton	$225-975
	BL	Bulova (gold)	$400-900
		(Gold filled)	$250-700
	BR	Bulova	$100-525
211	TL	Longines	$200-800
	TR	Bulova	$150-900
	BL	Benrus	$350-1200
212	TL	Bulova	$200-800
	TR	Bulova	$100-550
	BR	Benrus	$150-725
213	TL	Benrus	$100-425
	TR	Movado	$300-1025
	BL	Diwem	$250-800
214	TL	Wittnauer	$200-650
	BL	Bulova	$90-425
	BR	Orloff	$80-400
215	TL	Benrus	$110-650
	TR	Warren	$85-425
	BR	Patek Philippe	$35,000-45,000
216	TL	Universal	$250-900
	BR	Bulova	$95-425
217	TL	Hamilton	$110-700
	TR	Bulova	$90-450
	CL	Hamilton	$90-600
218	TL	Hamilton	$1000-2500
	TR	Longines	$375-1250
	B	Longines	$200-700
219	CR	Hamilton	$250-850
220	TL	Hamilton	$600-1850
	TR	Hamilton	$1500-4500
	BL	Hamilton	$500-1800
221	TL	Hamilton	$250-750
	CL	Hamilton	$150-700
	TR	Hamilton	$350-900
	BR	Hamilton	$250-750
222	TR	Hamilton	$150-800
	CL	Hamilton	$175-600
223	TL	Hamilton	$500-2500
	TR	Hamilton	$200-800
	BR	Hamilton	$200-800
224	TL	Hamilton	$200-700
	CL	Hamilton	$275-850
226	BL	Hamilton	$150-700
228	TL	Hamilton	$500-1200
	TR	Hamilton	$500-1200
	BL	Hamilton	$500-1800
229	TL	Hamilton	$300-900
	TR	Hamilton	$150-700
	BR	Hamilton	$350-900
		-w/bracelet	+$500
230	TR	Hamilton	$150-600
	BL	Hamilton	$150-650
231	TL	Hamilton	$450-850
	TR	Hamilton	$175-550
	BL	Hamilton	$175-550
232	TR	Hamilton	$300-1000
	BR	Longines	$400-1200
233	TL	Longines	$500-1300
	TR	Longines	$800-1800
	BL	Longines	$200-700
234	TL	Longines	$300-700
	BL	Longines	$300-900
	BR	Longines	$250-900
235	TR	Longines	$400-800
	BL	Longines	$500-900
	BR	Longines	$500-1000
236	TR	LeCoultre	$500-1800
	CL	LeCoultre	$300-900
	BR	LeCoultre	$300-900
237	T	LeCoultre	$450-950
	BL	LeCoultre	$300-800
	BR	Wittnauer	$750-1900
238	TL	Wittnauer	$150-650
	BR	Wittnauer	$90-450
239	T	Wittnauer	$90-400
	BR	Wittnauer	$95-500
240	TL	Elgin	$110-550
	BL	Elgin	$150-700
	BR	Elgin	$300-900
241	TL	Elgin	$100-400
	TR	Elgin	$150-500
	BL	Gruen	$125-600
242	TL	Gruen	$1100-1800
	BL	Benrus	$250-750
	BR	Gruen	$150-950
243	TR	Benrus	$150-850
	BL	Bulova	$150-550
	BR	Benrus	$130-550
244	TL	Bulova	$100-450
	TR	Bulova	$250-900
	B	Westbury	$150-500
245	TL	Borel	$85-450
	TC	Borel	$85-400
	TR	Borel	$85-600
	BR	Louvic	$125-400
246	TR	Ball	$150-600
	BL	Ball	$125-550
	BR	Unknown	$125-500
247	TL	Pierre Cardin	$150-600
	TC	Longines	$200-900
	TR	Zodiac	$150-700
	BL	Gotham	$110-500
	BR	Louis	$125-600
248	TL	Swiss	$125-400
	TR	Juvenia	$125-600
	BL	Louvic	$150-800
	BR	Sandoz	$125-600
249	TL	Unknown	$85-350
	TR	Vacheron & Constantin	$2000-4500
	BL	LIP	$240-750
	BR	Benrus	$400-1250
250	CL	Bulova	$135-425
251	CR	Bulova	$150-425
252	TL	Bulova	$125-400
	BL	Bulova	$100-350
253	TR	Bulova	$175-750
254	TR	Bulova	$250-700
	CL	Bulova	$150-550
255	TL	Bulova	$135-450
	CR	Bulova	$140-600
256	TL	Bulova	$140-500
	TR	Bulova	$150-525
	BL	Bulova	$150-600
257	T	Bulova	$150-700
259	T	Bulova	$150-575
	BR	Bulova	$400-1500
260	TL	Bulova	$150-450
	CR	Bulova	$400-1500
	BL	Bulova	$400-1500
261	TL	Bulova	$150-750
	BR	Movado	$500-1250
262	TL	Caravelle	$130-375
	TR	Gruen	$75-370
	BL	Longines	$250-800
263	TL	Gruen	$110-390
	TR	Caravelle	$120-600
	BR	Zodiac	$100-650

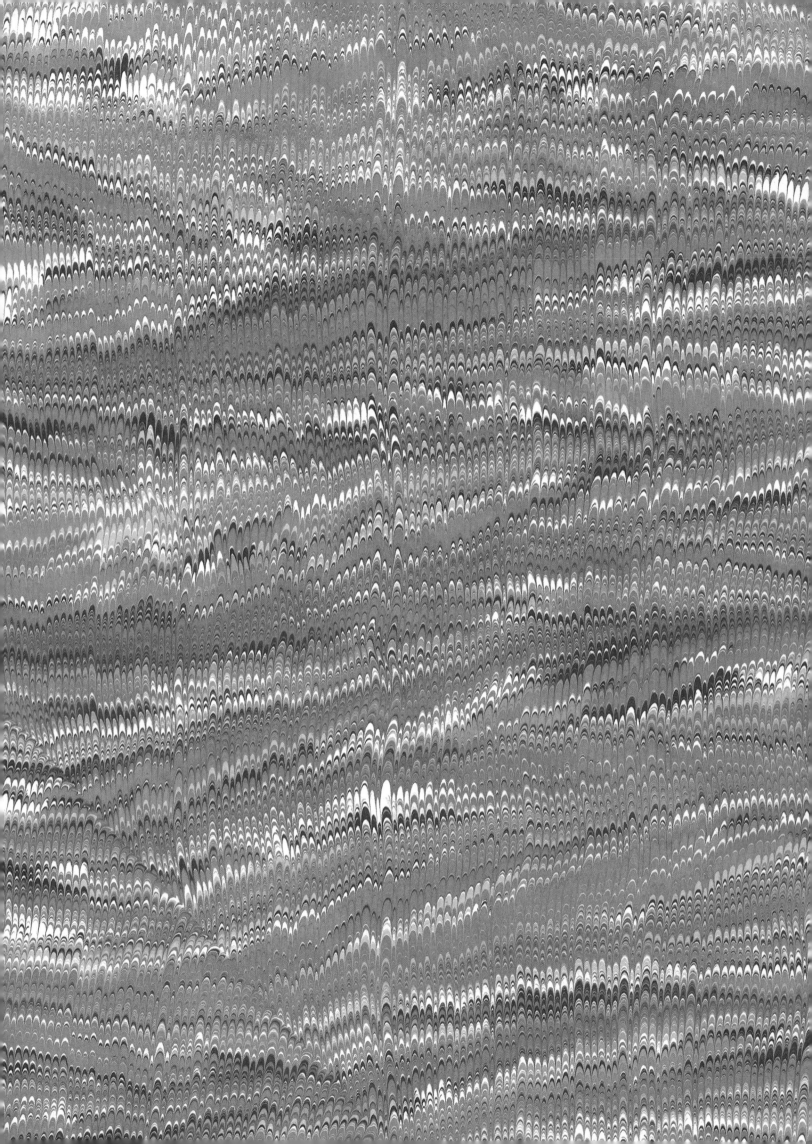